MYSTICAL THEOLOGY AND SOCIAL DISSENT

THE LITTMAN LIBRARY OF
JEWISH CIVILIZATION

MANAGING EDITOR
Connie Webber

Dedicated to the memory of
LOUIS THOMAS SIDNEY LITTMAN
*who founded the Littman Library for the love of God
and as an act of charity in memory of his father*
JOSEPH AARON LITTMAN
יהא זכרם ברוך

'*Get wisdom, get understanding:
Forsake her not and she shall preserve thee*'
PROV. 4: 5

*The Littman Library of Jewish Civilization is a registered UK charity
Registered charity no.* 1000784

Mystical Theology and Social Dissent

♦

The Life and Works of Judah Loew of Prague

♦

B Y R O N L. S H E R W I N

Oxford · Portland, Oregon
The Littman Library of Jewish Civilization

The Littman Library of Jewish Civilization
Chief Executive Officer: Ludo Craddock

PO Box 645, Oxford OX2 0UJ, UK

Published in the United States and Canada by
The Littman Library of Jewish Civilization
c/o ISBS, 920 N.E. 58th Avenue, Suite 300
Portland, Oregon 97213-3786

First published 1982 by Associated University Presses, Inc.,
on behalf of the Littman Library of Jewish Civilization

First issued in paperback 2006
First digital on-demand edition 2006

A catalogue record for this book is available from the British Library

Library of Congress cataloging-in-publication data

Sherwin, Byron L.
Mystical theology and social dissent
Bibliography: p   Includes index
1. Judah Loew ben Bezalel ca 1525–1609.
2. Rabbis—Czechoslovakia—Biography I Title
BM755.J8S45 296.8'33 [B] 80-67968   AACR2

ISBN 1–904113–50–8
ISBN 978–1–904113–50–8

Printed in Great Britain on acid-free paper by
Lightning Source UK, Milton Keynes

This book has been printed digitally and produced in a
standard specification in order to ensure its continuing availability

For Judith

Blessed are you, beyond
all women on earth. . . .
May God allow this to
glorify you and reward
you with blessings. . . .

The Book of Judith 13:18, 20

Contents

Acknowledgments

The present study was undertaken at the suggestion of my mentor, the late Abraham Joshua Heschel. He had always wanted to write a study on the thought of Judah Loew of Prague, but the pressure of other concerns never provided him the time necessary to do so. Unfortunately, Professor Heschel passed away shortly after I had begun my research for this book. I can only hope that he would have been pleased with the product of my labors.

I am especially grateful to Dr. Louis Jacobs of London for his continued interest in my work and for his encouraging me to publish the manuscript of this book. To Dr. David Goldstein, my thanks for his learned editorial suggestions.

It would be ungracious of me not to acknowledge the personal support, warm friendship, sagacious advice, and persistent patience of the following individuals while I was researching and writing this study: Dean Karl J. Weintraub of the University of Chicago; Dean Emeritus Martin Goldman of Spertus College of Judaica; Professors Arcadius Kahan, Ralph Lerner, and Brian Gerrish of the University of Chicago.

Without the technical and secretarial services of Patricia Mattox, Frieda Loux and Barbara Smith, I would not have been spared many hours of tedious work. Without the gracious assistance of Ernest Baum in deciphering many obscure German sources, many crucial secondary sources would have eluded me.

A special debt of gratitude, which can never be repaid, is due my parents, without whom this book would never have been written.

For having undeserved faith in my abilities and for generously supporting my scholarly activities, I owe more than words can convey to David and Joyce Leavitt. Their friendship is one of my most treasured possessions.

Finally, of my wife Judith, to whom this book is dedicated, I ask forgiveness for the many hours and months during which I was more attentive to Judah Loew than I was to her.

August, 1980
Chicago, Illinois.

Mystical Theology
and Social Dissent

1

Rabbi Loew in Legend

Prague: city of mystery, city of marvels.

Prague: its ghetto once teeming with Jews; now a captive city pregnant with memories, enveloped by shadows of a Jewish Atlantis. Its Jews are gone, but their presence remains. Though brutally murdered, their legends survive. By telling their tale, we resurrect their Atlantis. By reviving their legends, we awaken their spirits. Their souls haunt the old ghetto of Prague. Their presence pervades the old synagogue in Prague. For there they go to be with their master, the "Exalted" Judah Loew, called the "Maharal," rabbi of Prague. Though dead for generations, he *is* still rabbi of Prague. Though there have been rabbis *in* Prague, only he was and is rabbi *of* Prague. Revered by Jew and Gentile alike, Bohemians all consider him a symbol of providence over Prague.

An elderly Catholic woman creeps into the Jewish cemetery at night. Cautiously she approaches the grave of Judah Loew. In her hand is a slip of paper. Its contents could send her to prison if she is caught. Soviet soldiers surreptitiously observe her. Spies posing as her friends all know her mission. She must deposit the note in a crevice in his tombstone.

She unfolds the note and reads it again, "Rabbi of Prague, save us from our oppressors." Quickly she folds it and places it in a crack in the tombstone. Quietly she retreats back into the shadows. The Russian soldiers mock her superstition. But the Czechoslovakian collaborators know better. She believes in the legends of the Rabbi of Prague and so do they. Political dissidence can be fought and encountered, but a legend is immortal; it is immune to attack. Rooted in a blend of fact and imagination, the legends are true. Belief in their power makes them true.

In 1939 in Prague, there was a rabbi who believed in the legends. His belief saved his congregation from death and destruction. He

13

believed that the synagogue of the Exalted Rabbi Loew is inviolate; it cannot be destroyed.

The Nazis had already come to Prague. Seeking solace on the Sabbath, the Jews crowded into the synagogue to pray for redemption. While the prayers proceeded, the Nazis surrounded the synagogue. Machine-gun nests were set up outside. Dynamite was placed in the synagogue's basement. The Nazis informed the police, who then told the rabbi of the synagogue about the dynamite. The Nazis hoped the Jews would panic upon hearing the news of the dynamite and would trample each other as they fled the synagogue. The Nazis anticipated "target practice" for their gunners on the terrorized Jews.

But the rabbi, believing in the legends, proceeded with the service, not telling his people of their danger. When the service had ended, the people quietly left. The danger, unbeknown to them, had passed. The gunners were gone, thinking that the dynamite would save them the need of shooting the people. When all the worshippers had left, the rabbi discovered that the dynamite had indeed been set to explode. But a cap had become detached from the fuse, leaving the dynamite ineffective. [1]

Not only Bohemian Jews and Bohemian Gentiles believe in the present potency of the Rabbi of Prague. Amongst Hungarian Jews a story is told about the Maharal of Prague. According to this tale, after his death, Rabbi Loew was appointed by God to protect the Jews from oppression, as he had done during his lifetime. He would appear in visions to saintly and pious rabbis and would warn them of impending disaster. In the 1930s, it is said, Judah Loew appeared to a rabbi in Hungary and warned him of imminent catastrophe for his community unless he took them to a certain place of safety in Turkey. The rabbi obeyed what he was told in the vision and the community was spared.

In the synagogue of Prague, Rabbi Loew's chair still stands. Though great scholars and mystics have been rabbis in Prague, none has presumed to sit upon that chair. His presence is too keenly felt; the legends about him remain too potent. The many legends about Judah Loew are variations upon a single motif: his alleged magical abilities. The legends coalesce around two themes: (1) Judah Loew and the Emperor Rudolf II, and (2) the Maharal and the golem. The legends of Rudolf and Loew are the embellishment of history by legend while the legends of the golem represent an attempt to root legend in historical fact.

Two contemporary reports of Judah Loew's meeting with the quixotic Hapsburg have survived. The first is that of Loew's student, the chronicler and scientist David Ganz, who reports the date of the meeting as 3 Adar (February 13) 1592. Ganz claims that the emperor called for Rabbi Loew, greeted him cordially, and spoke to him face to face. The subject of the meeting according to Ganz is secret and confidential.[2]

A second account of the meeting is an eyewitness report by Rabbi Loew's son-in-law, Isaac Katz. According to Katz, the meeting occurred on 10 Adar (February 20) 1592. He recounts that both he himself and Rabbi Loew's brother, Sinai, accompanied Judah Loew to the palace for the meeting. Katz also insists upon the confidential nature of the meeting, but promises to reveal it "in due time." Katz does mention, however, that the following day he was informed that Judah Loew "had found unusual grace in the eyes of the emperor."[3]

One may only speculate as to the subject of the conversation between Rabbi Loew and the emperor. Though Katz never fulfilled his promise to reveal the subject of the discussion at a future time, he does mention that it was *nistarot*–i.e., secrets, mysteries. It may well be assumed that the subject of conversation was mysticism or the occult. This assumption is strengthened by consideration of the following data. First of all, Rudolf's interest in the mystical and the magical is well known. Indeed, it was by 1592 that Rudolf had become most unapproachable and most preoccupied with alchemy and mysticism. His specific interest in Jewish mysticism may have been considerable. One of Rudolf's closest confidants was Johann Pistorius, one of the leading Christian kabbalists of the day. A record dating from 1600 notes the emperor's interest in securing a copy of the early Jewish mystical tract *Sefer Yeẓirah*. Rudolf may have wanted to discuss matters of occultism and kabbalism with Rabbi Loew.[4] It may not be coincidental that almost without exception, the host of legends which were generated by this meeting all refer to some magical feat of Rabbi Loew's as the basis for the emperor's continued friendship and admiration. Consideration of a statement made by Yair Hayyim Bachrach, a great-great-grandson of Judah Loew, also lends credibility to the claim that occultism was the subject of Judah Loew's audience with Rudolf. In a catalogue of his writings (only the catalogue and not the writings survived), he records that in the text (not preserved) an account of Rabbi Loew's invitation to appear before Rudolf and a copy of the texts of the amulets Judah Loew prepared for the emperor would be provided.[5]

The aura of mystery and confidentiality which surrounded Loew's audience with Rudolf stimulated the popular Jewish imagination. A plethora of myths concerning Rabbi Loew's long-sustained, frequent meetings with his close friend and fellow occultist Rudolf developed as a result of the historic meeting.[6] Some of these meetings were said to have been attended by the eminent court astronomer, Tycho Brahe.[7] At one such meeting, Rabbi Loew is said to have demonstrated the use of a "magic lantern," a kind of rudimentary slide projector. At another meeting, Judah Loew is reported to have attempted to prove the lack of human free will to a skeptical Rudolf. Standing before a fence with two doors, Rudolf asked Loew to write down which door the emperor would choose to enter. Rabbi Loew wrote something on a slip of paper and handed it to one of the king's servants. The defiant Rudolf then broke through the wall and, without the use of either door, arrived at the other side. He then turned to the rabbi, believing his point that free will *did* exist to have been demonstrated. Loew, however, asked the emperor to read what was written on the slip of paper. Rudolf took the paper and read the following quotation from the Talmud, "The king will make a breach in the wall."[8]

Not only in Jewish legend, but also in Bohemian tales, does Judah Loew's presence persist. According to one of these legends, the first meeting between Rudolf and Loew took place not at the castle but on a bridge. When the expulsion of the Jews from Prague had been ordered by imperial decree, Rabbi Loew went to the castle to plead for his people. He was denied an audience with Rudolf. Knowing that to reach the castle the king must pass over a certain bridge, Rabbi Loew stationed himself on the bridge. When the king's splendid carriage came to the bridge, the drivers and the soldiers called to the rabbi to move aside so that they could pass. Loew was adamant. The soldiers then began to throw stones at him, but the stones immediately turned to roses. As the carriage was about to trample him underfoot, the horses abruptly stopped of their own accord. The astonished emperor invited the rabbi to the palace, where the decree was rescinded and a firm friendship was established.[9]

In another story about Judah Loew, which struck the popular Bohemian imagination, a rose also plays an important role. According to this tale, the angel of death hid himself in a rose which Rabbi Loew accepted from his favorite granddaughter. The angel of death was thereby able to circumvent the rabbi's magical powers which protected him from death. Not wanting to distress his granddaughter by rejecting her gift, the knowing rabbi put the rose to his nose whereupon the angel of death entered his body and claimed his soul. This legend inspired the sculpture by Ladislav Saloun of a tall, aged rabbi looking down at a young girl who is offering him a rose. At the foot of the statue is the figure of a beaten dog, symbolizing the oppressed Jews of Prague, looking up at Rabbi Loew for protection. In Prague, this sculpture stands in front of the City Hall. Only in Prague, of all capital cities of the world, does a sculpture of a rabbi stand before its city hall. During World War II, the statue was hidden from the Nazis by the Czechs. After the war, it was replaced. Such could not have been the case if it were not for the prominent place that Judah Loew holds in the popular Bohemian imagination.[10]

By far the most popular legend concerning Judah Loew is the legend of the golem. Unlike the legends of Loew and Rudolf, the golem legend is not based upon historical fact.

Although the golem legend has early roots in Jewish lore, it has become most closely identified with Rabbi Loew. According to the Talmud, the third-century Babylonian sage Rava created an artificial man by magic.[11] Medieval legends record that a female golem was created by the poet-philosopher Solomon Ibn Gabirol. A victim of a communicable skin disease, Ibn Gabirol had to live in complete isolation. He therefore created a female golem to serve his domestic needs. When he was denounced to the authorities for having created a woman for lewd purposes, he restored her to the elements from which she had been created.[12]

In medieval kabbalistic literature the golem is widely discussed. Creation of a golem was considered the mark of an adept kabbalist. Though a creature himself, man was presumed to have magical abilities with which to create artificial life through esoteric rituals based upon the *Sefer Yezirah,* or by invoking secret names and incantations. By penetrating the mystery of creation, by becoming himself a creator, the human being, the kabbalists believed, experiences the mystical rapture of oneness with the Creator. The creative experience thus becomes a conduit to mystical ecstasy.[13]

In the seventeenth century there was a widespread tradition that Rabbi Elijah of Chelm (d. 1583) had created an automaton by means of the *Sefer Yezirah.* By the eighteenth century this tradition had been transferred to the more prestigious Rabbi Loew.[14]

According to the various versions of the golem legend, Rabbi Loew created a huge, powerful, but not quite human creature (1) to be a servant in his home, (2) to protect the Jews of Prague from physical harm, (3) to assist him in countering accusations of ritual murder made against the Jews. It was only when the golem's power could no longer be controlled by Rabbi Loew, when his creation became destructive, that he was forced to destroy it.[15]

In recent years, reflections upon the golem legend have led to serious consideration of some of the implications of the relationship between man and machine, between a human creator and an artificial creation. Norbert Weiner, a pioneer in cybernetics, considers "the machine . . . to be the modern counterpart of the Golem of the Rabbi of Prague."[16] Thus, the golem legend is not only artistically evocative but morally provocative. It can alert us to the danger that the things we create to help us can potentially harm or annihilate us. As Gershom Scholem has noted, the golem legend can show us–specifically in the case of the computer–why we must have the wisdom to control the repositories of knowledge and power we have created. One may further speculate that it is not mere coincidence that the word "robot" emerged from the literary investigations into the modern human condition of the Czech Čapek brothers in their famous play *R.U.R.* Possibly influenced by the golem legend, the Čapeks, like Gustav Meyrink, may have been stimulated to enunciate their view that just as people can create machines which have the power to destroy them, so may people become machines, golems, robots, devoid of a soul, without conscience, lacking creativity.

The legends concerning Rabbi Loew, especially the legend of the golem, have inspired the work of a number of novelists, playwrights, and filmmakers. For example, there is some evidence that Goethe's ballad "The Sorcerer's Apprentice" was inspired by a visit to the synagogue in Prague where the remains of the golem are said to be stored. It has also been widely suggested that Mary Shelley's *Frankenstein* may have been influenced by the golem legend.

The legends about Rabbi Loew also inspired novels by Max Brod and Gustav Meyrink. In 1971, Abraham Rothberg's historical novel *Sword of the Golem,* based upon the life and legend of Judah Loew, appeared. The famous Hebrew author David Frischmann expressed the golem legend in short-story form.[17]

The legends of Rabbi Loew inspired the drama of the eminent Austrian playwright Rudolph Lothar. The first published play of H. Leivick, the great Yiddish playwright, was *The Golem.* Johannes Hess wrote a four-act "Kabbalistic drama," *The Rabbi from Prague, Rabbi Loew.* The Czech poet Hugo Salus published German verse, *The Exalted Rabbi Loew.*

Eugen D'Albert's opera *The Golem* and Joseph Achron's *The Golem Suite* attempted to capture Rabbi Loew for music and dance. Furthermore, attempts to represent Rabbi Loew and his legend have been made by the filmmakers as well as the literary artists. One of the classical examples of the late Expressionist period in films is the 1920 silent German classic, *The Golem*.

Despite the endeavors of artists to capture the spirit of Judah Loew of Prague, his actual presence eludes all these attempts. His legends attract us, but the facts of his life and the content of his teachings elude us. Eclipsed by the legends about him, his life and his thought remain enshrined in the tomes he composed. In the pages which follow, we shall try to unlock the secrets of his life and delineate the content of his teachings. We shall attempt to do what he did: to reveal the concealed. But, as for now, we can only do what the poet Jorge Luis Borges describes God as doing:

> At the hour of anguish
> and vague light
> He would rest his eyes on
> his Golem.
> And who can tell us
> what God felt,
> As He gazed on His
> rabbi in Prague?[18]

2

Judah Loew and Modern Jewish Scholarship

The power to revive the dead, once considered the exclusive domain of the prophet and the sorcerer, is now the task of the scholar and the researcher. Unfortunately, the price paid by the heroes of history for their resurrection is often the distortion of the facts of their lives and the nature of their teachings. Too often the image conjured up by the modern scholar represents a projection of his own mind rather than an accurate depiction of the subject of his scholarly seance. While enveloped by the shadows of death, the great souls of past generations remain elusive and free. However, once they become subjects of research, past masters are in danger of becoming mummified forever in the eternal purgatory of a "definitive study." While the researcher may be convinced he is freeing their spirits from limbo and obscurity, he may be simply etching their silhouettes in his own likeness. The portrait he draws may be replete with distortion. Thus, figures of past eras may become subject to the intellectual fashions and the social prejudices characteristic of the age and of the individual disturbing their eternal rest. Such has been the fate of the sixteenth-century rabbinic master Judah Loew ben Bezalel of Prague.

The founders of modern Jewish scholarship in the early nineteenth century preferred to leave dormant the souls of the intellectual and spiritual luminaries of Central and Eastern European Jewry. Stimulated in their studies by their concern for the social and political emancipation of the Jew in Western Europe, these pioneers of *Wissenschaft des Judentums* largely disassociated themselves from their "unenlightened" co-religionists in Central and Eastern Europe. The founders of the "Scientific Study of Judaism" stressed their cultural affinity not so much with the Jews of Eastern Europe, past and present, as with Western European Gentile culture. Convinced that a demonstration of the common concerns of Jewish culture and Western European culture would help win them political emancipation and would emulsify anti-Semitism, these scholars stressed the universalistic, rationalistic, and aesthetic aspects of Jewish historical experience and denigrated the mystical and nationalistic components of the Jewish cultural heritage which they associated with cultural isolation endemic to the ghetto experience of the pre-Enlightenment period. Many of the founders of *Juedische Wissenschaft* wished to demonstrate that in past ages the Jewish people had contributed culturally to the societies in which they resided and had not remained a pariah in a hostile cultural environment. Consequently, the models for their own lives and the subjects of their scholarly observations were largely bicultural Sefardic Jews rather than the unicultural Jews of Central and Eastern Europe. Since these scholars considered rationalism an indication of cultural achievement, studies abounded concerning the medieval Sefardic philosophers while the very legitimacy of the mystical tradition in Judaism was denied. [1]

These personal and intellectual prejudices of many nineteenth-century German Jewish scholars toward Central and Eastern European Jewry affected the shape modern Jewish scholarship was to take in subsequent years. Though some effort to assuage this situation was made by Russian and Polish Jewish scholarship in the late nineteenth and early twentieth centuries, these attempts were stunted by the advent of World War II. Even these initial undertakings, however, failed adequately to consider the place of the Jewish mystical tradition in the cultural heritage of Eastern and Central European Jewry. It was only as a result of the monumental scholarly efforts of Gershom Scholem, beginning in the 1920s, that the field of Jewish mysticism began to attain a respectable place within Jewish scholarly circles. However, Scholem's apparent continuation of the prejudice of German Jewish scholarship toward Eastern European Jewry and his personal commitment to a unique brand of secular Zionism stimulated him and his students to concentrate upon Jewish mysticism in Germany and Palestine and largely to disregard Jewish mystical speculation in Central and Eastern Europe, especially during the time of Judah Loew. Consequently, while Scholem has expended vast energies upon the Lurianic and Sabbatean movements of the sixteenth and seventeenth centuries, both essentially grounded in the Land of Israel, he pays virtually no attention to the Jewish mystical speculation which flourished in Europe at that time. While he posits strong links between Hasidism and Sabbateanism, he virtually neglects the possibility of Hasidic ideological roots in Central and Eastern Europe in the centuries immediately preceding its birth and growth. While Scholem has discussed Rabbi Loew's relationship to the golem legend, he has paid scant attention to the mystical theology of Judah Loew.

The sparse attention given Judah Loew in nineteenth-century Jewish scholarship yielded two reactions. Those who considered him an Eastern European by birth and a mystic by inclination abhorred him. Those who considered him German by birth and an enlightened, scientifically and philosophically minded Renaissance figure by inclination distorted his views and offered a portrait of what they had hoped he was rather than of what he actually was. An example of the first approach was Heinrich Graetz, while an example of the second was Solomon Judah Rapoport. The preeminent nineteenth-century Jewish historian Heinrich Graetz offers a very unflattering picture of Rabbi Loew, presumably on the assumption that Loew was a mystic. Rapoport, on the other hand, rejects the claim that Rabbi Loew was a mystic and offers a very laudatory description of Judah Loew as a scientist and mathematician.

Graetz's unflattering assessment of Rabbi Loew's thought was not based upon a careful reading of his works. Judah Loew's supposed involvement with the magic arts and his polemic against Azariah dei Rossi (who was apparently construed by Graetz and others to be the forerunner of *Wissenschaft des Judentums*) convinced Graetz that Rabbi Loew was the epitome of superstition, occultism, and mysticism. For Graetz, Loew represented everything modern Judaism should reject.[2] It is no wonder, therefore, that Graetz does not offer a very sympathetic portrait of Judah Loew.

Rapoport, as successor to Rabbi Loew as Chief Rabbi of Prague and undoubtedly influenced by the high opinion of Loew held in the Bohemian Jewish and Gentile imagination, could offer only a favorable evaluation. In order to do so, Rapoport felt compelled to disassociate Loew from mysticism. Rapoport, therefore, stresses Rabbi Loew's interest in astronomy and mathematics. With regard to the possibility of identifying Loew as a mystic, Rapoport asserts, "Knowledge of the mysteries called 'kabbala' made no impression upon him [Rabbi Loew] at all." On the basis of what is known about Rapoport, one may claim that his attempt to minimize the mystical element in Judah Loew's work is a reflection of his own rationalistic intellectual orientation.

Rapoport's evaluation, like that of Graetz, does not seem to be grounded in a careful or extensive reading of Loew's work. Rapoport's position, however, seems to have influenced the portrait of Rabbi Loew sketched by Nathan Grün, in the only attempt at a critical biography of Judah Loew. While Grün does not deny the existence of a kabbalistic tinge in Judah Loew's thought, he does tend to minimize its importance. Like Rapoport, Grün stresses Rabbi Loew's interest in science, especially in astronomy.

The attempts of Rapoport and Grün to deny Judah Loew's involvement with mysticism and Graetz's assertion of such involvement, besides expressing their own proclivity for the rational, appear to be reactions to the portrait drawn of Rabbi Loew in legend.[3] In Jewish and Bohemian legend, Rabbi Loew is venerated as a master of what Jewish mystics call *kabbalah ma'asit* or "practical mysticism."

Jewish mystics and historians of Jewish mysticism distinguish between two manifestations of Jewish mysticism: *kabbalah ma'asit* and *kabbalah iyyunit,* "practical mysticism" and "speculative mysticism." Practical mysticism is concerned with mystical experiences and with magic. Speculative mysticism is "mystical theology," an attempt to present a structured, coherent, if not a systematized account of esoteric knowledge drawn from tradition, experience, and history.[4]

The Rabbi Loew of legend is the champion of practical mysticism. The Judah Loew of speculative mysticism has yet to be uncovered. Graetz's and Rapoport's writings may have discouraged scholars from seeking him. Until the 1950s, Jewish scholarship took little interest in the writings of Judah Loew, specifically, their theological and mystical content. Indeed, even some scholars who did take an interest in Rabbi Loew in the 1950s and 1960s sought to minimize if not to disregard the influences of Jewish mysticism upon his work.[5] It is a desideratum, therefore, to evaluate the totality of Rabbi Loew's available literary legacy in order to reconstruct his theological system and to see whether his theology may be considered a mystical theology, an example of "speculative kabbalah." Since previous studies of Judah Loew generally have disregarded his theology, concentrating rather upon the legends concerning him or upon his theories of education or his notions of morality, the following discussion must assume a dual task. It must both formulate Rabbi Loew's theology and attempt to isolate the mystical element therein. Thereby, it will hopefully be demonstrated that the legendary master of "practical kabbalah" is actually a master of "speculative kabbalah." Furthermore, a concerted effort will be made to reconstruct Rabbi Loew's theological categories in *his* terms and not in what we might wish his terms to be. In the present study of Judah Loew of Prague, no attempt will be made to disguise his militant mysticism, his anti-philosophical prejudices or the extremely chauvinistic components of his theological system. Where apologetic concerns condition the shape of some of modern Jewish scholarship, they ought to be replaced with intellectually honest analysis and objective presentation. We would then be compelled to recognize that Jewish religious thought is by no means as universalistic and rationalistic as it is often made out to be.

The chapters which follow will attempt to reconstruct the facts of Judah Loew's life, the content of his thought, and his social concerns. Chapters 3 and 4 will attempt to reconstruct Judah Loew's biography and his bibliography. The absence of any sustained attempt to do so, since that of Nathan Grün in 1885 transforms what is desirable into a necessity. Chapters 5 through 13 will attempt to reconstruct Judah Loew's major theological categories from his massive, though unsystematic writings. Though he did not write in a systematic fashion, the discussion below will hopefully demonstrate that a coherent theological system does emerge from a consideration of Loew's literary legacy. Specifically, chapters 6 through 9 will discuss his views concerning what are generally considered the three major issues in Jewish theological discourse: God, Torah, and Israel; chapters 10 through 12 will discuss Judah Loew's theological anthropology, his notion of messianism and other eschatological concerns. Chapter 13 will discuss the relationship of his mystical theology to his social concerns.

3

The Man Behind the Legends: The Life of Judah Loew

Speculation must replace documentation regarding many of the details of Judah Loew's life. The legends woven from reports of his alleged deeds have eclipsed his actual deeds. Neither the date nor the place of Loew's birth may be established with certainty. Where and how he spent his early years are obscure. Why he moved from country to country, from city to city, during his middle and later years is more often a matter for conjecture than a matter of fact.

Though Judah Loew seems to have been born in Posnań (Posen, Poland), there is some evidence that he might have been born in Worms (Germany).[1] Though the year of his birth cannot be determined, it can be established with some certainty that he was born no earlier than 1512 and no later than 1526.[2]

Loew's family had its roots in three cities: Worms, Posnań, and Prague. Loew's grandfather, Hayyim, lived in Worms, at least during his later life. Loew's father, Bezalel, also lived there, at least during his youth. Later in his life, Bezalel apparently joined the masses of Jews who fled eastward from persecution-ridden late fifteenth-century Germany.[3] Bezalel seems to have arrived in Posnań sometime before 1520.[4] Because he undoubtedly had family in Prague, it is not unlikely that Bezalel stopped in Prague on his eventual eastward trek to Posnań.

Bezalel's great-grandfather, and apparent namesake for his famous son, had lived in Prague. Judah the Elder, as he is known, died in Prague in 1440. From the inscription on his tombstone it may be surmised that Judah attained prominence as a talmudist and as a mystic.[5] Though it is not clear whether Judah the Elder served the Jewish community in any official capacity, it can be established that his nephew, Avigdor ben Isaac Kara (d. 1439), served as Chief Rabbi of Prague.[6] Regarding Kara, a Jewish author, writing in 1470, wrote:

> A development of the highest consequence was brought about by Rabbi Avigdor Kara, of blessed memory, who lived in Prague the capital of Bohemia. The King of the land [apparently, Wenceslas IV] took a liking to him and this grew into a feeling of intense love, until the king learned from him to acknowledge the true monotheism of the Jewish faith. Shortly afterwards the king passed away. As leader he had appointed a man named Hush Lanu [i.e., John Hus].[7]

This text, written by Rabbi Jacob Mollin, undoubtedly refers to Wenceslas's initial support of Hus in an attempt to diminish German and papal influence upon the Czech people. It is not coincidental that Rabbi Jacob links the king's support of Hus to his friendship for Rabbi Avigdor, since Loew's ancestor influenced the Hussites and composed hymns and prayers in Hebrew and German, stressing the unity of God which were incorporated by the Hussites into their liturgy.

Whether Judah Loew spent his childhood in Posnań or in Prague cannot be determined.[8] Where and by whom he was taught cannot be known. Nowhere in his writing does he reveal the identity of his teachers.[9] Nowhere in his work does he discuss his youth.

According to a family tradition, Loew married a woman from Prague, named Pearl, when he was thirty-two years of age and when she was twenty-eight. This comparatively "late marriage" (for their time and place) was ascribed to a reversal in Pearl's father's financial situation for the worse soon after the engagement of Pearl to Judah. When, through a stroke of luck, Pearl's father recovered his wealth, the patient Judah Loew claimed his bride.[10]

It is only with 1553 that we know with any certainty where Judah Loew was and what he was doing. According to the contemporary chronicler, David Ganz, Judah Loew served as rabbi of Nikolsburg and Chief Rabbi of Moravia between 1553 and 1573.[11] As such, he was only the second incumbent to hold that post. His predecessor, Mordecai Moses Eles, was the first to hold the post of Chief Rabbi of Moravia, a position instituted by Emperor Maximilian II.[12]

It was in Moravia that Judah Loew's abilities as a community leader became manifest. His organizational abilities and the force of his personality and scholarship made a profound and lasting impact upon Moravian Jewry. Under Loew's direction, an attempt was made to collect the statutes of the various local communities of Moravia and to reissue them in an organized form, sanctioned for popular use by the centrally recognized authority of the chief rabbi. This activity all but established a constitution for Moravian Jewry. Such things as tax reform and the standardization of the election of county elders were achieved. There is some evidence that, while in Moravia, Loew attempted to institute educational reforms. Exactly how successful he was in this endeavor, which was close to his heart throughout his life, is unclear. [13]

While in Moravia, Judah Loew attempted to lessen conversation during religious services by instituting a prayer in honor of those who refrained from profane conversation during the prayer service. This was a constant concern of his which he expressed later in Prague. [14] Another constant concern of Loew, which will be discussed in greater detail below, was the use by Jews of Gentile wine. Already in Moravia he attempted to encourage his co-religionists to observe the religious prohibition against imbibing wine produced or handled by non-Jews. [15]

Besides instituting the recitation of certain benedictions, Loew also standardized certain customs in Moravia. One example of this was his decision on the order of preference for people receiving the honor of being called to the Torah. [16] Another example was his standardization of the matchmaker's fee. Rather than setting a flat fee, as had apparently been the previous custom, Loew set a fee that would be contingent upon the size of the bride's dowry. [17]

In 1572, the year before his departure from Moravia for Prague, Loew presided over a meeting of representatives of all the Jewish communities of Moravia. The synod took place at Lundenburg (Břeclav). What was discussed there is unknown. The meeting may have been called in connection with a wave of anti-Jewish sentiment and activity then sweeping Moravia. [18] The synod may have been part of an attempt by Loew to conclude matters in Moravia before departing for Prague.

A most telling document relevant to Judah Loew's relationship with the Moravian Jewish community is a letter from a former student of his, identified simply as "Israel." The letter came to Loew as a plea for his intercession in the "Nadler" affair. (We shall discuss "Nadlerism" in a later chapter.) Suffice it here to say that "Nadlerism" was apparently a widespread outbreak of senseless and even malicious attempts at defamation of character. Rabbi Loew fought it throughout his life. Over fifteen years after he had left his rabbinic post in Moravia, a rash of these libels broke out throughout Moravia. In a pleading letter, saturated with extraor-dinarily exorbitant praise for Rabbi Loew and replete with claims of desperation because of the local rabbis' failure to lead in this matter, Loew's former student turns to his teacher as a final hope and as an established, powerful authority who undoubtedly could stem the abuse of Nadlerism. If Loew would take a public stand against Nadlerism, Israel asserts, his views would be accepted by the Moravian Jewish community without question.[19]

In 1573 Judah Loew left his position as Chief Rabbi of Moravia to assume residence at Prague as a private citizen. Why he did so is unclear and is therefore open to conjecture and speculation.

Loew may have left Moravia for a variety of reasons. His wife may have induced him to move to Prague to be closer to her family. Plague and pogrom may have been inducements enough to con-vince Loew to quit Nikolsburg. Rabbi Loew may have been unhappy with the results of the conference in Lundenburg. He may have wanted to introduce too many changes and reforms, espe-cially in the area of education, and had seen his proposals rebuffed. He may have believed he would be able to do more in Prague to put into practice the pedagogic theories so basic to his thought. Perhaps the eminent Jewish financier of Prague, Mordecai Meisels, induced him to come with the promise of support for his educational reforms.

Meisels supported and sustained Rabbi Loew's school in Prague, the "Klaus," and the position which Loew assumed when he came to Prague in 1573 was director of the Klaus.

Judah Loew may have come to Prague to free himself from the preoccupations which plagued a "chief rabbi" and to concentrate on teaching, studying, and writing. It may be that he came to Prague to be at a center of culture and scholarship rather than to be a "pioneer" in Moravia. The threats of expulsion, plagues, and massacres which had characterized Jewish life in Bohemia were all in the past by 1573. A quarter century of growth and development had begun for Prague Jewry. This may have been the kind of atmosphere Loew sought in contrast to the unsettled, harsh quality of Jewish life in Moravia and which had characterized his life before his move to Prague. In the more tranquil atmosphere of Prague he might do his writing, his teaching and his research.[20] Thus, Judah Loew came to Prague during the short-lived "Golden Age" of Prague Jewry.

When in 1567 Maximilian II issued an imperial charter ensuring Bohemian Jewry the right of domicile, this Golden Era of Prague

Jewry began. Maximilian's visit to the Prague ghetto in 1571 reassured the Jews of the continued friendship and protection of the Hapsburg rulers, despite the persistent ill will of the Bohemian Chamber toward the Jews. This new period of security for Prague Jewry came in the wake of a tumultuous recent past. As late as the 1540s Prague Jewry was small, generally poor, and undistinguished in scholarship. Internal conflict among the few wealthy families that were there required the arbitrational skills of the famous Josel of Rosheim. Threats of expulsion and decrees of expulsions, some cancelled and others carried out, characterized the unstable life of Prague Jewry from 1507 until 1567. In 1507, King Vladislav II consented to the expulsion of the Jews. Though the order was rescinded in 1508, it marked the beginning of a threatening period for Prague Jewry's right of domicile.

In 1520 the Prague Town Council asked for a writ of expulsion. In 1526 Ferdinand assured the Jews that there would be no expulsion. Finally, the king, forced to yield to the pressures of the Bohemian Chamber, ordered the Jews to leave in 1541. When the king did not execute this order of the Chamber, pogroms broke out in November 1541. Having no other choice, Ferdinand finally accepted 1543 as the date for expulsion. In April of that year, the majority of Prague Jewry left for permanent residence in Poland. Only a few somehow managed to stay. By 1544 Prague Jewry numbered only sixty-two families or about 200 people. Though the decree of expulsion was in effect annulled by 1549, when 280 adults were given "Permits of Residence," by 1557 a new ban of expulsion was issued. According to a possibly fictional report, the Prague printer Mordecai Zemah went to Rome and enrolled Pius IV's interest, which helped precipitate the cancellation of the decree. Despite a royal order not to harm the Jews, murdering of Jews and looting of their possessions occurred again in 1558. Throughout this period mob lootings, book confiscation, burning, and censoring were common occurrences. In 1559, for example, approximately 175 pounds of books were confiscated for inspection and were transported to Vienna.

The Jews were caught between two pincers in the power struggle between the king and the Bohemian Chamber. They were continually suspected of a secret alliance with the Turkish enemies of the empire. Favored by the often unpopular Catholic Hapsburgs, the Jews were often in the disfavor of the Bohemian nobility and people. The continual instigation of orders of expulsion by the Chamber demonstrates this.

The fire at Prague in 1541 which destroyed many public records centralized and increased the power of Ferdinand I, the first Hapsburg king of Bohemia. The Chamber and the Czech nobility apparently believed this fire was instigated by the king; however, they tried to blame the Jews for the fire. A forced confession, which was extracted from two unfortunate Jews, gave the Chamber the excuse for persuading Ferdinand to carry out their order for the expulsion of the Jews. Caught in the struggle for power between foreign king and native nobles, the Jewish pariah minority paid the price of the scapegoat–expulsion. It is not coincidental, therefore, that 1618, which marks the final break between the Protestant Estates of Bohemia and the Catholic Hapsburgs, also may be considered the end of the short-lived Golden Age of Prague Jewry.

Though the early half of the sixteenth century had been replete with massacres, expulsions, book burnings, and internal strife for the Jewish community in Prague, by the time Judah Loew arrived in 1573 all of this was in the past. Until a decade after Loew's death in 1609, Prague Jewry flourished. Thus, Prague in 1573 had much to offer Rabbi Loew, who may have been seeking a respite from his hectic and possibly endangered life in Moravia.[21]

Though he had no official rabbinical post in Prague during the years 1573-84, Rabbi Loew's presence in Prague nevertheless was felt by the Jewish community. Besides any effect his directorship of the Klaus might have had, Loew influenced Jewish Prague during those years in a number of ways. He established societies for the study of the Mishnah. The existence of these societies eventually spread throughout European Jewry.[22] In 1564, the *Ḥevra Kadisha* of Prague was established. It was this group of lay people who would undertake responsibility for the dead and prepare them for burial. About a decade after its founding it was recognized that to ensure the continuation of this valuable society, statutes had to be drafted. While the chief rabbi of a community usually drafts these statutes, such was not the case here. The then Chief Rabbi of Prague, Isaac Melnik, was not asked to do so, but rather the newly arrived Judah Loew. This demonstrates the high esteem and influence Loew commanded even during his early years at Prague.[23]

It was also during these years that Loew began to publish his works. In 1578 his commentary to the Torah was published in Prague. This was the first and most popular of a long list of works.

On May 3 (11 Iyyar), 1583, after thirty years of service as Chief Rabbi of Prague, Isaac Melnik died. That fall, on the Sabbath of Repentance, Judah Loew was invited to deliver the sermon at the

Old-New Synagogue, a privilege generally reserved for the Chief Rabbi of Prague. Besides its other features, which included a paean to the deference owed scholars, a harsh admonition concerning congregational conversation during the delivery of the sermon, an outline of the proper treatment of the poor, and a denunciation of the evils of sensual living, this sermon also included a public denunciation and excommunication of those guilty of "Nadlerism." Though this sermon was manifestly sincere, morally courageous, and homiletically classical, it was unsuccessful in persuading the leaders of Prague Jewry to elect Judah Loew the next Chief Rabbi of Prague. The contents of this sermon, in addition to Loew's harsh indictment of contemporary education in his already published works, coupled with the bold nature of his communal activities in Moravia and in Prague, did not win him adequate support among the elders charged with the responsibility of choosing the next Chief Rabbi of Prague.[24] Instead of Loew, his brother-in-law, Isaac Hayot, was elected Chief Rabbi of Prague. That the latter's tenure in office lasted only three and a half years may reflect his status as a minority or compromise candidate.[25]

Isaac Hayot was the scion of a prominent family of Jewish Prague. Thus, his candidacy may have been successful because he was a "favorite son" of Prague. It is also likely that Hayot was chosen because he represented a position supportive of the teachings of Jacob Pollak with regard to the then explosive issue of *pilpul* while Loew represented a powerful dissenting voice on this issue.[26]

Pilpul was a method of rabbinic scholarship which had permeated Jewish education on all levels by Rabbi Loew's day. It sought to sharpen the student's mind by introducing him to the hair-splitting world of casuistry and qualification. Throughout his career Judah Loew opposed the *pilpul.* He believed it was pedagogically dangerous because it, in effect, had made mental sharpness a pedagogical end in itself, rather than a means to textual comprehension. It kept students and teachers preoccupied with sterile mental gymnastics rather than providing an education which offered knowledge of the *content* of the sources of classical Judaica. It overemphasized form at the expense of content. It was a danger to Jewish education, to the development of the Jewish adult and consequently, for Loew, a threat to the essence and future of Judaism itself.[27] As much as Loew was an opponent of *pilpul,* so was Hayot its staunch defender. Hayot went so far as to compose a paean of adoration to pilpulistic scholarship.[28]

Though it can be established with some certainty that Judah Loew continued to serve as director of the Klaus from 1588 until 1592, when he departed Prague to become Chief Rabbi of Posnań, his whereabouts during the years 1584 and 1587 are in doubt. It would appear, however, that from 1584 until the summer of 1587, Loew served as Chief Rabbi of Posnań.[29] During the summer of 1587, he seems to have returned to Prague via Prossnitz (Moravia).[30] From the late summer of 1587 until the spring of 1592, Rabbi Loew once again served as director of the Klaus in Prague. His return to Prague at this time may have been encouraged by Hayot's recent resignation as Chief Rabbi of Prague. It may not be coincidental that Hayot's next recorded place of residence is Prossnitz.[31]

With the position of Chief Rabbi of Prague now vacant, Judah Loew was in effect Chief Rabbi of Prague, though his official appointment to that post was still lacking.[32]

In 1589, on the Great Sabbath (i.e., the Sabbath preceding Passover), Rabbi Loew preached to the Jewish community of Prague. In this sermon, among other things, he bemoaned the lack of communal leadership, reiterated his insistence upon certain kinds of reforms in religious education, condemned usury, and pleaded for Jewish unity.

Although this sermon was slightly more conciliatory than his last public sermon at Prague and notwithstanding the added fame and prestige that Loew now commanded, he once more was denied the office of chief rabbi. Mordecai Jaffe was named Chief Rabbi of Prague.

The years in Prague between 1588 and 1592 were eventful ones for Judah Loew. In 1592 an event occurred which secured for him a singular place in Jewish legend if not in Jewish history; namely, his aforementioned audience with the quixotic Hapsburg king, Rudolf II.[33]

Loew's audience with Rudolf in 1592 and Maximilian II's visit to the Prague ghetto in 1571 were considered events of great moment by the Prague Jewish community. Legends were engendered by both occasions. One may speculate as to why such was the case.

As was noted, the Jews were often caught in the middle of the power struggle between the emperor and the Bohemian nobility. An example of this, discussed above, is the struggle, more than a generation long, between Ferdinand and the Bohemian Chamber over the question of the expulsion of the Jews.

To a large degree, the very existence of the Jewish community depended on the good graces of the king. In Bohemia, as elsewhere in Europe, the nobles opposed the king, whose continual attempt at centralization of economic and political power they perceived as a fundamental threat to their own power. The Jews, often regarded by the citizenry, especially by the emerging middle class, as both pariah and economic threat, were despised accordingly. Such was the case in Bohemia. Spurned by most of the people on economic and religious grounds, always suspected of a secret allegiance to the powerful, menacing archenemy of Christendom–the Turks–the Jews were often considered a potential fifth column and an economic threat to the citizenry of Bohemia. Realizing that their protection lay neither in the populace nor in the nobility, the Jews of Bohemia, as elsewhere, sought out the favor of the king and emperor as their guardian and protector.

In Loew's day the Jews of Bohemia were in an uncertain position. Having recently witnessed the expulsion of the Jews from Iberia, where they had served as counselors to kings and princes, having experienced recent edicts of expulsion in Bohemia itself, having been subject to suppression in Moravia, the insecure Jewish population of Bohemia must have viewed every kindness of the emperor as an event of great significance. Every such event reinforced the belief which they hoped to be true, i.e., that they enjoyed the imperial favor. They knew that their very existence depended upon the pleasure of the king.

It is therefore comprehensible why Maximilian's visit to Prague and Loew's visit with Rudolf became events of such significance. They reinforced hopes and dampened insecurities grounded not in paranoia but in bitter experiences of the recent past. Considering these historical and psychological conditions, it should not be surprising that Loew takes a very strong promonarchical stance in his writings. Judah Loew's friend and benefactor, Mordecai Meisels, knew that a strong king meant a more secure Jewish community. Meisels knew that his substantial loans to the Austrian crown to aid in the war effort against the Ottoman Empire could only serve to allay doubts of a Jewish conspiracy with the Turks. He used his enormous wealth to attain these ends.

Only some eight or nine months after his meeting with Rudolf, on (4 Iyyar) 16 April, Loew left Prague once more and assumed the office of Chief Rabbi of Poland, a position he apparently also had held between 1584 and 1587. Why Loew left Prague for what is probably his birthplace is unsure. It has been suggested that he left as the result of Rudolf's ill will toward him subsequent to their meeting.[34] There is, however, no evidence that such was the case. None of the accounts of this meeting, contemporary or otherwise, provides credence for this theory. Furthermore, if Loew was in danger, it is doubtful whether he would have waited two months before making his exit. It might be that his impending departure was a reason for his audience and not the converse. He may have been unhappy with having been passed over again for the post of Chief Rabbi of Prague and waited for an acceptable offer to come his way. When the offer from Posnań came, he accepted it. The offer may have come before his departure from Prague, thus either stimulating Rudolf to want to see Loew before the latter's departure; or the decision to leave Prague for Posnań may be totally unrelated to the audience with Rudolf. In either case, there is no reason to assume that the audience with the emperor was the reason for Loew's departure for Posnań.[35]

On the Pentecost festival, after his arrival in Posnań, Loew preached his (subsequently published) sermons *On the Torah* and *On the Commandments.* In these sermons Loew records a rare but telling autobiographical statement. He notes:

> Since I began to think independently and I reflected upon the current conduct of scholarship and pedagogy, I realized that it [the process of Jewish education] was being improperly handled. This is not the way of our sacred ancestors; it is a deviation wanting in every value. Therefore, I strengthened myself as a lion, these many years, to correct what I have thought to be wrong. But my contemporaries disagreed with me, following the rule of the majority. Some time ago, I had wished to write to Poland and Russia to delineate what needed to be defined, but I did not do so; but my strength now is as my vitality was then. Perhaps some will take counsel from me. . . . Perhaps I will save one in a thousand. . . . Though we have written these things in numerous places, we have seen fit to reiterate them [here]. Their value is great, their importance is clear and the abuse they receive is considerable.

This passage discloses Loew's awareness of the radical nature of his views, especially in the area of Jewish education. His reticence throughout his works to reveal the names of his teachers may be because of his denial of their views on educational and other matters. Loew claims independence of thought not from his tradition, but from the many and varied abuses he perceived to have affected that tradition in his own day. He calls, not for a denial of tradition, but for an assertion of the authenticity of tradition in the face of what he considers to be the bastardization and the violation of tradition, sanctioned only by popular misconceptions and incompetent, mediocre leadership. Judah Loew wanted nothing less than a reformation of Judaism, a return by Judaism to its authentic roots. He was consequently a threat to a variety of establishments within Jewish community life. This may explain both his double rejection as Chief Rabbi of Prague and why he delivered these lengthy and explicit sermons so soon after assuming his new position in Posnań.

Throughout these sermons Loew reiterated general motifs and particular themes, central to his work (discussed below), such as: the Torah as a metaphysical entity, observance of the commandments as a means to human perfection, the metaphysical reality and particularity of the people of Israel, the metaphysical and physical distinctions between Jew and Gentile, the equal rights of rich and poor, the need for reform in education, the dangers of *pilpul*, the centrality of the Mishnah in Jewish literature and study, the low level of contemporary learning, the undesirability of codifying Jewish law, the sparseness of rabbinic leadership, the current laxity in observing the restriction on imbibing Gentile wine, and the Messianic hope.

How long Judah Loew served as Chief Rabbi of Posnań is unclear. By the spring (17 Iyyar) of 1597 he had already returned to Prague, for on that date he delivered a eulogy at the funeral of Akiva Ginzberg of Frankfurt in Prague. Within about a year of his arrival, Judah Loew's long anticipation of being named Chief Rabbi of Prague became a reality. It may not be coincidence that as he became Chief Rabbi of Prague, his predecessor in that position, Mordecai Jaffe, became his successor as Chief Rabbi of Poland. Apparently, they exchanged positions with the approval of the committee at Prague responsible for the election of a chief rabbi.[36]

According to the inscription on Loew's tombstone, he was "head of the Jewish community of Prague for more than ten years." Since he died in August of 1609, this would place his election sometime before the summer of 1599.[37]

Judah Loew apparently wanted his son, Bezalel, to follow him as Chief Rabbi of Prague and requested the community to name his son as his deputy with rights of succession. The community opposed this. Bezalel then left Prague for Kolin (Bohemia), where he served as rabbi. Soon after arriving there in 1600, Bezalel died. Loew was shaken by this loss.[38]

In March of 1601 Judah Loew suffered a second personal loss. His close friend and benefactor, Mordecai Meisels, died. Meisels, apparently aware of his terminal condition, about a fortnight before his death asked Loew and two distinguished lay leaders of Prague to witness his last will and testament. According to this document, Loew was to receive a considerable sum to distribute to the poor. After Meisels' death, his widow withheld the funds from Loew. The trustworthiness of Emperor Rudolf, who had been close to Meisels and who had guaranteed the execution of his will by imperial decree in 1592, was impugned when Meisels's fortune was confiscated in the name of the crown.[39]

In 1604, battered by age, disappointment, and grief, Loew requested that an assistant be named to aid him. Ephraim Lenczycz was appointed.[40] After Loew's death, Rabbi Ephraim succeeded him and his tenure of office reflected many views which Loew held dear. Many of Rabbi Ephraim's educational policies, attacks on communal abuses, et cetera, echoed those which Judah Loew had pioneered courageously in Prague.

Judah Loew died on August 12 (18 Elul), 1609. Only a few days before his death, Loew had written an approbation to a volume by one of his students, Issachar Baer of Eulenberg, which attempted to put his educational theories into effect. Loew thus lived to see in Ephraim Lenczycz and in the work of his student the beginning of his hopes for educational and communal reform. Pearl, Judah Loew's companion in life, survived him less than a year, dying in the spring of 1610.[41] Thus the "Exalted Rabbi Loew" ("*Der Höhe Rabbi Löw*"), the "Lion of Prague" left this world to become a model for posterity and a hero for makers of legend.

Judah and Pearl Loew were survived by five of their seven children. As has already been mentioned, their only son, Bezalel, died in 1600. Their eldest daughter, Leah, had married Isaac Katz and had died childless. Katz then married their second daughter, Vogele. Himself a prominent scholar, and scion of an important rabbinic family, Isaac Katz succeeded his father-in-law as Chief Rabbi of Moravia when Rabbi Loew left there for Prague in 1573. He also apparently served as Judah Loew's secretary for a time. When Loew had his historic meeting with Emperor Rudolf II, Isaac accompanied him. Besides a laudatory poetic introduction to Loew's *Sermon on the Torah,* Isaac Katz wrote a number of other works. Isaac's son, Hayyim, who apparently succeeded him as Chief Rabbi of Moravia, then served in Prague, Frankfurt, and Posnań. Another son, Naftali, served as Chief Rabbi of Prossnitz and eventually of Moravia, apparently succeeding his brother in that position. From this it becomes apparent that Judah Loew's family established a network of rabbinic leadership in communities he had served, such as Prague, Moravia, and Posnań. Judah Loew's uncle, Jacob of Worms, had served as Chief Rabbi of Frankfurt, a post eventually assumed by Loew's grandson, Hayyim Katz, and by others of his descendants.[42]

Loew's third daughter, Gitel, married Rabbi Samson Brandeis, who served the Jewish community of Prague. There is some evidence that Justice Louis Brandeis was a descendant of this couple. The fourth daughter, Rachel, married Abraham Valerstein Ha-Levi. His fifth daughter, Tela, married Hirsch Sabatka; and his sixth daughter, Varealina, married Hayyim, who served the Jewish community in Prague. Amongst Judah Loew's prominent rabbinical descendants were the aforementioned Yair Hayyim Bachrach and the founder of Habad or Lubavitch Hasidism, Schneur Zalman of Liady.[43]

Having sketched the events of Judah Loew's life, we now turn to a consideration of his works.

4

Judah Loew: Writings and Sources

Judah Loew was a prolific writer. Though all his works have not survived, an extensive mass of material numbering almost a dozen major works have been preserved and published. The latest edition of the works of Rabbi Loew, though it numbers some eighteen volumes, does not represent his total literary output.[1] In the following pages an attempt will be made to outline the nature and the scope of Judah Loew's literary work.[2]

Rabbi Loew's first published work was the *Gur Aryeh* [The Lion's Whelp]. It was issued by the press of Mordecai ben Gerson Katz at Prague in 1578.[3] The title is drawn from Genesis (49:10), where Judah, Jacob's son, is described as a "lion's whelp." Judah Loew apparently chose this title as it alludes to his own name, "Judah." This multivolume work is a supercommentary on Solomon ben Isaac's (Rashi) eleventh-century commentary to the Pentateuch. Loew's work is one of a number of such commentaries composed by members of his generation. A similar commentary, the *Be'er Mayim Hayyim,* was written by his brother, Hayyim of Friedberg (Germany).[4] In the *Gur Aryeh* Loew expresses ideas which are expanded and developed in his later works. Apparently, one of his purposes in composing this work was to defend Rashi from the criticisms leveled at him in the supercommentary of the thirteenth-century Moses ben Nahman ("Ramban" or Nahmanides).[5] Furthermore, there is some evidence that Loew also wrote a second, more analytic, less popular supercommentary to Rashi which did not survive.[6]

In 1582 Loew's second published work appeared. This book was not issued at Prague but at Cracow without the name of its author. It is entitled *Gevurot Ha-Shem.*[7] Why Loew published the work anonymously and in Poland is not certain.[8] Three possibilities present themselves: Loew may have feared the Bohemian censors.

He may have believed that the work should stand on its own and not on its author's name. He may have sought anonymity because of the views expressed therein. Whatever the reason, this work represents the beginning of an important phase in Loew's literary career. At the end of the introduction to this work, Loew outlines the titles and contents of six projected works.[9] The titles are based upon the verse, "Yours, God, are the greatness [*Ha-Gedulah*], the power [*Ha-Gevurah*], the glory [*Ha-Tiferet*], the eternity [*Ha-Nezah*] and the majesty [*Ha-Hod*]; for all that is in the heaven and upon the earth [*Ba-Shamayim u-va-arez*] is Thine" (I Chron. 29:11). These projected works would discuss theological and (to a lesser extent) halakhic problems relating to the religious holidays of the Jewish yearly cycle; as follows:

(1) *Sefer Ha-Gedulah*–On the Sabbath
(2) *Sefer Ha-Gevurah*–On Passover and the Exodus
(3) *Sefer Tiferet*–On Pentecost
(4) *Sefer Nezah*–On the Ninth of Av
(5) *Sefer Ha-Hod*–On Tabernacles
(6) *Sefer Shamayim Va-Arez*–On the Jewish New Year and Day of Atonement.

Loew justified his publishing the projected second volume first on the basis of the precedence of the Exodus over the Sabbath.

Of the six projected works, only three survived; albeit with slightly changed titles. Besides *Gevurot Ha Shem*, *Tiferet Yisrael* and *Nezah Yisrael* were eventually published.[10] Two suggestions have been offered to explain the fate of the other four projected works. According to one, the works, in either partial or total form, were destroyed while in manuscript by a fire which ravaged Prague in 1689.[11] According to a second, after writing the three volumes mentioned, Loew abandoned the rest of the project in order to undertake another endeavor; namely, an exposition of the aggadic materials in the Talmud.[12] The evidence, it has been claimed, supports the second suggestion. Although there are many cross-references within Loew's works, no references are made to these projected three works. It would thus appear that these works were not written and then destroyed; they simply were never written.[13] Another possibility, however, presents itself. First of all, the fact of a fire in Prague would only ensure the destruction of the manuscripts (if they existed) if they were then (1689) at Prague. However, they may have been somewhere else. Secondly, while it is true that Loew has cross-references to all his published works throughout his writings, it is not accurate to say that he never mentions any of these three "projected" works in his published writings. Both in his *Neẓaḥ Yisrael* and in his multivolume exposition of the aggadic materials in the Talmud (*Ḥidushei Aggadot*), Loew notes that a given issue "will be explained, with God's help, in *Sefer Ha-Gedulah.*"[14] From these apparently overlooked sources, one may conclude that while Loew may never actually have written any of the three "missing" projected works, he did not abandon his plan to complete at least one of them, i.e., *Sefer Ha-Gedulah.* The suggestion that he abandoned these projected works to compose *Ḥidushei Aggadot* is rejected by a citation from that very text. For in the *Ḥidushei Aggadot* itself Loew reveals his intention to complete at least one more of the projected series. Though it is true that Loew never actually makes a cross-reference to that particular work, there is no proof that he never wrote it. Besides the evidence that he always intended to write this volume, there is also a report dating from 1927 that in 1904 a manuscript of the *Sefer Ha-Gedulah* was offered for sale by Chaim Sharfstein of Minz.[15] There is, therefore, reason to believe that Loew never relented on his original plan and that he may have written all or part of a fourth book in his projected series of six volumes.

In 1600, besides the aforementioned *Neẓaḥ Yisrael,* Loew published two additional works on two holidays, not intended as part of the original series: *Or Ḥadash* on Purim, the Feast of Lots, and *Ner Miẓvah* on Ḥanukah, the Festival of Lights.[16] The title *Or Ḥadash* is drawn from a description of Purim found in the Bible and embellished upon by the Talmud.[17] It also refers to the "new light"; i.e., the Messianic Age, which Rabbi Loew hoped would soon be a reality.[18] The title *Ner Miẓvah* derives from a verse in Proverbs (6:23).[19]

Loew also wrote two works on the moral and religious values of Judaism. *Derekh Ha-Ḥayyim* was published in 1589.[20] The title is drawn from the same verse as is the title of his aforementioned *Ner Miẓvah* (i.e., Prov. 6:23).[21] The volume is written as a commentary to the mishnaic moralistic tract, *Pirkei Avot.* In 1595, a large work on specific moral and religious virtues was published.[22] The title, *Netivot Olam,* derives from Jeremiah (6:16).[23] In 1600, Loew published a polemical defense of rabbinic literature. This work, *Be'er Ha-Golah* (Well of the Exile), is Loew's attempt "to roll the stone from the mouth of the well in order to uncover the living waters below."[24] This is Loew's attempt to demonstrate the validity and the vitality of rabbinic literature and its traditions in the face of contemporary attacks from a variety of camps.[25] It is intended to serve as a complement to *Tiferet Yisrael*. While the latter work was written as an analysis of a number of issues relating to the written tradition, the *Be'er Ha-Golah* was intended as a discussion of issues relating to the oral tradition as well as for the purpose of "defending" the ancient masters from libel.[26]

Five of Loew's sermons were published. Though probably delivered in Yiddish in a terser form, they apparently were rendered into Hebrew and then expanded for publication.[27] His *Sermon for the Sabbath of Penitence* (1584) and his *Sermon for the Great Sabbath* (1589) were both delivered at Prague. Two sermons were delivered at Posnań (1592): *On the Torah* and *On the Commandments.* In addition, a lengthy eulogy for Akiba Ginzberg delivered at Prague (1597) also was published.[28] Loew's extensive *Ḥidushei Aggadot* has been published only recently from manuscript.[29]

From what must have been extensive writings on Jewish religious law only scanty documents have survived. From what must have been many responsa only one has been preserved and published during Loew's lifetime, namely, the *Responsum on the Deserted Wife.*[30] Loew's novellae to Jacob ben Asher's legal code, *Arba'ah Turim*, have enjoyed little popularity.[31]

It has already been suggested that Loew wrote the *Responsum on the Deserted Wife* during his ministry at Posnań, which began in 1592. The issue discussed in this text is a most difficult and agonizing one over which much has been written in the history of Jewish law. The problem of the deserted wife (Hebrew: *agunah*) refers to a married woman whose husband is presumed dead but whose death cannot be established with certainty. She is therefore "tied" and cannot remarry as she is still considered married to her husband as long as certain proof of his death is not forthcoming. The absence of a statute of limitations in Jewish law only serves to exacerbate this already difficult problem.

Since much of Jewish history was marked by continual geographical dislocation, persecutions, massacres, etc., this problem was a frequent one. It engendered an agonizing choice for the rabbinical authorities involved in the decision of whether to "untie" deserted wives. That Loew deals with an instance of this problem is not surprising. That of all his responsa only this one survived is also not surprising. A lenient view on such a weighty subject by such a prominent authority as Judah Loew would be sought as a precedent by future generations. Because of the importance of the issue and the prominence of Rabbi Loew, many copies of the responsum were made. It was not long in manuscript and was printed almost immediately upon its composition. This may account for its fortuitous survival.

According to the reported facts of this rather complicated case, a woman's husband was considered dead on the basis of testimony given by a single Gentile witness who testified "in his naiveté" (le-fi tumo). Loew upheld the testimony as being sufficient to establish the death of the woman's husband, thus permitting her remarriage. Loew's comparatively lenient view was by no means upheld by subsequent authorities.[32]

Though the *Responsum on the Deserted Wife* is the only responsum of Rabbi Loew published during his lifetime, another of his responsa, published after his death, has been preserved. In the *Bayit Ḥadash,* a collection of the responsa of Joel Sirkes (d. 1640), a responsum of Judah Loew has been preserved. In this responsum, Loew replies to a question from Sirkes concerning a dispute between a debtor and the guarantors of the payment of a promissory note.[33]

Though few of Rabbi Loew's writings exclusively devoted to legal matters have survived, considerable documentation concerning his legal views on a wide variety of matters has been preserved. In the previous chapter a number of examples of Loew's communal-halakhic activity in Moravia, Bohemia, and Poland have been noted. His halakhic views relating to the "Nadler" calumny and the "Gentile wine" (*yeyn nesekh*) controversy will be discussed below. The controversial nature of his just-mentioned *Responsum on the Deserted Wife* has been discussed. It should also be noted that sprinkled throughout his works are discussions of a variety of other halakhic problems. Suffice it here to mention but a few. In the *Gevurot Ha-Shem,* for example, halakhic discussion of Passover-related issues abound. One specific issue which merits mention is the following. While it is customary for one to drink four cups of wine at the traditional Passover meal (*seder*), Loew follows a "minority view" of the talmudic authorities and claims that one ought to drink a fifth cup. He claims that the fifth cup is not simply "permitted" as others had claimed, but is "obligatory."[34]

In the *Tiferet Yisrael* as well, a number of halakhic issues are discussed. One issue is worthy of mention, as it is quoted by subsequent literature. According to Loew, if, in the course of reading the Torah, a mistake is found in the text, one need not, indeed one should not, stop the reading and take out a second Torah. Loew's view on this matter was not widely accepted.[35]

In the *Derekh Ha-Ḥayyim,* Loew takes a position on the question of the age at which a male reaches complete majority. His view was later challenged by Zevi Ashkenazi. According to Loew, a child does not attain complete majority at thirteen as is generally assumed in Jewish law, but at twenty years of age. In Loew's words, "The Court on High does not inflict punishment until the individual has attained an age at which complete adulthood has been attained; i.e., a state in which the form of the individual is independent of the influence of matter."[36] According to Ashkenazi the child becomes totally responsible at thirteen. For Ashkenazi, the child has attained his majority at that age and then becomes liable for the consequences of all his deeds.[37]

Each of the above three examples is culled from halakhic views stated by Loew in his printed works. It is important to note, however, that legal views are attributed to Loew by others which cannot be found in his surviving published works. Two examples follow.

In a collection of his own responsa, Ashkenazi includes a responsum of Loew's great-grandson, Naftali Katz of Frankfurt. In this text, Katz records Rabbi Loew's view that a chicken found to have no heart may be considered fit for human consumption according to the Jewish dietary laws. The assumption upon which the decision rests is that when the chicken was cut open after having been slaughtered, the heart (which was present when the animal was killed) must have then fallen out and been subsequently devoured by a cat. Loew is claimed to have assumed that since an animal must have a heart to live, the chicken must have had a heart originally. The chicken, therefore, was not deformed and was fit for consumption. Rabbi Loew's position on this matter was challenged by subsequent authorities as it differed from a number of other decisions on the matter in Jewish legal literature.[38]

In a second instance also relating to the Jewish dietary laws, Rabbi Loew is reported by another one of his descendants, Samuel Bachrach, to have considered a peacock permissible for consumption (*kasher*).[39]

A number of what may have been many of Loew's endorsements to various contemporary works have also been preserved. One such approbation was given to Abraham of Bredfeld's *Torah Or,* apparently in 1602.[40] Rabbi Loew's last literary task was writing such an endorsement, a few days before his death, to Issachar Eulenberg's textbook *Sefer Be'er Sheva.*[41] As noted above, Loew also appears as a signatory to Mordecai Meisels's will and as an underwriting authority on the book of community minutes from the Moravian town of Prossnitz.

Though extensive, the above-named works probably do not represent the entire scope of Rabbi Loew's literary productivity. There are indications that he authored other works that are either lost or simply remain obscure and unpublished. For example, according to Loew's great-great-grandson, Yair Hayyim Bachrach (d. 1702), only a miniscule representation of Judah Loew's total literary work has been published. By the end of the seventeenth century, from which Bachrach's report apparently dates, all of Loew's currently known major works except *Ḥidushei Aggadot* had already been published. If Bachrach's report is accurate, the quantity of Loew's unknown and unpublished work must be considerable.[42] We shall presently discuss why there is reason to believe such is the case and what the nature of these lost or hidden works may be.

A variety of sources refer to reputed works by Judah Loew other than those mentioned above. According to the inscription on Loew's tombstone, he is claimed to have written more than fifteen works including a collection of responsa and a commentary, apparently halakhic in content, on the entire Talmud.[43] Second, a collection of his responsa appears to have once existed, but is presently lost. Perles, reporting what he may have seen or what he may have known from a family tradition, claims Rabbi Loew wrote many responsa. Perles states that these responsa were lost in the fire that ravaged Prague in 1689. Because of Perles's proximity to that time and place, one has little reason to challenge his view in this regard. References to Loew's views on halakhic issues, not discussed anywhere in his known writings, are found elsewhere, quoted by his contemporaries and by those who came after him.[44] These may refer to his once-extant responsa. It is indeed difficult to assume that an active rabbinic leader in three communities– Moravia, Bohemia, and Poland–would not have written numerous responsa on the many halakhic issues that must have been forced on his attention.

Perles also notes that Loew had possessed a complete copy of the Talmud to which he and his son-in-law, Isaac Katz, had written glosses. (The glosses in Katz's handwriting may have been taken in dictation from Loew.) Perles notes further that all but two tractates were lost and that they were in the possession of his brother, David Perles. He identifies the two tractates as being *Sukkah* and *Eruvin*.

The fate of the manuscript of *Sukkah* remains unknown. However, the fate of the manuscript on *Eruvin* may be determined. In 1862, Joseph Saul Nathanson of Lemberg (Lwow) wrote an approbation to what he claimed were Loew's *Novellae on Tractates Shabbat, Eruvin and Pesaḥim*. In the approbation he notes that the work under discussion is being published from manuscripts.[45] Though the Oxford manuscript of *Ḥidushei Aggadot* is missing *Eruvin* and *Pesaḥim*, it does contain *Shabbat*. The text of the 1862 edition and the published text of the Oxford manuscript on the tractate *Shabbat* compare favorably, though not exactly. There is reason to believe, therefore, that the 1862 edition resolves the problem of the disposition of the contents of the manuscript referred to by Perles, at least with regard to *Eruvin*. The other tractate, *Pesaḥim*, it would appear, is also a part of the incomplete version of *Ḥidushei Aggadot*.

According to another report, Loew composed a *gemara* for the extensive sections of two orders of the Mishnah which have none, i.e., *Seeds* and *Purities*. Loew apparently composed this work from selections drawn from the entire corpus of talmudic literature. When the daring Hasidic leader, Gershon Hanokh of Radzyn attempted the identical project late in the nineteenth century, the usually anti-Hasidic Joseph Saul Nathanson of Lwow defended him on the grounds that such a project was not an affront to tradition as it had already been accomplished by Loew. According to Nathanson, Loew's manuscript perished in a fire. Nathanson may be referring to the 1689 fire at Prague.[46]

The codex of the Oppenheimer Library records three additional treatises by Judah Loew.[47] The first, *Ḥidushei Aggadot*, mentioned above, has been published from manuscripts originally part of the Oppenheimer collection now at Oxford. The other two remain unknown. One is a treatise on varied halakhic matters such as the laws of the *mezuzah*, writing the *megillah*, and matters dealing with the sacrificial cult. The second consists of glosses to the talmudic commentaries of Isaac Al-Fasi and Mordecai ben Hillel. Manuscripts of these and still unknown works of Loew may yet appear. In addition, one may assume that a number of manuscripts of Rabbi Loew's work perished during the European Holocaust (1939-45). It is reported, for example, that the manuscript collection of the Hasidic community of Stolin (Lithuania) contained a manuscript of one of Loew's works.[48]

To this point, the names and the editions of Loew's published works have been noted. Speculation concerning the existence and

the nature of his unpublished works has been offered. Some observations relating to those works are now in order before proceeding
to discuss and to analyze their content. One is tempted to try to
uncover a development in Rabbi Loew's thought by assuming that
the order in which his works were published represents the order in
which they were written and consequently reflects the progession
which his thinking underwent over the years, especially from 1578
to 1600, when most of his works were published. A closer look at
the text of the works themselves will reveal that such an assumption
cannot be made; the order of publication does not represent the
order of composition.[49]

On the basis of a careful scrutiny of Loew's writings, it may be
suggested that he:

1. probably wrote *Gevurot Ha-Shem* first, before 1578;
2. completed *Gur Aryeh* by 1578;
3. began *Derekh Ha-Hayyim* before 1578 and completed most
    of it by 1583;
4. wrote and delivered his *Sermon for the Sabbath of Penitence*
    in 1583 and published it in 1584;
5. by 1584 had probably completed *Beer Ha-Golah;*
6. by 1586 completed *Hidushei Aggadot;* since he makes fre-
    quent reference therein to *Tiferet Yisrael,* it is likely that
    by 1586 he had completed *Tiferet Yisrael* as well;
7. in 1589 published his sermon, recently delivered;
8. probably wrote *Netivot Olam* between 1593 and 1595;
9. wrote *Or Hadash* at an undeterminable time before 1600;
    possible references to it in *Derekh Ha-Hayyim* and in the
    Sermon for the Great Sabbath, both published in 1589,
    indicate that it may have been written before that date.[50]

What emerges from a careful examination of Loew's writing is
that one cannot assume that the order in which Loew's works were
published was the order in which they were written. Furthermore,
one cannot establish the order in which Loew composed his works
with any certainty; nor can one ascertain when he wrote each of his
works. Nevertheless, one may offer the aforementioned suggestions as to the possible order of their composition. Thus, one can
only suggest, but not conclusively demonstrate, the development of
Judah Loew's thought.[51]

A close look at the contents of a number of Loew's works
fortifies the claim that he continually edited, reworked, and sup-
plemented his manuscripts until their publication. A careful
analysis of *Gevurot Ha-Shem,* for example, reveals that chapter 47

seems to be the original end of the book while the subsequent chapters were added to the original manuscript.[52] A chapter in one of Loew's works, abruptly beginning "Thus says Judah Loew ben Bezalel," may indicate an interpolation of an addition by the author into an already written manuscript. Loew introduces chapters this way in a number of his books.[53] A close comparison of the table of contents of the *Netivot Olam* and the contents of that work will show certain discrepancies. A chapter placed toward the end of the book may be referred to in an early chapter as being "discussed below" while a chapter placed early in the book may refer to a chapter placed toward the end of the book as being "discussed above." This would suggest that Loew continually reedited and rearranged the contents and the structure of this work until it reached its final printed form, which contained the aforementioned discrepancies in internal reference. Similar discrepancies appear when Loew, in one of his works, refers in one citation to one of his other works as already having been completed, while in another citation refers to it as yet to be completed. These inconsistencies seem to demonstrate that his individual works were not composed separately or individually, but that he continually worked on his manuscripts, a number at a time, unconcerned about removing inner discrepancies for the final printed editions. A look at the manuscript of *Ḥidushei Aggadot,* written in Loew's own hand, would also reveal that he continually reworked his writings, striking out already written sections and adding new material.[54] Furthermore, the classical homiletical style, employed by Rabbi Loew in a number of his works, suggests an originally oral nature to some of his written works.[55] He may have dictated some of the sections of some of his books. The *Derekh Ha-Ḥayyim,* for example, might be a compendium of the transcripts of sermons delivered over the course of many years by Rabbi Loew on the *Ethics of the Fathers.* As it was customary to study a different chapter of that work each Sabbath during certain periods of the year, it is conceivable that Loew taught the *Ethics of the Fathers* or preached on its text each week during the spring and summer over the course of a number of years, after which he collected a large amount of material which he later collected in a volume which became the *Derekh Ha-Ḥayyim.*[56] If this were the case, much of the repetition of ideas which characterizes the content of that work would be accounted for. The repetition might have originally been intended as a pedagogic aid for listeners, not needed by readers.

Judah Loew's writings are vast in content, scope, and style. One finds biblical exegesis, talmudic commentary, homiletical expressions, polemics, apologetics, poetry, social commentary, and much more.[57] The nature of the sources from which he drew to compose his works and to help formulate his ideas will now be discussed.

To understand an artist it is helpful to appreciate the nature of the medium with which he or she works. To understand a scholar such as Judah Loew, an awareness of his sources should prove helpful.[58]

It is difficult to present a complete picture of Rabbi Loew's sources. In his writings Loew does not identify all the sources he used in composing them. In the case of some of his sources, therefore, Loew's hint to a given work becomes our conjecture that he utilized the said work. In other instances it is difficult if not impossible to determine his sources. Often, when attempting to refute a position, Loew will cite the source of that position. However, when adopting someone's view as his own, Loew often presents it as his own, leaving the identification of the source to oblivion at the worst and to conjecture at the best. Fortunately, however, Loew does provide his reader with extensive information concerning his sources, happily leaving identification through conjecture for the minority rather than the majority of his sources. At present the intention is only to note his sources. Loew's attitudes toward these sources and the philosophy of Judaism he constructed with them will be the subject of much discussion in future chapters.

Judah Loew was thoroughly at home in biblical, mishnaic, midrashic, and talmudic sources. While an exacting knowledge of talmudic and even of midrashic sources might be expected of a sixteenth-century Ashkenazic scholar such as Rabbi Loew, a careful knowledge of Scripture could not be readily assumed of one in his time and place.

As the author of a supercommentary to the Torah, Rabbi Loew was also at home in the world of biblical exegesis and commentary. He especially mentions the names of his fellow commentators with whom he was wont to disagree, especially Abraham Ibn Ezra (1089-1164), Moses ben Nahman (Ramban) (1194-1270), David Kimhi (1160?-1235?), and Elijah Mizrahi (ca. 1450-1526). He also has occasion to mention other commentators such as Samuel ben Meir (Rashbam), and Hezekiah ben Manoah (Hizkuni) (thirteenth-century).[59] In his commentary to the Talmud (*Hidushei Aggadot*) and elsewhere, Loew has occasion to refer to the commentaries of his predecessors. He refers to Isaac ben Jacob

Al-Fasi (Rif) (d. 1103), Asher ben Yehiel (Rosh) (ca. 1250-1327), Solomon ben Abraham Aderet (d. 1310), Mordecai ben Hillel (d. 1298), Yom Tov ben Abraham Ishbili (Ritba) (1250-1330), Nissim Gerondi (Ran) (d. 1381), Jacob ben Solomon Ibn Habib (*Eyn Ya'akov*).

In Loew's writings relating to issues of Jewish law, he cites many authorities and sources; for example, the halakhic views of Isaac ben Jacob Al-Fasi, Asher ben Yehiel, Mordecai ben Hillel, Nissim Gerondi, Samuel ben Meir, Solomon ben Isaac (eleventh-century) in their respective commentaries to the Talmud.[60] He cites the halakhic views in the codes or digests of Jewish law by Hai Gaon (*She'iltot*), Moses Maimonides (1135-1204) (*Sefer Ha-Mizvot, Mishneh Torah*), Moses of Coucy (Semag) (thirteenth century), Jacob ben Asher ben Yehiel (Turim), and Joseph Karo (sixteenth-century).[61] He mentions views found in the following commentaries to the various codes: Abraham ben David's (Rabad) *Hasagot* (glosses), Joseph Karo's *Magid Mishnah*, Meyer Cohen's *Hagahot Maimoniot*, Shem Tov ben Abraham's *Migdal Oz* and Eliezer Menahem's *Avi Ha-Ezri* to Maimonides' *Mishneh Torah;* Joseph Karo's *Bet Yosef* to Jacob ben Asher's *Turim.*[62] Loew also quotes the halakhic views of individuals not mentioned above, such as Jacob Tam of Orléans (d. 1171), Isaac ben Sheset (d. 1408), Moses ben Nahman (Ramban).[63]

Loew refers extensively to medieval Jewish philosophical literature. He makes reference to the writings of Saadya Gaon (892-942), Gersonides (Levi ben Gerson) (1288-1344), Abraham Shalom (d. 1492), and Joseph Albo (1380-1444).[64] Rabbi Loew also shows a total familiarity with the philosophical and non-philosophical works of Moses Maimonides.[65] His use of certain Hebrew expressions pecular to the writings of Judah Ha-Levi indicates that Rabbi Loew was familiar with Ha-Levi's *Kuzari.*[66] There is some indication that Loew utilized the philosophical works of Solomon Ibn Gabirol.[67] There is also ample evidence to establish the influence of Isaac Arama's work upon Rabbi Loew.[68]

Though Rabbi Loew was at home in medieval Jewish philosophical literature, he seemed more at ease in Jewish mystical literature. He quotes from such classics of Jewish mysticism as *Otiyot d' Rabbi Akiva,*[69] *Sefer Yezirah,*[70] *Sefer Ha-Bahir,*[71] (Meir Ibn Gabbai's) *Avodat Ha-Kodesh,*[72] (Perez ben Yizhak Gerondi's) *Ma'arekhet ha-Elohut,*[73] and of course the Zohar.[74] Rabbi Loew considered Nahmanides to be "a divine kabbalist and great master" and quotes from a number of his works.[75] There is some indication that Loew was acquainted with the work of Moses Cordovero (1522-70) and Isaac Ibn Latif.[76] It is doubtful that he was aware of the mystical teachings of his contemporary, Isaac Luria (1534-72).

Whether Rabbi Loew was directly familiar with the classics of ancient philosophy and science is unclear. Which languages he knew besides Hebrew and Yiddish cannot be ascertained with any surety. Though Loew does mention a number of Aristotle's works, e.g., *Physics, De Caelo,* it is likely that he knew of these works indirectly, i.e., from classics of medieval Jewish philosophy, especially the works of Maimonides and Abraham Shalom, rather than in their original sources. The same would hold for his references, by name, to Plato and to Averroës.[77]

Loew also refers to such works as Menahem ben Saruk's grammatical treatise *Mahberet,*[78] Josippon's history,[79] David Kimhi's grammatical work *Sefer Ha-Shorashim,*[80] the anonymously written moralistic tract *Orhot Zaddikim* or *Sefer Middot,*[81] the historical chronicle *Seder Olam,*[82] and Nathan ben Yehiel's "dictionary" of non-Hebrew words in ancient Jewish literature called the *Arukh.*[83]

Loew makes reference to Abraham of Prague. This may be Abraham Kara, Loew's distant relative and former Chief Rabbi of Prague.[84] In this case Loew may be recounting an oral rather than a literary source.

Judah Loew does not confine his citations to past literature. He cites a number of the works of his contemporaries, usually to challenge their views. Loew refers approvingly to the explanations of certain biblical verses by his brother, Hayyim ben Bezalel of Friedberg. He may be referring to the latter's supercommentary on the Torah, *Be'er Mayim Hayyim.*[85] Loew harshly attacks the views of Azariah dei Rossi's "recent work" *Me'or Einayim.*[86] Loew takes the defensive and then the offensive against Eliezer Ashkenazi's attack in *Ma'aseh Ha-Shem.*[87] He challenges a number of the views of Don Isaac Abravanel (1437-1508).[88] Though Rabbi Loew does not mention him or his work by name, it is clear that he also takes issue with certain views of Moses Isserles (d. 1572) in his *Torat Ha-Olah.*[89]

The previous chapter attempted to reconstruct the life of Judah Loew. The present chapter has been concerned with the nature and scope of his works. Having discussed the life and works of Judah Loew, it remains to examine the content of those works.

5

Judah Loew and the Jewish Mystical Tradition: Introductory Remarks

Though there have been many attempts to define "mysticism," no conceptually embracing or historically adequate definition has been formulated. Most attempts at definition are either too vague or too broad.[1] They would apply to religious experience as a whole, rather than to a specific variety of religious experience; or they would not prove historically accurate if applied to particular historical manifestations usually described as "mysticism." For example, to define "mysticism" as "intimate consciousness of the divine presence" or "a conscious relation with the absolute" or "direct intuition or experience of God" would equate religious experience with mystical experience.[2] Such definitions would be reductionist; they would reduce religion to mysticism. To be sure, the mystic might assent to such a possibility. The mystic may be content to assume religion is mysticism or that mysticism is simply religion in its most intense expression. However, such a definition might not satisfy the cultural historian or the historian of religion who views mysticism as an expression of religion, as an element *within* the history of religion, but not as religion itself. Attempts to describe mysticism as the attainment of a state of *unio mystica* (mystical union with God) also do not suffice.[3] While possibly applicable to a variety of expressions of Christian mysticism and Eastern mysticism, such a definition is all but irrelevant to Jewish mysticism, where the mystic strives for an ecstatic view of God or for "cleaving" to God, but does not usually even conceive of the possibility of becoming one with God.[4] It might be advisable, therefore, to recognize the faults and the inaccuracies of purely speculative definitions of "mysticism." It might prove more productive to accept the claim that there is no "mysticism" in the abstract and therefore there can be no possible definition of "mysticism" in the abstract.[5] It may be useful to assume that, while there may be points of comparison between particular expressions of one mystical tradition and another, "there is no mysticism as such, there is only the mysticism of a particular religious system."[6] The claim, therefore, that a given historical figure was a mystic would mean that the person's life and thought expressed characteristics of the mysticism of that particular religious tradition from which he emerged. Consequently, the claim that Judah Loew of Prague was a mystic must be examined through an analysis of his relationship with the Jewish mystical tradition. While the following chapters will explore Rabbi Loew's relationship to the Jewish mystical tradition which preceded him, the remainder of the present chapter will briefly discuss his influence upon the Jewish mystical tradition which succeeded him.

Judah Loew's writings made a significant impact upon the two major trends in the history of Jewish mysticism which flourished after his death: Sabbateanism and Hasidism. One may discover Loew's influences in the writings of Nathan of Gaza, the principal Sabbatean theologian. Nathan's idea of salvation by faith rather than by deeds, an atypical notion in the history of Jewish messianism, may be traced directly to Loew's treatise on messianism, the *Neẓaḥ Yisrael* (chapter 29).[7] After Shabbatai Zevi's conversion from Judaism to Islam, Sabbateans culled Judah Loew's books, searching for some anticipation of their "Messiah's" unexpected conversion. They claimed that Rabbi Loew had cryptically predicted that the Messiah would be bound to the world of Islam.[8] More profound and direct than his influence on Sabbateanism was Judah Loew's impact upon Hasidism.

Abraham Isaac Kook (d. 1935), considered by many the last great Jewish mystic and himself profoundly influenced by the thought of Judah Loew, considered the Maharal to be the "father of Hasidism."[9] Gershom Scholem, the preeminent contemporary historian of Jewish mysticism, considers Loew "the first Hasidic writer." Scholem suggests that Rabbi Loew's successful attempt at expressing kabbalistic ideas in a popular jargon, without the use of technical kabbalistic terminology, accounts for his popularity in some Hasidic circles.[10] Loew's books served as models for Hasidic writers, especially of the Przysucha-Kotsk school, of how to express "concealed" thoughts in a "revealed" idiom.[11]

Not only his literary style, but also many of Rabbi Loew's attitudes and views echo throughout Hasidic literature. His abhorrence of the sterility of pilpulistic talmudism, of mental gymnastics as an end in itself, endeared him to many Hasidic masters.[12] One finds in Loew's writings a foreshadowing of the pivotal Hasidic notions of *devekut* ("cleaving" to God) and of the *zaddik,* the religious leader.[13] Though the specific and direct influence of Rabbi Loew upon Beshtian Hasidism is difficult to identify, his impact upon a number of later Hasidic masters is well documented. Israel of Koznitz (d. 1814), known in Hasidic literature as "the second Baal Shem Tov," was "particularly fascinated by the personality of Judah ben Bezalel Loew of Prague."[14] He encouraged his wealthy friends, such as Moses Muskat, to underwrite the cost of reprinting Loew's works.[15] In his own writings, the Maggid of Koznitz attempted to explain and to correlate Rabbi Loew's teachings with those of the Zohar and other works of the classical Jewish mystical tradition.[16] Israel of Koznitz also wrote a commentary to Loew's *Gevurot Ha-Shem* entitled *Geulat Yisrael.*

Hasidic interest in Judah Loew reached its acme in the Przysucha-Kotsk school. One may suggest that both Simha Bunam of Przysucha's and Mendel of Kotsk's interest in the Maharal was stimulated by Israel of Koznitz.[17] Bunam and his disciple, Mendel of Kotsk, made study of Loew's works a basis for an understanding of Hasidism.[18] Bunam believed that every individual should have both an earthly mentor and a heavenly mentor. He considered Rabbi Loew his heavenly mentor.[19] In one source which credits Bunam with spreading Rabbi Loew's teachings, the rabbi of Przysucha is quoted as saying the following on a visit to Judah Loew's grave, "Know that I have spread your ideas. Until I did so many failed to appreciate your thoughts. But now, you are praised even more than Rabbi Hayyim Vital."[20] According to another source, Bunam was accustomed to recite a selection from Rabbi Loew's writings before saying his prayers.[21] In his later life, when he had become blind, Simha Bunam would have his students read to him, primarily from two sources: the Talmud and the writings of Judah Loew.[22] Isaac Meir of Ger, Bunam's disciple and Mendel of Kotsk's successor, is quoted as saying, "Only with Bunam did the world begin to appreciate the sweetness of Rabbi Loew's words."[23]

Historians of Hasidism agree that Rabbi Loew's impact upon Bunam's enigmatic disciple, Mendel Menahem Morgenstern of Kotsk, was overwhelming and profound.[24] Abraham of Sochaczew, the Kotsker's son-in-law, claimed that Rabbi Mendel's novellae on Talmud and Jewish law were influenced by the approach of Rabbi Loew.[25] Rabbi Mendel, who was not generous with his compliments, lauded Rabbi Loew's works. He is reported to have admonished Nahum Israel of Lipna, one of his closest disciples, not to read any Hasidic books, but to study only the writings of Rabbi Loew,[26] To those of his students who wished to attain a keen intellectual apprehension of Talmud and Jewish legal codes, the Rabbi of Kotsk insisted that they study the works of Rabbi Loew.[27] The Rabbi of Kotsk apparently believed Rabbi Loew's books to contain profound and complex ideas. For when his disciple Yehiel Meyer of Gostinin once entered his study, anxious to seek counsel on how to write a book modeled after those of Rabbi Loew, the Kotsker replied, "You could not even understand the Maharal's gossip."[28] In response to Rabbi Yehiel's complaint that Rabbi Loew was often repetitious in his works, Rabbi Mendel is supposed to have replied, "We labor simply to understand him while you complain he is repetitious."[29] Abraham of Sochaczew, Rabbi Mendel's son-in-law, echoes his father's and his father-in-law's esteem for Rabbi Loew. Rabbi Abraham's father is said to have remarked that "the Maharal of Prague has brains even in his feet.[30] When on his deathbed, Rabbi Abraham is reported to have ordered Rabbi Loew's book on moral values, *Netivot Olam* to be brought to him. He turned to the section *yisurim* (heavenly afflictions) and died.[31]

Besides the Przysucha-Kotsk school, one may discern some influence of Judah Loew upon at least two additional Hasidic figures: Shneur Zalman of Liady and Gershon Hanokh Leiner of Radzyn (d. 1891). Loew's influence on the former may be partially due to the fact that his family claimed Rabbi Loew as one of their ancestors.[32] Gershon Hanokh's apparent admiration for Rabbi Loew may have come to him indirectly from Rabbi Mendel of Kotsk, as Rabbi Gershon was a descendent of Mordecai Joseph of Izbicza, a disciple of Rabbi Mendel of Kotsk. The controversial rabbi of Radzyn may have been influenced by Rabbi Loew in his daring attempt to construct a *gemara* to the Mishnaic order *Taharot,* a section of the Talmud to which there is no *gemara.*[33]

Though the present discussion has merely suggested Judah Loew's impact upon Sabbateanism and Hasidism, fully to examine the extent of his influence upon them would undoubtedly prove a massive, though rewarding experience.

In the chapters which follow, an attempt will be made to reconstruct Judah Loew's theology and to examine the relationship of that theology to the texts and ideas which constitute the history of Jewish mystical speculation until his time. The remainder of the present section of this study will discuss Judah Loew's views regarding what are generally considered the three major concepts in Jewish theology: God, Torah, and Israel. The third section will round out the presentation of his theology with a consideration of his views regarding the nature of man and an analysis of his eschatological concerns. Hopefully, by discussion's end, the reader will find himself informed as to the content of Judah Loew's theology and convinced of its essentially mystical nature.

6

The Nature of God

The medieval Jewish philosophers were not content only to *believe* that God exists; they insisted upon *knowing* that God exists. They therefore attempted to demonstrate that which they already believed, i.e., the existence of God.[1] The Jewish mystics, however, assumed God's existence as the single irrefutable reality. Human existence and the world's existence, they claimed, may be illusions, but not His existence. The medieval Jewish mystics therefore did not attempt to prove God exists. Judah Loew, who was aware of the attempts of Maimonides and others to demonstrate the existence of God, and who accepted Joseph Albo's claim that belief in the existence of God is one of the three essential principles of the Jewish faith, never attempts to demonstrate the existence of God.[2] Like the mystics, he assumes God as the only certain existent and never conceives of demonstrating His existence.[3]

Loew viewed the attempts by Jewish philosophers to demonstrate the existence of God as a needless endeavor and as a potential threat to already affirmed religious beliefs. He specifically discusses Maimonides' demonstration of the existence of God.[4] According to Loew, Maimonides' demonstration for the existence of God is based upon faulty and even heretical assumptions. It cannot be taken seriously, therefore, as a means of buttressing religious belief. Maimonides assumes the existence of eternal motion, a doctrine which is in opposition to faith, in order to demonstrate the existence of God, which is the basis of religious faith. This use of falsehood to prove truth is logically a mistake and religiously a travesty. Rabbi Loew writes:

> Behold, Maimonides built the foundation of his demonstration upon the assumption of [eternal] motion. But this is in opposition to the faith. We do not assent to this assumption. Since we cannot assent to the assumption, the entire demonstration collapses.[5]

Philosophical demonstrations of God's existence led not only to the conclusion that God exists, but to the inference that a God characterized by distinct attributes exists. Consequently, a central concern of the medieval Jewish philosophical tradition was predication of divine attributes.[6]

For the medieval Jewish philosopher, predication of divine attributes meant: What can one logically and grammatically predicate of "God"? Maimonides' problem, for example, was: How can one speak about a being about which nothing can be said? Maimonides' solution, therefore, was drawn from logic and grammar.

For Loew, Maimonides' problem is a pseudo-problem. Predication of divine attributes does not predicate attributes of "God," but describes human perceptions of God. Not God, but our perceptions of God are the product of predicating divine attributes.[7]

In claiming that man never knows what God is and cannot, therefore, predicate attributes of God, Rabbi Loew reiterates what has been termed the "mystical agnosticism" of the kabbalists. He, like them, claims that God in Himself lies beyond any speculative comprehension or even ecstatic apprehension.[8] Loew writes:

> One who believes in God, believes in the existence of something, but does not know its nature. He only believes as one who knows nothing of the nature of the object of his belief, except that its nature is obscure and concealed.[9]

Thus, for Rabbi Loew, one does not predicate divine attributes. One only relates human perceptions of the divine as inherited from tradition, as grounded in precedent. God's essence remains unknowable. Man never knows what He is. He only knows what God is perceived to be. Only the divine attributes utilized by Jewish tradition are proper. Other attributes are not proper. By tradition, Rabbi Loew primarily meant the mystical tradition. Correct attribution is to be derived from the kabbalists, and not the philosophers.

The philosopher's attempt at predication of attributes, because it assumes it is stating something about the nature of God, leads to many problems which, according to Rabbi Loew, could be avoided were the realization made that predication of attributes has our concepts rather than God's essence as its referent. For the philosopher who believes himself positing predicates which relate to the divine essence, a shift from one predicate to another would indicate an alteration in the nature of God. Since such an alteration would infer change in the divine nature and, therefore, would imply imperfection in God, the predication of many divine attributes produced a difficult problem for the philosopher. Not so for Judah Loew, who understood shifts in predication to be an indication not that God has changed, but only that our understanding of Him has. God remains above human knowledge, which is constantly in flux. For Loew, therefore, the only thing that may be said or known about God's essence is that we know nothing about it. All one may know, all one can say is that "He is a 'simple,' distinct from all beings."[10]

Amongst the essential attributes of God, predicated by medieval Jewish philosophers, was "knowledge" or "wisdom." This claim led to a conclusion, which the philosophers had to circumvent by means of additional argumentative gymnastics, namely, that a change in God's knowledge implied a change in His essence, which in turn meant a compromising of God's perfection. Positing the attribute of divine knowledge engendered a host of problems such as: Does God know future contingents? Is human choice in conflict with divine omniscience and/or divine omnipotence?, etc.[11] Rabbi Loew suggested that this nest of philosophical perplexity could simply be eliminated by denying the assumption that knowledge is an essential attribute of God and by considering it instead to be an attribution of action. In effect, without mentioning Maimonides by name, Loew adapts a Maimonidean response–attributes of action– to a problem which he identified with the philosophers in general and with Maimonides in particular. Loew assumes Maimonides' claim that attributes of action may be posited without stating any information concerning essence of the subject, in this case, God.[12]

In *Gevurot Ha-Shem* (1582), Judah Loew rebuffed what he considered the philosophical position on attribution, specifically that of Gersonides, which identified the divine intellect with the divine essence.[13] Immediately after the publication of *Gevurot Ha-Shem,* Eliezer Ashkenazi (1513-86) published a rebuttal of Loew's position. Ashkenazi's rationalist bent irked Loew into a response.[14] Rabbi Loew's rejoinder is found in the fifth chapter of *Derekh Ha-Hayyim* (1589).[15] Without mentioning Ashkenazi by name, Loew reveals enough information to allow his reader to be aware of the identity of his antagonist. After reiterating his views, stated in *Gevurot Ha-Shem*, concerning the philosopher's mistaken identity of divine knowledge and will with the divine essence, Loew relates:[16]

Behold I have heard that there was a certain individual in Poland who read that which I have written in my book *Gevurot Ha-Shem*. He filled his mouth, without limit, with disputation and disseminated vanity and lies. All of his efforts were aimed at honoring himself before others who themselves are ignorant, as is characteristic of the present generation. For they read works not imbued with the spirit of the sages, works which are of a tertiary variety of knowledge. With all this he defamed me because I had claimed that God's knowledge is not His essence, but rather one of His actions.

Loew's conceptual joust with Ashkenazi is significant not simply because it provides an opportunity to discuss problems such as the predication of divine attributes and the reconciliation of divine omniscience with human free will. It also provides Loew with the opportunity to answer his critic in order to widen the scope of his argument. Loew views his polemic with Ashkenazi not simply as an argument between two scholars on a specific theological issue. Rather, he interprets the attack upon himself as being paradigmatic of the challenge posed by Jewish philosophy to Jewish tradition in general and to the Jewish mystical tradition in particular. The thrust of the rationalist Ashkenazi stimulates Loew to demonstrate the centrality of the Jewish mystical tradition to his thought.

Ashkenazi's position is grounded in the assumption that God cannot do the impossible. He cannot, for example, duplicate Himself. He cannot know future events because, "if He knew future events, that knowledge would contradict His former knowledge when He created man with absolute free will." Ashkenazi does not perceive God's inability to do the impossible as a limitation of His omnipotence or omniscience. He infers that the logically impossible cannot exist; and, therefore, to claim that God cannot do what cannot logically be done is no limitation upon divine perfection.

Loew denies the validity of Ashkenazi's premises. To say there are things God cannot do is to limit Him. Limiting God to the *logically* possible is limiting God to the laws of logic. For Loew the mystic, God transcends all, including human logic.

Loew's attack on Ashkenazi was launched for reasons similar to those which stimulated his attack upon another contemporary, Azariah dei Rossi.[17] Like dei Rossi, Ashkenazi called for a critical, historical reevaluation of Jewish tradition. Indeed, dei Rossi even lauded Ashkenazi by name for the nobility of his humanistic efforts. According to dei Rossi, who had met Ashkenazi in Italy, he was "the outstanding authority of his generation."[18] To Rabbi

Loew, who considered the sacred literature, the Torah, the tradition, above question, the possibilities raised by Ashkenazi and dei Rossi were unthinkable. For Loew, who believed it was his task to defend tradition from its disclaimers, Ashkenazi and dei Rossi were at the vanguard of the opposition. While Rabbi Loew stressed faith, Ashkenazi claimed that faith does not ensure knowledge or certainty, and that the former is meaningless without the latter. In a proto-Cartesian vein, Ashkenazi encourages the believer to doubt his faith in order eventually to fortify his faith with intellectual certainty.[19] Loew considered this approach potentially harmful and destructive, rather than supportive of faith.

Ashkenazi took the medieval Jewish philosophical tradition to its extreme. He doubted all. He attempted rationally to demonstrate all. Ashkenazi therefore posed an essential threat to Loew's vision of Judaism. While Loew could have as easily redirected his argument on the issue of predication of attributes and divine foreknowledge against Gersonides, as he had in *Gevurot Ha-Shem*, he nevertheless chose to direct his remarks in *Derekh Ha-Ḥayyim* against Ashkenazi. Rationalism was a threat. Maimonides and Gersonides were threats. However, extreme rationalism and contemporary rationalism, coupled with the utilization of new critical tools with which to dissect the literary sources of tradition, posed an acute and immediate threat to Rabbi Loew and to his vision of Jewish religious belief. While Loew polemicizes against Maimonides and Gersonides, he virulently, almost libellously, attacks Ashkenazi and dei Rossi because they, unlike the medievals, posed a vital and immediate threat to his world view. What appears, therefore, as a discussion of the question of the predication of divine attributes and the age-old problem of reconciling divine omniscience with human freedom is in actuality only the pretext for discussion of what was for Judah Loew a more pivotal issue. Loew's clash with Ashkenazi provides an insight into the dispute between the Jewish rationalist tradition and the Jewish mystical tradition, each taken to its extreme. For Loew, the two cannot be reconciled and he makes no attempt at reconciliation. For Loew, Jewish tradition is Jewish *mystical* tradition. Jewish philosophy and rationalism are useless distortions of Judaism, unworthy of legitimacy or even toleration. In Judah Loew's words:

> There are men of an analytic bent of mind who follow their reason. They are called "philosophers." They wish to enlighten themselves concerning the order and reality of things until they

find truth. But they are foolish and walk in darkness. If they really had an interest in wisdom they would acknowledge revelation as their root-principle and would no longer grope in darkness.[20]

Since Loew believed Jewish tradition to be the ultimate source of truth, he could not understand why an individual already possessing truth would seek truth through the inadequate means of empirical observation and human reason. The Gentiles, who in Loew's view were not in possession of truth as revealed in the Torah and passed down by Jewish tradition, had a viable motivation to concern themselves with philosophy. The Torah and its proper interpretation by Jewish tradition were not available to them. The Gentiles, therefore, have no recourse but to attempt to apprehend truth by means of philosophical speculation. But why should Jews already possessing truth seek a corrupted truth in philosophy? Loew refuses to accept what he understood to be Maimonides' claim that truth may be apprehended by means of individual speculation. When one already possesses truth which derives from a supernatural source, one need not and one ought not rely upon penultimate truth gained by natural means such as rational speculation and empirical observation.[21]

Rather than relying upon their reason and their senses in their quest for truth, the Jewish philosophers should have consulted the "honored works" of the masters of the Jewish mystical tradition. By so doing, Loew insists, they would have been directed toward truth and would not have sunk into error.

For Loew, the failure of the Jewish philosophers in general and of Ashkenazi in particular with regard to the predication of divine attributes was in their not having followed the example of the Jewish mystics. The philosophers' analogy of God and the human intellect was misguided. Had they followed the example of the mystics who drew an analogy between God and the human soul, the philosophers would have obviated many of their difficulties.

According to Rabbi Loew, the essence of the human soul is unknown. All one knows of the soul are its activities, which in no way indicate its essence. God therefore ought to be compared to the human soul, which is the unknowable essence of man. God is the soul of existence, whose actions are known, but whose essence remains unknown.[22] Loew writes, "The sages of the Truth referred to the Holy One, Blessed be He, as a soul because . . . He, may He be blessed, is a soul in relationship to his attributes which are the emanations."

Loew refers specifically to the analogy of God to the soul, as found in Meir Ibn Gabbai's *Avodat Ha-Kodesh* (1568), which has been described as "perhaps the finest account of kabbalistic speculation before the resurgence of the kabbalah in Safed."[23] According to Ibn Gabbai, who echoes earlier motifs in Jewish mystical literature, God manifests Himself by means of emanations out of His essence. This essence remains unknowable and unchanged; it relates to its emanations as flames of a variety of colors emitted by a coal relate to the coal. As the coal and its flames form one organic unity, so does the divine essence and its emanations. The theory of emanation, therefore, does not infer disunity or multiplicity within God.[24] Ibn Gabbai anticipates Loew's position that the Jewish mystical tradition is Jewish tradition, originating in that which was communicated to Moses at Sinai and conveyed from teacher to student since then. Philosophy, on the other hand, claims Ibn Gabbai, is simply the attempt of individual intellectual speculation (assumed less truthworthy than tradition) to attain a variety of knowledge which cannot be attained by such means.

Rabbi Loew's mention of Ibn Gabbai alludes to the following citation in Ibn Gabbai's *Avodat Ha-Kodesh:*[25]

Not only in the activity of natural forces such as the sun and fire is this phenomenon found [i.e., the ability of one entity to engender a variety of different actions which are unrelated to its essence. Ibn Gabbai, without mentioning Maimonides by name, borrows his example. The essence of fire is heat, but one who saw only the products of the actions of fire, which are very different, could not ascertain the essence of fire simply from its actions. Fire whitens metals, reddens other metals and blackens wood. Yet the essence of fire is not whiteness, blackness or redness].[26]
...The sages of the Truth [i.e., the kabbalists] called the Holy One blessed be He "the soul of a soul." For He, may He be blessed, is a soul [in relation] to His attributes which are emanated from His light. They–these emanations–are souls because that which is above is a soul for that which is below it. Each one [is a soul] for its mate and they [all] are united in an essential unity. The substance of this analogy is such as that the human soul is one and we cannot perceive its essence but only its actions which are manifest in the limbs of the body, so–with vast differences– we are unable to perceive God except through His actions, done by means of His attributes. And just as the body cannot perform any movement without the soul which gives it vitality and purpose, so there can be no activity for the [divine] attributes if they are not present in a total unity with that from which they

emanated. Therefore, every "simple" entity, such as the soul, is one and its faculties are one with it. They are the essence of the soul and though its names vary according to the change in its actions... [some examples are given] the faculties [still] originate in the essence of the simple soul. Similarly, the *sefirot* are united in the essence of the Creator, may He be blessed. The multiplicity and the change reflect a change in activity which coalesce in the unity of the Creator. The only change which occurs is in the estimation of the recipients [i.e., man].

After noting Ibn Gabbai's analogy, Rabbi Loew reiterates his view that the Jewish mystical tradition represents the basis of Jewish religious faith and that philosophy leads to a distortion of that faith. He rebuffs the suggestion that philosophy and mysticism convey the same insights but in a different idiom. In this, Judah Loew seems to be disclaiming Moses Isserles's identification of philosophy and mysticism as well as restating Moses Cordovero's insistence upon the vital distinctions between them.[27] It is not surprising, therefore, to find Loew noting the idea of the *sefirot*, since Cordovero had indicated the doctrine of the *sefirot* to be the major difference between the teachings of the philosophers and the teachings of the mystics.[28]

Rabbi Loew, at this point, refers to Ibn Gabbai once again. The different terms used for God, the number of the *sefirot*, imply no multiplicity within God. Only God's actions seem to change, relative to the perceptions of human beings. God does not change essentially.

Rabbi Loew follows the mystics' understanding of God as an inscrutable essence, from which emanate ten *sefirot* which manifest the divine personality, though not the divine essence.[29] These *sefirot* tell us not what God is, but only what He does and how He appears to us. As the philosophers' problems with predication of divine attributes are all engendered, according to Rabbi Loew, by positing attributes of essence, awareness of the kabbalistic alternative would have obviated their difficulties. "Of what use are the things they [the philosophers] say?" writes Judah Loew. "Once one assumes God is a 'simple,' one must conclude that nothing, not even negative attributes, may be predicated of Him." Attributing no essential attributes to God, while predicating attributes of action of God identified as the *sefirot*, obviates the difficulties. For these *sefirot*, as all of the attributes we predicate of God, reflect not *His* reality, but *ours*. "It is impossible to ascribe to God, attributes from other than [those related to] this world." According to Rabbi Loew (elsewhere in *Derekh Ha-Ḥayyim*):

It is known that this material world is like a garment for the separate [i.e., supernatural] world. Just as a description of a garment does not essentially describe the wearer of the garment, but only how the garment may be described, so is God, may He be praised, described in the material world according to [the characteristics of] the material world.[30]

Continuing his discussion of Ashkenazi (in chapter 5 of *Derekh Ha-Ḥayyim*), Loew gives his readers the impression that Hasdai Crescas had shared the insight of the mystics that God is described in terms of this world and not as He is in His essence. Loew also seems to attribute to Crescas the view that the *via negativa* is an undesirable way of predicating divine attributes.

Why Loew cites a philosopher–i.e., Crescas–against a philosopher–i.e., Ashkenazi–is also problematic. Perhaps he did not identify Crescas as a philosopher, for by philosopher Loew seems to refer to the Aristoteleans and the thrust of Crescas's thought is a brutal critique of Jewish Aristoteleanism.[31]

Loew does not quote Crescas directly but relates his position as stated in *Neve Shalom*, a philosophical work by a fifteenth-century Jewish philosopher who lived in Spain, named Abraham Shalom.[32]

Whether Loew directly knew Crescas's philosophical treatise *Or Ha-Shem* is uncertain. However, Loew correctly identifies Crescas's denial of the cogency of the *via negativa* as embodied in Maimonides' thought. Crescas believed that the semantic displacement brought about by means of negative attribution is indeed logically equivalent to the affirmation of knowledge of the divine essence. Crescas dismisses the *via negativa* and opts for the predication of positive attributes. Taking a position on these positive attributes similar in principle to that of the kabbalists on the *sefirot*, Crescas argues that predicating positive attributes of God does not imply a compound subject, and hence does not compromise God's simplicity, if these qualities are understood to be interconnected and bound to the subject by inner necessity. Crescas's attributes, like the kabbalists' *sefirot*, are positive attributes which are understood to be qualities distinct from the essence of the subject, in this case God.[33] It is interesting that as an example of the relationship of God's unknowable essence to His knowable, positive attributes, Crescas utilizes the analogy later repeated by Ibn Gabbai (noted above) of the coal and the flames emitting from it. For the mystics, just as flames of different colors emit from a coal, so do the *sefirot*, which represent different qualities, emit from a single source. For Crescas:

Just as essence cannot be conceived without existence, nor existence without essence, so the attribute cannot be conceived without its subject nor the subject without its attribute; and all the attributes are comprehended in absolute goodness which is the sum total of all perfections.[34]

Both Crescas and Ibn Gabbai draw this analogy from a common source, the *Sefer Yezirah*, a pivotal work in early Jewish mystical literature which evoked the interest of both medieval Jewish rationalists and mystics.

Loew accurately reports Crescas's view that negative predication of divine attributes is not viable. The position which Loew implies Crescas held–that our predicates are drawn from the created world–is not one which Crescas may be said to have held. It ought to be remembered, however, that Rabbi Loew does not cite Crescas directly, but indirectly through Abraham Shalom's presentation of Crescas's views. It should also be noted that Shalom does not do justice to Crescas's position, either in his presentation of that position or in his critique of it.

Shalom's description of Crescas's position on attribution of positive, essential attributes is correct, though not complete. He correctly interprets Crescas's position as an attack on Maimonides' theory of negative attribution and attempts to defend Maimonides from Crescas's attack. He therefore correctly portrays Crescas's complete opposition to negative attributes, not very clearly expressed in Crescas's own writing.[35] The impression one gets from Rabbi Loew–that Crescas also held that our predicates for divine attribution are drawn from the world–is caused by the ambiguity of Loew's language and represents neither the position held by Crescas nor that represented by Shalom as being the position held by Crescas.

The question still remains why Loew quoted Crescas from Shalom's writings rather than directly. A number of possibilities present themselves. The easiest thing to assume is that Loew quotes Crescas indirectly because Crescas's original work, especially his *Or Ha-Shem*, was unavailable to him. This would explain why Loew quoted Crescas indirectly; however, it would not explain why he chose Shalom's anti-Crescas work as his source for presenting Crescas's position.

While Loew's reasons for quoting Crescas from Shalom's work cannot be known with any certainty and while the unavailability of Crescas's work to Loew is the most reasonable explanation, another possibility may be considered. In the text under analysis, Loew is stressing two major motifs: the speciousness of negative attribution and the refutation of a position, which may be assumed to be that of Moses Isserles, which describes the kabbalistic and the philosophical traditions as being essentially identical. Awareness of Loew's concern with these two motifs may explain his decision to bring Shalom into the discussion; for Shalom not only advocates negative attribution, but insists upon it. In his defense of the *via negativa* he takes the position to an extreme which insists that all divine attributes "must be negative."[36] Shalom also argues that certain teachings essential to the mystics have parallels in the teachings of the philosophers. Specifically, he refers to the doctrine of the *sefirot,* discussed in the section of Rabbi Loew's writings under consideration. He identifies the ten *sefirot* with the ten celestial intelligences described by the philosophers.[37] This identification is a gross distortion of the kabbalists' idea of the *sefirot* as understood by Rabbi Loew. For Shalom, unlike Loew, the *sefirot* are neither God nor attributes of God, but distinct beings apart from God.

It is this kind of incorrect identification between mystical and philosophical doctrines which Loew may have had in mind when he decided to link his discussion of the relationship of philosophy to mysticism with his discussion of the attribution of divine predicates. In his insistence upon a sharp distinction between philosophy and mysticism, Judah Loew may have had Abraham Shalom clearly in mind.

Returning to his polemic with Ashkenazi, Rabbi Loew rhetorically asks why Ashkenazi did not refer to the teachings of a second mystical treatise, *Ma'arekhet Ha-Elohut.* If he had done so, he would have learned the true teachings of Jewish faith on the nature of God and would not have been led astray. Loew refers specifically to the seventh chapter of this mystical text, written anonymously in the early fourteenth century and first published in 1558.[38] According to this text, the *sefirot* relate to their source as rays of the sun relate to the sun. Their emanation does not imply a diminishing of their source, nor does it reveal the essence of their source.

According to Rabbi Loew, the *sefirot* of the kabbalists and Crescas's predication of divine attributes provide a manner in which positive attributes may be predicated of God without revealing His essence and without compromising His simplicity. Had the philosophers recognized and utilized this manner of predication of divine attributes, Rabbi Loew claims, they would not have had to devise their circuitous manner of predicating divine attributes, specifically by negative attributes. Judah Loew sums up his pro-kabbalistic position as follows:

> The kabbalists ascribed [positive] attributes to Him [i.e., God] which do not add [any qualities to His essence]. The kabbalists called these by the general term–*sefirot*. It is hereby explained to you that the sages of the kabbalah dispute the philosophers concerning this very matter. For according to the kabbalists there are essential attributes of God. Even so, according to the structure of the *sefirot* which include: *hokhmah, binah* (and the remaining *sefirot*), they [the *sefirot*] are only attributes [of God] and do not represent His essence at all. . . . What he [Ashkenazi?] wrote, claiming that they [the philosophers] removed attributes from God, because if He had attributes they would be added to His essence [and therefore would compromise His simplicity], has already been clearly refuted by Rabbi Hasdai [Crescas] as is explained in the book *Neve Shalom*.

Rabbi Loew's presentation of the God-idea by means of the peculiarly kabbalistic notion of the *sefirot* demonstrates his identification with the kabbalists. Rabbi Loew mentions the *sefirot* many times in his work both overtly and implicitly. The *sefirot* reflect ultimate reality as well as the reality of the physical universe. The *sefirot,* for example, reflect God the Macrocosm; however, they also reflect man the microcosm. Just as the *sefirot* are described in a configuration approximating human form, so do the limbs of man correspond to the *sefirot*. The five pairs of organs–two eyes, two ears, two hands, two legs, and penis and mouth–are identified by Rabbi Loew with the ten *sefirot*.[39] In so doing, he is following well-established kabbalistic precedent, which identifies the limbs of the human body with the *sefirot*.[40]

In the kabbalistic mode of biblical and talmudic exegesis, Rabbi Loew understood certain classical texts to refer, on a symbolic level, to happenings in the realm of the *sefirot*. According to one text, for example, "Ten miracles were wrought for our ancestors in the Temple in Jerusalem" (Av. 5:7). According to Loew, these ten miracles correspond to the ten *sefirot*.[41] "Abraham faced ten tests of his faith" (Av. 5:4). Rabbi Loew interprets each of the tests of faith as corresponding to one of the *sefirot*.[42]

Rabbi Loew interprets various parts of the liturgy as corresponding to certain of the *sefirot*. [43] He sometimes explicitly and sometimes implicitly follows the kabbalistic method of identifying
biblical characters, especially the Patriarchs, and Matriarchs, and
David, with various *sefirot*. [44] He identifies different areas of Jewish
literature–Bible, Mishnah, Talmud–with individual *sefirot*. [45]
Following the pattern of the kabbalists, he identifies right and left
with male and female, good and potentially impure sides of the
structure of the *sefirot*. Like the kabbalists, he assumes that evil,
change, and fragmentation in "this world" derive from the "left
side" of the *sefirot*. [46]

One may conclude from the above discussion of Judah Loew's
views on the nature of God that his position on this question derives
from and is expressive of the idea of God as it had been developed
in Jewish mystical literature until his time. Whether Rabbi Loew's
views concerning predication of divine attributes are cogent or not
is not at issue here. Whether Loew fairly or accurately presented
the position of medieval Jewish philosophy in general, or of
Ashkenazi in particular, is not the thrust of the present analysis.
What is of importance here is the question of Judah Loew's attitude
toward the Jewish mystical and the Jewish philosophical traditions,
as they relate to the predication of divine attributes.

What this analysis has attempted to demonstrate is that, for
Loew, Jewish tradition is Jewish mystical tradition; that Jewish
medieval philosophy, culminating for Loew in the writings of
Eliezer Ashkenazi, is an unnecessary and inauthentic threat to
what Loew perceived Judaism to be. Rabbi Loew emerges from the
present analysis as one who felt obliged to articulate the kabbalistic
idea of God in the face of what he perceived as a vital threat to
tradition from the philosophers. While Loew often chooses to
enunciate kabbalistic ideas in non-kabbalistic terminology, such is
not the case in the text analyzed above. When provoked by the
rationalist Ashkenazi, Loew the mystic unabashedly appears. [47]
Thus, while representatives of the Jewish philosophical tradition,
such as Maimonides, Gersonides, and Ashkenazi, considered
philosophical speculation a religious obligation, Rabbi Loew perceived it as a gateway to heresy. [48] While some medieval Jewish
philosophers believed philosophical analysis a means toward
attaining a true and accurate understanding of the Torah, Loew
believed it a means of disfiguring the content of Jewish tradition.

Judah Loew considered philosophy to be either superfluous
or antithetical to religious tradition. While some of his

contemporaries held philosophy and mysticism to be two means of expressing the same religious truth, Loew claimed that only the Jewish mystical tradition and not the Jewish philosophical tradition may claim validity and authenticity.[49] In the following passage, Rabbi Loew enunciates his attitude to both philosophy and mysticism. The stance he takes here permeates all of his work:

> In summation it can be stated that these people [the philosophers] challenge the entire Jewish mystical tradition. Whosoever perceives this knows that everything is grounded in the foundation of the wisdom of the mystical tradition (*kabbalah*) . . . Individuals who heed their [i.e., the philosophers'] teachings which have now–because of our sins–become wide-spread, have concluded that these teachings are as if they derived from Mosaic tradition. They are shocked if one challenges them. When they [the philosophers] study kabbalah they accommodate its teachings [to philosophy] and indicate that they [i.e., philosophy and kabbalah] are true. They do not realize that they are attempting to reconcile two things which are contradictory and opposite. The philosophers claim that only terminology distinguishes [the two world-views], that the same thing is said in the language of the kabbalists as that which is said in the language of the philosophers–as if this would resolve the contradictions between them! All of this is the result of the folly of individuals who do not understand; if they knew and understood these things, they would know that they [i.e. kabbalah and philosophy] are diametrically opposed.[50]

Thus, for Judah Loew, the attempt to submit religious truth to rational analysis is doomed to failure. Jewish tradition, specifically Jewish mystical tradition, is the gateway to supernal, ultimate truth. Jewish philosophy at its best can only hope to provide penultimate truth. But, as its worst, Jewish philosophy is a gateway to heresy. For Judah Loew, neither rationality nor philosophical inquiry can determine truth or falsity; only tradition–specifically Jewish mystical tradition–can do so. Faith, grounded in tradition, is the criterion by which the doctrines of philosophy are to be examined. Tradition measures philosophy; philosophy cannot evaluate tradition.

7

The Nature of the Torah

Judah Loew understands the Torah to be an intermediary between opposites, a synthesis of opposites. For Loew, the Torah serves as a link between the divine realm and the human realm, between the supernatural and the natural dimensions of existence. To comprehend Rabbi Loew's description of the nature of the Torah, therefore, one must first grasp his theory of opposites.

According to Loew, there are two kinds of opposites: "complementary" and "contradictory," the mutually inclusive and the mutually exclusive.[1] These two varieties of opposites are reflected in two kinds of relationships "form" may have to "matter." Form (*zurah*) may be implanted within matter (*homer*); or it may exist together with matter, but remain essentially apart from it.[2] When form is implanted within matter it is affected by the condition of that matter. When form exists together with matter, what happens to that matter leaves the form unaffected.

Everything consists of form and matter.[3] What is one thing's form may be another thing's matter. What is one thing's matter may be another thing's form. Only God is ultimately form. There is no form of which He is its matter. Only His form does not essentially require corresponding matter.[4]

Everything, except God, exists in a condition of dialectical opposition. Only God is truly one. Everything else exists in a state of fragmented disunity.[5] While God transcends all disunity, He is both the source and the resolution of all disunity and of all fragmentation.[6] The existence of any entity except God implies the existence of another entity which either complements it or contrasts with it.[7]

According to Loew, complementary opposites share some essential quality in common. Incomplete when apart, they are whole when together. The existence of one implies coexistence with the other. One is form befitting a peculiar kind of matter. The other is matter receptive only to a peculiar type of form. Once together, matter and form strive for the variety of perfection peculiar to their own nature. For complementary opposites, matter cannot be perfected unless its corresponding form has also been perfected. Similarly, form depends upon the perfection of its corresponding matter in order to attain its own perfection.[8]

Besides complementary opposites, there are also contradictory opposites. While complementary opposites are mutually inclusive, contradictory opposites are mutually exclusive. For contradictory opposites the existence of one *logically* implies the existence of the other; however, the *presence* of one requires the obliteration of the other. There can be no coexistence, no relationship, no mutuality of essence or purpose between contradictory opposites. One is form and the other is matter. In this case, form and matter do not coalesce, but are essentially inhospitable one to the other. They are at odds. The strength of one implies the weakness of the other. The relationship is accidental, not essential. Form can exist without its matter and should strive to do so.[9] Their only possibility for reconciliation is by means of an intermediary. They cannot directly reconcile; however, indirectly, in an entity which represents a synthesis of both of them, which embodies elements of each of them, indirect reconciliation can occur. The imposition of a third entity, an intermediary, may produce a synthesis between an otherwise irreconcilable thesis and antithesis.[10]

For purposes of clarification, examples of these two kinds of opposites will presently be given. An example of the role of the intermediary as synthesis of irreconcilable opposites will then be offered. The relationship of Loew's theory of opposites to his view of the nature of the Torah will then be examined.

Male and female are examples of complementary opposites. The male is form; the female is matter. One cannot exist without the other. Male implies female and female implies male. Man needs woman and woman needs man. Both need each other to achieve the quality of perfection peculiar to each. Apart, they are incomplete, bereft of all opportunity for perfection. Together, they are of a single essence. Together, they provide each other with an opportunity to realize the purpose of their individual existences. Pulling in separate directions, their existence can never be truly actualized. Only tension, disharmony, and imperfection would prevail. But pulling together toward their common goal they can achieve perfection.[11]

There are many contradictory pairs of opposites; for example: the material and the spiritual, the natural realm and the supernatural realm, the righteous and the wicked, "this world" and the World to Come, the Jew and the Gentile. These pairs of opposites are not unrelated. The material, the temporal, the changeable, the physical, the natural, the "this-worldly," and the Gentile are related concepts, as are the spiritual, the intellectual, the supernatural, and the other-worldly and the Jew. Each class is internally coherent and exclusive of the other class.

The body is material. Like all material entities, it is subject to change and corruption. It dwells in the dimensions of time and space. It is attached to the material world, the world of motion, "this world" (*olam ha-zeh*). Privation, sin, imperfection characterize this dimension of existence. "This-worldly" existence typifies Gentile existence. It exemplifies the accidental, the temporal, the potential, the fragmented, as opposed to the essential, the eternal, the actualized, the unified.[12] The intellect (*seikhel*), on the other hand, is spiritual. Like all spiritual entities, it transcends change and corruption, time and space. It typifies the essential, the actual, the World to Come. For Loew, the essence of the Jew epitomizes this dimension of timeless, eternal, spiritual existence. These two dimensions of existence: material and spiritual, "this-worldly" and "next-worldly," temporal and eternal, Jew and Gentile represent examples of irreconcilable, contradictory opposites. The vitality of one implies the weakness of the other. The ascent of one implies the descent of the other. The victory of one means the defeat of the other. When the body (*guf*) is weakened, the intellect (*seikhel*) is strengthened.[13] When the power of Esau or Amalek triumphs, the vitality of Israel is diminished.[14] If the Jew, symbolized by fire, attempts reconciliation with the Gentile, symbolized by water, only obliteration and not reconciliation can ensue. Water can extinguish fire. Fire can cause water to evaporate.[15] According to the biblical narrative Esau (Edom) and Jacob (Israel) were twins who fought even in their mother's womb. For Loew, Esau represents the Gentile, the "this-worldly." Jacob symbolizes the Jew, the "other-worldly." The twins fought in the womb out of necessity. When two irreconcilable opposites came together, conflict must ensue.[16] According to the Talmud, Solomon's marriage to Pharaoh's daughter eventually led to his demise. This, too, was inevitable. Solomon represents Israel while Pharaoh represents Esau (Edom). The two, by their nature cannot coexist. Their attempt at reconciliation must out of necessity lead to the demise of one. Solomon's demise came about because he attempted reconciliation with his contradictory opposite.[17] Similarly, Loew reads the biblical injunction upon the Jews to obliterate Amalek according to his theory of contradictory opposites. The biblical Book of Esther is read in a similar vein. Following the tradition identifying Haman with Esau and Amalek, Rabbi Loew contends that the clash between Mordecai and Haman, Israel and Amalek, had of necessity to result in the obliteration of one or the other. Coexistence could not be possible.[18]

Contradictory opposites must remain as thesis and antithesis, irreconcilable, distinct, separate, and apart. Though direct relationship is not possible, the coalescence of qualities of each in a third entity is possible. In a separate entity, by means of a synthesis, indirect coexistence may obtain. What may not be attained by two entities may obtain in a third entity.

The notion of synthesis in an intermediary or "center" (*emza*) is vital to Loew's thought.[19] He often utilizes this notion to explain important concepts and to elucidate the "inner meaning" of biblical and rabbinic texts. Loew's interpretation of the biblical story of Cain and Abel provides an example of this theory of contradictory opposites and their reconciliation in a synthesis.[20]

According to biblical law one is forbidden to wear a garment containing wool and linen (Deut. 22:11). Flax, Loew argues, being a product of the farmer, is the irreconcilable opposite of wool, which is the product of the sheepherder. As linen, a derivative of flax, is the opposite of wool, so is the farmer the opposite of the sheepherder. Having established this dichotomy, Loew applies it to the biblical story of Cain and Abel. Cain was a sheepherder and Abel was a flax farmer. Being irreconcilable, contradictory opposites, it was only to be expected that one would kill the other. It was impossible for them to coexist. However, once Abel was dead, Cain no longer had a corresponding opposite. Since the existence of everything implies the existence of its opposite, Abel had to be replaced. Since replacing Abel with another contradictory opposite would have yielded the identical result–the annihilation of one of the brothers–Cain was provided with another alternative. Another brother, Seth, was born to replace Abel. But rather than being Cain's contradictory opposite, Seth represented a synthesis between Cain and Abel. Cain could, therefore, coexist with Seth.

In the course of his writings, Loew gives many other examples of syntheses, some of which will be discussed in some detail below. The Patriarch Jacob, for example, is considered the synthesis between the earlier Patriarchs Abraham and Isaac.[21] The Messianic Era is the synthesis between "this world" and the World to Come. The "middle world" (*olam ha-emza'i*) is the synthesis between the material, lower world and the supernal, spiritual world.[22] Man is the synthesis between the animal and the angel. The psyche (*nefesh*) is the synthesis between the body and the intellect (*seikhel*).

The intermediary or the synthesis represents the third entity in a series, i.e., thesis, antithesis, and synthesis. For Loew, who believed that numbers have a quiddity, a reality, a nature of their own, this was not coincidence.[23] Like many mystics, Loew believed that the odd numbers in general, and the number "three" in particular, have a special significance.[24] This significance, he believed, is exemplified by the synthesis. Jacob, who represented the synthesis of Abraham and Isaac's qualities, was the third Patriarch.[25] The revelation of Sinai, which represents the classical example of synthesis between spiritual and physical, man and God, occurred on the third day of the third month. Moses, the intermediary between man and God, who for Loew represents a synthesis between man and God, was the third child in his family (after Aaron and Miriam) and was from the third tribe of Israel, Levi (after Reuben and Simeon).[26] The number "three," which symbolizes the synthesis, represents perfection, completion, and unity. The third entity insures unity between two opposites. For example, two juxtaposed lines represent a lack of unity; however, the imposition of a third line composes a triangle, which represents unity, completeness.[27]

The number "one," which represents the thesis, is perfect in itself as it is indivisible. The number "two," however, which represents the irreconcilable antithesis, is divisible and consequently has no real existence. Hell, which represents the privation of existence, is designated by the number "two." The number "three," representing the synthesis, is the first multiple, single-digit, indivisible number. Loew identifies it with sanctity and perfection. While the number "two" represents irreconcilable fragmentation, the number "three" represents unity. It is the first "complete number."[28]

From what has already been said, it should be apparent that Loew's theory of opposites and his notion of synthesis are keys to attaining a comprehensive understanding of his thought. Some implications these theories hold for comprehending his views on a number of issues will be examined in future chapters. In the present chapter, however, discussion will be confined to the implications of these ideas for Judah Loew's understanding of the nature of the Torah.

The Torah links corporeal man with the incorporeal God. The Torah is an intermediary (*emza'i*) between God and man.[29] The Torah is the knot between the upper and the lower dimensions of existence.[30] By linking God and man, the Torah provides the opportunity for human fulfillment, human perfection, human relationship with the divine.[31]

According to Loew, the goal of religious existence is for one to attain an intimate relationship with the divine, a cleaving *(devekut)* to God. This cleaving, however, necessitates the bringing together of two opposites–man and God. To accomplish this goal, therefore, an intermediary consisting of both spiritual and physical dimensions is required. The Torah is such an intermediary.[32]

The Torah may be construed as a synthesis between the natural and the supernatural, the material and the spiritual, because it embraces elements of both dimensions. In its essence, the Torah is spiritual. In its manifestation, the Torah relates to the physical dimension. The spiritual aspect is essential while the physical dimension is accidental.

The supernatural dimension of the Torah relates to qualities associated with the spiritual realm. The Torah is identified with the *sefirot.*[33] Like the *sefirot,* "the Torah, which is the origin of all," emanated from God.[34] In fact, it is the first emanation from, and the first effect of the divine essence.[35] "Just as a daughter issues from the essence of her father, so the Torah [issues from the essence of God].[36]

Judah Loew frequently describes the Torah as "a tree rooted in God." The use of this simile is undoubtedly drawn from the kabbalistic identification of the sefirotic construct with a tree, the roots of which emanate out of the divine essence.[37]

Following the pattern of the earlier kabbalists, Loew identifies the essence of the Torah with the *sefirah* of "Divine Knowledge" (*hokhmah*) as well as the *sefirah* of "Glory" (*tiferet*).[38] It is no coincidence that Loew's volume on the Torah and revelation is entitled *Tiferet Yisrael.* Like all of his major works, the title of this work contains the name of one of the *sefirot.*

Rabbi Loew identifies the Torah with the "divine intellect" which the kabbalists often identified with the *sefirah* of "Divine Knowledge" (*hokhmah*).[39] As an essentially supernatural entity, the Torah enjoys characteristics peculiar to the supernatural realm. It is a distinct, separate, intellectual (*sikhli*) entity. It is transtemporal, eternal, static. As such, Loew identifies the Torah with the "next-worldly," the *Olam Ha-Ba.* In his words, "As those who are wise and understand [i.e., mystics] know, the Torah is itself the *Olam Ha-Ba.*" According to Zoharic literature, the *Olam Ha-Ba* is identical with the *sefirah* of "Divine Knowledge."[40]

Only because the Torah also has another side to its nature is it able to function as an intermediary between man and God. "The Torah has two distinct dimensions. From one, it has a relationship with man, but from the other it enjoys no relationship with man [but only with God]."[41]

Though man is essentially undeserving of the Torah, part of it becomes his because of divine grace. The essence of the Torah, as the essence of God, remains inscrutable from the perspective of man. Just as the *sefirot* are the outer manifestations of the inscrutable God, and the human body the outer garb of the inscrutable soul, so is an outer garb required for the Torah to become manifest in the physical realm.

"The Torah, itself," writes Loew, "cannot come into the [i.e., this] world without a[n] [outer] garb . . . just as the soul cannot exist in the world without a body which is the garb of the soul."[42]

Without this garb to shield the meeting of the two opposites–essentially physical man and the essentially spiritual Torah–obliteration would ensue. The Torah would not be able to play its role as intermediary between the man and God.

The above-noted comparison between the essence of the Torah and its outer manifestations with the human soul and the human body seems to be drawn from the following statement in the Zohar:

> Rabbi Simeon said: If a man looks upon the Torah as merely a book presenting narratives and everyday matters, alas for him! Such a torah, one treating with everyday concerns, and indeed a more excellent one, we too, even we could compile. More than that, in the possession of the rulers of the world there are books of even greater merit, and these we could emulate if we wished to compile some such torah. But the Torah, in all of its words, holds supernal truths and sublime secrets.
>
> See how precisely balanced are the upper and the lower worlds. Israel here below is balanced by the angels on high, concerning whom it stands written: "who makest thy angels into winds" [Ps. 104:4]. For when the angels descend to earth they don earthly garments, else they could neither abide in the world, nor could it bear to have them. But if this is so with the angels, then how much more so it must be with the Torah: the Torah it was that created the angels and created all the worlds and through Torah are all sustained. The world could not endure the Torah if she had not garbed herself in garments of this world.

Thus the tales related in the Torah are simply her outer garments, and woe to the man who regards that outer garb as the Torah itself, for such a man will be deprived of a portion in the next world. Thus David said: "Open Thou mine eyes, that I may behold wondrous things out of Thy Law" [Ps. 119:18], that is to say, the things that are underneath. See now. The most visible part of a man are the clothes that he has on, and they who lack understanding, when they look at the man, are apt not to see more in him than these clothes. In reality, however, it is the body of the man that constitutes the pride of his body.

So it is with the Torah. Its narrations which relate to things of the world constitute the garments which clothe the body of the Torah; and that body is composed of the Torah's precepts, *gufei-torah* [bodies, major principles]. People without understanding see only the narrations, the garment; those somewhat more penetrating see also the body. But the truly wise, those who serve the most high King and stood on mount Sinai, pierce all the way through to the soul, to the true Torah, which is the root principle of all. These same will in the future be vouchsafed to penetrate to the very soul of the soul of the Torah.

See now how it is like this in the highest world, with garment, body, soul and super-soul. The outer garments are the heavens and all therein, the body is the Community of Israel and it is the recipient of the soul, that is "the Glory of Israel"; and the soul of the soul is the Ancient Holy One. All of these are conjoined one within the other.

Woe to the sinners who look upon the Torah as simply tales pertaining to things of the world, seeing thus only the outer garment. But the righteous whose gaze penetrates to the very Torah, happy are they. Just as wine must be in a jar to keep, so the Torah must be contained in an outer garment. That garment is made up of tales and stories; but we, we are bound to penetrate beyond.[43]

For Loew, the Torah, though essentially spiritual, also has a material, "this-worldly" dimension. The narratives of Scripture reflect this dimension as do the commandments. By means of the commandments, which represent the fusing of the spiritual and the material, the human and the divine, the Torah can function as an intermediary between God and man, and can lead man to God.

According to Rabbi Loew, the spiritual Torah requires a material form, a "physical carrier," a "body," in order for it to become efficacious in "this world."[44] Though the essence of the Torah, which emanated from the divine essence, is totally spiritual, the commandments represent an amalgamation of the spiritual and the physical aspects of the Torah. The commandments are the "center," the liaison between man and God. In Loew's words, "man and the [essence of the] Torah are two distinct entities, unrelated one to the other."[45] "Man is corporeal [homri] while the Torah is 'simple intellect' [seikhel pashut]."[46] The commandment (mizvah), however, relies upon human activity, that is, activity related to the human body and to corporeality. "By means of this [i.e., the commandments], the [essentially] intellectual Torah becomes fitting for man."[47]

Thus, the essence of the Torah, being intellectual (sikhli) in nature, relates to the human intellect (seikhel). The commandments, on the other hand, relate to the body which is physical and which governs the concrete, physical activities performed by the body.[48]

The physical form the Torah assumes in "this world"–the biblical narratives and the commandments–reflect "this world." Human perfection in "this world" by means of the commandments means the realization of "this world" (i.e., of the material dimension of existence). This is the essence of the messianic fulfillment. It does not mean, however, that man is free of the commandments or that he has a grasp of the essential content of the Torah. In "this world," the essence of the Torah must elude man.[49]

Though they have a physical dimension, the commandments also have a spiritual quality. In that performance of the commandments brings man closer to God, the commandments themselves cannot be totally physical and material in nature.[50] Though the commandments are laws, they are a peculiar variety of law–divine law. They cannot, therefore, be compared with other varieties of law. They cannot be justified by human reason.[51]

Loew lists what he considers the three varieties of law in an ascending order of importance: rational or natural, conventional, and divine. According to Loew, the third variety, unlike the first two, represents the supernatural, the metaphysical.

By drawing an analogy between certain of the commandments and natural law, by thereby equating the product of revelation with the product of reason, Saadya attempts to offer a rational defense for at least some of the commandments. Loew rejects this approach. Like Albo, he asserts that all of the divine commandments transcend the natural, the rational, and the conventional.[52]

Having made an essential distinction between law grounded in revelation and other varieties of law, Loew concludes the impossibility, if not the absurdity, of an attempt to examine the suprarational by means of the rational. He adamantly rejects what he perceived as an attempt to reduce or to compare the revealed commandments to natural or to conventional laws with a view to analyzing them according to a rationalist criterion. He rejects the reductionist attempt to construe the Torah as a book of science, ethics, or natural law. For once that is done, one is drawn to assent to the conclusion Loew fervently opposed, namely, that Torah and its commandments may be examined according to the methods peculiar to science, logic, etc.[53] For Loew, the Torah is divine, it is a metaphysical, supranatural entity. Any attempt to relegate it to the physical, natural realm is to compromise it and to distort it. One need not, nor should one, attempt to offer a rational defense; even if such an approach would yield correct conclusions, such results would be peripheral, penultimate. According to Loew, such findings might represent *a* reason, but not *the* reason for religious observance. "How," Loew rhetorically queries, "can one attempt to offer reasons for that which derives from the supernatural dimension when one cannot even explain all that which occurs in the natural dimension of existence?"[54]

According to Loew, the basic assumption upon which the attempt to discover a rational justification for the religious commandments is based is faulty. That assumption is that the commandments, like natural law and convention, are primarily aimed at fulfilling human needs. The attempt to justify the commandments rationally is to demonstrate their utility for human beings. Loew categorically rejects this approach to Jewish religious law. For Loew, the commandments are theocentric in origin and meaning. In contrast to those who seek rational explanations for the commandments, Loew seeks none, for none can be known with any certainty. He writes, "From the teachings of our sages it appears incorrect to assert that God gave the commandments for the sake of the recipient, i.e., man. They are simply decrees from the divine."[55]

For Judah Loew the reasons for observance elude man. They should not be sought out. They cannot be known. Man must be content with the knowledge that in some manner which he cannot apprehend, observing the commandments brings him closer to the divine. The way to God is the way of God. The commandments are similar to royal decrees; as such, they must be obeyed without question. Their individual purpose, their relative importance, one to the other, cannot be known by human beings. Such information may only be known to the King and Commander.

By virtue of its spiritual dimension, the Torah evokes the spiritual potential in man. Without the Torah, specifically without the commandments, the human being would be a prisoner of the natural realm. Without the commandments, he would not be distinguishable from other natural creatures, e.g., from animals. Without the Torah, man would be bereft of all possible relationship with God. Without the Torah, he would be inextricably bound to the temporal, to the natural. He would die and nothing would remain. The commandments of the Torah elevate man out of the natural realm.[56] By means of the Torah, man may become attached to the transtemporal realm. By means of the Torah, he may acquire permanence, eternal life.[57] One may summarize Judah Loew's position on this issue with his own words:

> By means of the Torah the celestial and the terrestrial are joined. . . .[58] By means of the Torah, Israel may cleave to God and may be liberated from [the conditions of] the material world. . . . By means of the Torah man realizes his "separate intellect" [seikhel nivdal], distinct from matter. Then, he becomes a perfect and beneficent creature, worthy of existence. The perfection of man's essence, therefore, only occurs by means of the Torah. There is no other [means by which to attain it].[59]

As the Torah is an intermediary between man and God, a synthesis of the physical and the spiritual, the human and the divine, so is Moses such a synthesis, such an intermediary. It was not a coincidence, therefore, that the Torah was revealed to Israel through Moses. Though talmudic and medieval Jewish literature described Moses in the highest human superlatives, considerable caution was exercised lest the figure of Moses become magnified beyond human proportions, lest qualities of divinity be ascribed to the greatest prophet in Jewish tradition.[60] Even Maimonides, for example, who counts the belief in the supremacy of Moses over all past and future prophets as a basic principle of Judaism, who elevates Moses over the Messiah, ascribes no divine qualities to him.[61]

Unlike many of his talmudic and medieval predecessors, Judah Loew does not hesitate to ascribe spiritual, even divine qualities to Moses. As the intermediary between God and man, Moses necessarily emerges as a synthesis of God and man. Loew's theory of synthesis logically requires the Torah, which is the intermediary between man and God and a synthesis of materiality and spirituality, to be given by a person who also exemplifies these qualities.

Rabbi Loew attempts to defend the validity of his bold position by appealing to a verse in Scripture and to a precedent in rabbinic literature for interpreting that verse as he does. Psalm 90 begins with the verse–"A prayer of Moses *ish-ha-elohim.*" This Hebrew phrase is usually translated "the man of God." Loew, however, translates it literally to mean "the man-God." His precedent for such a translation, besides the literal meaning of the words themselves, is an interpretation found in the *Midrash on Psalms.* Relating to this verse, Rabbi Abin said: "From his middle and above Moses was called 'God,' and from his middle and below he was a man."[62] With this text apparently in mind, Judah Loew writes:

[Because the Torah is peculiarly unique it was only fitting that it be given by Moses who was also peculiarly unique.][63] And because of Moses' high quality and the uniqueness of him as a prophet it [the Torah] is called by his name [i.e., *Torat Mosheh*– Moses' Torah]. For though this man, Moses, was from the terrestrial realm [*min ha-taḥtonim*], he was most highly exalted so that Scripture describes him as being "a little lower than the divine" [Ps. 8:5]. Concerning him Scripture [also says], "Who [else] ascended to heaven and [subsequently] descended?" [Prov. 30:4]. Therefore, since Moses was of the terrestrial and of the heavenly as it is said–Moses is called the man-God–from his waist downward he was man and from his waist upward he was God– one must necessarily conclude that he was like an intermediary [*emza'i*] between the celestial and the terrestrial, for an intermediary is fused [*mezuraf*] to both [elements]. Therefore, in that "he ascended to heaven and descended," Moses is judged as an intermediary, as it is written–I [Moses] stand between God and you [i.e., the people of Israel]. Consequently, the [Hebrew] letter "mem" which is the first letter of Moses' name is the middle [*emza'it*] letter in the [Hebrew] alphabet.[64]

Thus, just as the Torah is the intermediary between man and God and a synthesis of the celestial and the terrestrial, so is Moses, who brings the Torah to man in general and to Israel in particular. Just as the Torah, as synthesis, is symbolized by the number "three," so is Moses, who is the third child in a family belonging to the third tribe and who receives the Torah on the third day of the third month.[65] Just as the Torah may bring man into a state of perfection and actuality, so does Moses by transmitting the Torah to Israel.[66] Just as the essence of the Torah is spiritual and its manifestations are material, its essence form and its expression matter, its spiritual aspect essential and its physical aspect accidental, so according to

Rabbi Loew is Moses' essence, spiritual and holy.[67] Like the Torah, which emanates from God, "Moses' soul was of the holiest of holies. It emanated from the highest heights and renewed the world."[68] Like the essence of the Torah, Moses' essence is distinct divine form.[69] Moses' essence, like that of the Torah, assumed physical form, and, like the Torah's essence, Moses' essence remained "distinct from matter."[70]

Thus, for Judah Loew, the Torah represents a synthesis of the spiritual and the physical, of God and the world. Moses represents a synthesis of the spiritual and the physical, of God and man.[71] These two intermediaries are means of explaining how the otherwise contradictory opposites of God and the world, of God and man, may be related one to the other. Only a synthesis may link such opposites. The Torah and Moses, being such syntheses, can effect such a relationship.

8

Jew and Gentile:
Theoretical Considerations

As the previous chapter noted, Judah Loew considered Moses to be a "man-God," a synthesis of the human and the divine. While any other individual man is a particular example of his species, Moses is a species in and of himself. While other human beings share a common rung on the "chain of being," Moses occupies his own rung.

According to Rabbi Loew, Moses was essentially different from all other human beings.[1] While the souls of other men are implanted within their bodies and are, therefore, subject to the vicissitudes of the body, Moses' soul was distinct from his body. His soul was "a holy of holies, [which] had emanated from the most exalted rung."[2] While other men are somewhat influenced by matter, Moses was essentially pure form, distinct from the influences of matter.[3] Moses simultaneously represented a "distinct level of divinity" and a unique variety of humanity.[4] Whereas other men are particular effects of a particular cause–their parents–not so Moses. Natural men have a natural cause; Moses, however, was not a natural man and could not therefore have a natural cause.

Moses' soul preexisted the creation of the world. He was created by God. His parents only served to bring him *into* this world. While the essence of other men is derived from their parents, while the nature of other men would differ had they had other parents, such was not true of Moses. Amram and Jochebed were the parents of Moses' brother, Aaron. They determined Aaron's nature, but not that of Moses. Who Moses' parents were was accidental. His essence preceded his existence. It transcended his biological parents.[5]

As the sole member of a class of being, it was Moses' function to serve as the form for the class of beings immediately below. For Rabbi Loew, that class is the people of Israel. In other words, Moses is the form of which the people Israel is the matter. Moses is the essence of which Israel is the accident. As Israel's form, it was Moses' task to make them a people by giving them the Torah, "the Torah of Moses." It was to be Moses' task, determined at creation, to provide his matter with purpose, with distinct identity and with the means of attaining perfection–i.e., the Torah. Furthermore, of the two types of relationship form may have to matter–form implanted within matter and form detached from matter–the relationship between Moses and Israel is of the latter variety; Moses' relationship to Israel is that of form detached from its matter. In relation to Israel, Moses is "separately divine" (*nivdal elohi*). It is his task to perfect his matter, to give it form, purpose, direction, and actuality. Consequently, Israel became a people only through Moses. Before Moses, Israel was matter devoid of form.[6]

The covenant made with Abraham, renewed by Isaac and later by Jacob, was a covenant made between God and an individual, not between God and a people. Only with the Exodus led by Moses and only with the Torah of Moses did Israel become a people. Egypt was the womb out of which Israel would be born. When Israel was in Egypt, it existed only in potential. With the Exodus, its existence became reality; Israel was born. Before the Exodus, Israel was dominated by matter. With the Exodus, Israel secured its own distinct form.[7]

According to Rabbi Loew, the genesis of the people of Israel was not accidental. What happens to individuals may be accidental, but an event such as the Exodus, embellished with miracles and climaxed by the theophany at Sinai, experienced by an entire people, could not be accidental. As these events of liberation and revelation are unique, the people thus created must be unique.[8] As the Torah is eternal and as the Giver of the Torah is eternal, so is the recipient of the Torah eternal.[9]

Israel was not redeemed from Egypt, fashioned as a people and given the Torah because of its merits, nor because of the merits of the Patriarchs of Israel. Israel became a people and is sustained as a people because of divine grace.[10] Israel's peculiar receptivity to the revelation at Sinai was because of the innate quality of the souls of its members, a factor which essentially differentiates it from other peoples.[11]

Throughout his writings Rabbi Loew insists that God's choice of Israel cannot be rationally justified. It was not a quid pro quo but an act rooted in divine mystery and in divine passion. It may well be that Rabbi Loew's opting for election by grace rather than for election for merit was part of his attempt to rebut Christian claims that the sins of Israel caused God to reject them just as the merit of their ancestors caused God to elect them. By claiming election by grace, the question of whether Israel's election was related to their merits or demerits becomes irrelevant. Election by grace relies solely upon the divine initiative. It is unrelated to human action. Therefore, Israel's degraded state in the world need not imply that it has been rejected by God, that its election has been terminated. As long as the election was never contingent upon deeds, it cannot be assumed terminated because of human deeds. The dejected state of Israel in "this world" testifies to its election and not its rejection by God. The power of the Gentile peoples in "this world" only demonstrates that while "this world" is the province of the Gentiles, the World to Come, the super- natural dimension, is the realm of Israel. The Gentiles achieve their perfection in the temporal realm. Israel's perfection, its fulfillment, is vouchsafed for the World to Come. For Rabbi Loew, the material and social conditions of Israel in "this world" do not testify to divine rejection engendered by sin. Israel's dejection in "this world" can only affirm one's faith in the divine election of Israel by divine grace. [12]

In response to those who claim Israel's dispersal throughout the world is an indication of divine rejection, Rabbi Loew offers a sharp retort. Israel's continued existence, despite hostile condi- tions, only testifies to the providential cause of Israel's continued existence. [13] In the identical situation any other people would have vanished. [14]

Since the election of Israel is rooted in grace, it can neither be terminated nor superseded; the election of Israel is eternal. [15] Since sin is accidental to Israel's essence, it cannot, therefore, affect the elected status of that essence. While for other peoples, sin may affect their essence, not so for Israel. The election of Israel, which is eternal, cannot be canceled by that which is accidental. [16]

Like many of his forebears and like many of his contemporaries, Rabbi Loew uses two analogies to express the notion of the eternal election of Israel. The first of these compares the relationship of God to Israel to that of husband and wife. The second compares the relationship of God to Israel to that of father to child.

In comparing the relationship of God to Israel to that of husband to wife, Rabbi Loew introduces an image found elsewhere in sixteenth-century Jewish literature, for example, in the writings of his brother, Rabbi Hayyim of Friedberg.[17] For purposes of polemics, it did not suffice to refer to Israel as being like a wife in its relationship to God, since a wife may be divorced. Rabbi Loew therefore compares God's relationship to Israel to a particular kind of wife, specifically, to one who cannot be divorced.

According to a talmudic passage, Israel did not accept the Torah at Sinai by choice. God coerced Israel into assent by offering a choice of acceptance or death. According to this text, upon which Rabbi Loew has occasion to comment, "The Holy One, blessed be He, overturned the mountain [i.e., Sinai] upon them like an [inverted] cask and said to them–If you accept the Torah, it will be well; if not, here shall be your burial."[18] Loew utilizes this coercion motif as the basis for his analogy comparing Israel to a wife betrothed to her husband by rape. According to Jewish law, a man who coerces a woman into marriage by raping her can never divorce her. Similarly, God forced Israel into the covenant by means of a combination of divine grace and divine passion. Divine duress of Israel means that the covenant with Israel is eternal. It can never be superseded, nor can it be canceled. God and Israel are eternally bound one to the other in a variety of wedlock from which there can neither be divorce nor annulment.[19]

A second motif utilized by Rabbi Loew, also found in polemical literature, is that which compares the relationship of God to Israel to that of a father to a son. Just as a father-and-son relationship is eternal, so the relationship of God with Israel endures forever. Just as a father's love for his son should not be conditional upon the son's deeds, so God's love for Israel should not be conditional upon their merits nor upon their demerits. By nature love of a father for a son exceeds that of a son for a father.[20] Furthermore, claims Rabbi Loew, the biblical description of Israel as God's "firstborn son" demonstrates the unique and irrevocable status of Israel in relation to God. While there may be many sons, there can only be one firstborn son. Israel's status as firstborn son is to be interpreted as symbolizing its unique and exalted status over the other "sons," i.e., over other peoples. God's relationship to Israel is governed by His love, while His relationship to other peoples is dependent upon *their* deeds.[21]

According to Rabbi Loew, the eternal duration of Israel's election is assured by divine grace and is ensured by the natural order. Following a talmudic view, he connects the continuation of creation to the acceptance by Israel of the revelation at Sinai. The Talmud says, "The Holy One, blessed be He, stipulated with the works of creation and said to them–If Israel accepts the Torah you shall continue to exist; if not, I will revert you back into Nothingness and void."[22] Rabbi Loew interprets the talmudic view to mean that the Exodus and the revelation at Sinai were the climax of creation. Without these events, by means of which Israel became a people, creation would never have been completed. Without them the creation would have been undone. Judah Loew writes:

> The Exodus from Egypt effected the complete perfection of the world. The world was not complete until the Exodus when Israel became a people. Therefore, the completion of Israel is tantamount to the completion of the world.[23]

Since the existence of the world is only assured by the continued existence of Israel as an elected people, it is inconceivable for that election to be canceled; termination of election would mean the termination of creation, the end of the world. Furthermore, because so much depends upon Israel, their liberation from Egypt, their experience of revelation at Sinai, and their continued elected status could not have been dependent upon something so contingent, so tenuous as their deeds. It can only be assured by something as permanent as divine grace. Israel's existence as an elected people is not simply a historical phenomenon but a fact of nature. It is part of the "order of the world" and as such it commands a permanent status. It is an immutable condition of existence.[24]

Despite fierce persecutions and continuous attempts to annihilate Israel, Rabbi Loew continually emphasizes the eternity of Israel. It may be assumed that Loew's statements in this regard are both expressions of his philosophy of Jewish history as well as views directed to his contemporaries to explain their present plight. For example, in discussing Haman, who attempted to destroy the Jews in biblical times, he notes that a person such as Haman who wanted to destroy the eternal people of Israel may be compared to a person who throws a stone at an impregnable metal wall. The stone cannot destroy the wall. It can, however, richochet and destroy the one who throws it.[25] Rabbi Loew's consideration of the fact that Haman, who wanted to destroy the Jews, himself met destruction, led him to reflect upon the Christian claim that God's providence had deserted Israel. Rabbi Loew asserts that the redemption of Israel from their present state of degradation is vouchsafed by recalling precedents in which God's saving power was manifest. Loew recalls that at the beginning of God's relationship with the patriarchs of Israel, He saved individuals from destruction. Alluding to a rabbinic legend, he notes that God saved Abraham from a fiery furnace. Noting biblical texts, he mentions that God saved Isaac from slaughter, Jacob from the angel, Moses from Pharaoh. After Israel became a people, God saved them at the Red Sea. In the time of Mordecai and Esther He saved Israel from Haman. Finally, in a rhetorical question, with definite polemical overtones directed against Christianity, Judah Loew writes: "And from the Cross is He not able to save?"[26] Rabbi Loew is apparently arguing that Israel's expectation of a complete redemption in the future is grounded in a memory of many past redemptions. However, the Christian claim of election and its expectation for a future complete redemption is based upon one event where divine intervention, where redemption, was absent.

According to Judah Loew, each people has a unique national essence, a particular contribution to make to sustain the order of the world. Each people has its own "form" which it is obliged to perfect. This "form" expresses itself in a variety of national characteristics. Each people has its own language, its own food, its own dress, its own land. Each people therefore should have the freedom to express these characteristics. Each people should be granted national self-determination. The suppression of one people by another is a violation of the "natural order"; genocide perverts the order of creation. The attempt of members of one people to assimilate the mannerisms peculiar to any other people is a violation of the "natural order."[27]

Rabbi Loew relates his plea for national self-determination and his insistence upon unique national characteristics to the predicament of the Jewish people in his day. For Loew, the continued alienation of the people of Israel from their land and from their heritage is an unnatural state of affairs.[28] The acceptance by Jews of Gentile customs, foods, and languages is a violation of their unique essence.

For Judah Loew, each people may be considered a unique "species" of human being, a separate, distinguishable rung on the "chain of being." In this "chain of being," Moses is the form of Israel and Israel is the form of the world.[29] As such, Israel's eternal existence is essential to the existence of the world and to the other peoples of the world while the existence of other people is accidental.[30] In Loew's words:

> The matter is as we have explained. Unlike the Gentiles, Israel was created in essence by God. Though the Gentiles were also created by God, their creation was not essential. For the essence of Creation was Israel. The creation of the [other] nations only follows from the creation in essence which is Israel. It is as if the creation of the nations was accidental and only follows from the formation of the essence of creation.[31]

As the form of which other peoples are the matter, Israel may relate to other peoples in one of the two ways form may relate to matter. Israel may relate to other peoples as form implanted within its corresponding matter; or as form essentially unrelated to its corresponding matter. In other words, Israel's relationship with the Gentiles may be one of complementary or of contradictory opposition.

As was noted in the previous chapter, Judah Loew offers the relationship of male and female as an example of form (male) in relationship to its corresponding, complementing matter (female). He utilizes this analogy to describe the relationship of Israel to the other peoples of the world. The relationship of Israel to *some* of the other peoples of the world is like that of male to female. Just as a man may be married to many women but a woman may not be married to more than one man, so may form be implanted in many individual examples of matter while matter, being passive, may not accept more than one individual form at one time. Similarly, Israel may be the form of many nations, but other nations may not be the form of Israel or of each other. Following this analogy Loew insists that, since it is natural for man to rule woman, the present state, in which Israel is ruled by the Gentile peoples, is unnatural and will eventually cease in the Messianic Age, when the natural order will be restored.[32]

Rabbi Loew does not consider all peoples as being able to relate to Israel as complementary opposites. In fact, he mentions few who may do so. In his discussion of the Exodus, for example, Loew relates that Israel could dwell in Egypt only because Israel and Egypt are complementary opposites. The form of Israel is compatible with the matter of Egypt. Consequently, when Israel left Egypt, Israel became pure form. It became form independent of matter. It became a people.[33] Similarly, the relationship of Israel to "the people of Ishmael" (i.e., the Arabs) is one of complementary opposites. Israel may coexist with the descendants of Isaac's brother, Ishmael.[34]

According to Rabbi Loew, the world, like the human being, has two aspects, a natural one and a supernatural one. The former is its matter; the latter is its form. The matter of man is his body; the form of man is his intellect. The matter of the world is the Gentiles; the form of the world is Israel. In order to attain perfection, an individual must ensure a proper relationship between his form and his matter, between his intellect and his body. In order for perfection of the world–the Messianic Era–to begin, a proper relationship must obtain between Israel and the other peoples of the world. Just as human perfection in "this world" cannot be complete without perfection of the body, so perfection of the world may not be complete without the perfection of the other nations of the world. Just as intellectual perfection alone would be an incomplete variety of perfection in this material world, so would the perfection of Israel alone be incomplete in this natural world. Intellectual perfection is perfection of only part of man, not of the whole man. Similarly, perfection of Israel is a desirable goal, but it would represent only a partial, incomplete variety of perfection.[35]

Besides those peoples who may relate to Israel as complementary opposites, with coexistence a possibility, there are those peoples who may relate to Israel only as contradictory opposites with which coexistence and relationship are impossible. Though the relationship between Israel and some of the nations is like that of male to female, the relationship of Israel to Amalek is compared to that of male to male. As biblical law forbids homosexuality, coexistence with Amalek becomes prohibited. Amalek is an example of a contradictory opposite of Israel. Coexistence could only spell annihilation of one or the other.[36]

A second people, to which Israel relates as a contradictory opposite, is Edom (Esau). The ascendance of Edom means the descent of Israel. The ultimate triumph of Edom implies the destruction of Israel.[37] Edom and Amalek are not two separate peoples but are essentially one and the same. Israel can coexist with all the nations of the world except their archenemy, their historical foe, Esau-Amalek. This identification of Esau with Amalek is found in Rabbi Loew's discussion of the festival of Purim, the Feast of Lots.

According to the biblical account in the Book of Esther, Haman wished to exterminate the people of Israel. Following precedents established by rabbinic legend, Loew identifies Haman as a descendant of Amalek who in turn is identified as a descendant of Esau.[38] Mordecai the Jew and Haman the Amalekite represent contradictory opposites which cannot coexist. Haman must destroy Mordecai, Amalek must destroy Israel, or, Mordecai must destroy Haman, Israel must destroy Amalek.[39] Just as Moses had to vanquish Amalek in his day, so did Mordecai need to vanquish Amalek, symbolized by Haman.[40] The bouts between Israel and Amalek in the time of Moses and later in the time of Mordecai and Esther are simply episodes in the ongoing conflict between Israel and Esau, the ancestor of Amalek. This battle began in Rebecca's womb and will not be concluded until the messianic redemption.

According to Rabbi Loew, the biblical narrative which describes Jacob and Esau fighting in their mother's womb is an account of a physical and of a metaphysical reality. Israel and Esau represent contradictory opposites. The two, by their nature, must fight until one ultimately destroys the other.[41]

It may be assumed with some certainty that these references to Esau, Edom, and Amalek are not simply exercises in biblical exegesis or metaphysical speculation, but are statements directed at contemporary sociohistorical conditions. Identification of Esau, Edom, and Amalek with the archenemy of the people of Israel is rooted in the biblical narrative. Through the centuries, however, these biblical characters were identified with various historical foes of Jewry. Already in rabbinic literature, during the Roman occupation of Palestine, Esau-Edom was identified with the Roman Empire and Haman was identified with a variety of Roman emperors. In early medieval Jewish literature Esau-Edom is identified with the historical successors to Rome, i.e., Christendom.[42] By Rabbi Loew's time, the identification of the biblical character of Esau with Christendom was well established. Therefore, when Judah Loew draws his physical and metaphysical distinctions between Israel and Esau, he is making a distinction between Jew and Christian.

Seen in its historical setting, Loew's distinction between Israel and Esau emerges as his attempt to explain certain sociohistorical conditions. For Loew, as for most of classical Judaica, the essential question is: How can one reconcile theological assumption with historical reality? How can one harmonize the theory of the Jews as an elected people with the reality of the Jews as a despised, persecuted, humiliated people? Specifically, in Judah Loew's generation, the immediate problem was to offer some explanation for the recent expulsion of the Jews from Spain and Portugal at the end of the fifteenth century. This traumatic event had a profound influence on sixteenth-century Jewish thought in general and on sixteenth-century Jewish mystical speculation in particular. Indeed, the sixteenth-century Lurianic school of Jewish mysticism provided a new interpretation of Jewish existence as a reaction to this event.[43]

Though he does not clearly articulate his position, perhaps because of its potentially dangerous implications, Rabbi Loew's view that Ishmael is a complementary opposite of Israel while Edom is a contradictory opposite of Israel may express his formulation of a response to the expulsion of the Jews from Spain and Portugal. As Edom is traditionally identified with Christendom, Ishmael is traditionally identified with Islam. The expulsion from Spain was simultaneous with the completion of the "reconquest" of Iberia by the Christians from the Moslems. For Loew, therefore, the expulsion of the Jews is simply the physical and historical expression of a metaphysical reality. As long as Islam ruled Iberia, the Jews could stay, since Israel may coexist with Ishmael. However, once Edom took control, a clash was inevitable since coexistence is impossible. In the case of the Jews of Iberia, exile was the result (certainly a better result than physical extermination). For Rabbi Loew to have clearly enunciated this position would have been dangerous since at this time the empire of the Catholic Hapsburgs was at war with the Moslem Turks. The Jews were continually suspected of being sympathetic to the Turkish enemy. Rabbi Loew was required, therefore, to veil his allusions.

Loew's many references to irreconcilable distinctions between Jews and Gentiles (especially Christians) posed no immediate threat to himself or to the Jewish community. These references were essential to his theodicy and were neither politically nor militarily subversive. His insistence upon these distinctions was crystalized in his halakhic stances on a number of issues (considered in the following chapter), which served as the basis of his insistence upon the social isolation of the Jewish community from the Christian community. Loew believed social isolation to be a necessary condition for the preservation of the unique qualities of the Jewish people and for the conservation of their essential integrity. The Gentile community, which apparently also favored a self-contained, socially isolated Jewish community, could find little threatening in this view. Nor could his claim that Edom-Christendom would eventually be obliterated, while Israel would reign triumphant, be considered an immediate threat to the political order of his time and place. For Loew continually claimed that the eventual triumph of Israel would occur in messianic and not in historical times. Until messianic times, he cautioned, Jews must obey the civil authorities. In fact, he often states that in "this world" it is proper for the Gentiles to reign supreme in economics and politics. "This world" is the domain of Esau. Gentile domination in "this world" is a historical given, an ontological reality. It is part of the plan of existence.

In the chapter which follows, Judah Loew's views concerning the Jewish people and its relationship to other peoples will be explored further by means of an analysis of the application of his theoretical considerations to two concrete problems in Jewish religious law (*halakhah*): Jewish use of Gentile wine and religious conversion.

9

Jew and Gentile:
Halakhic Concretizations

Wine

A constant halakhic preoccupation of Judah Loew was Jewish use of Gentile wine. He discusses this issue, at the slightest pretext, in a number of his writings. It may be instructive, therefore, to speculate as to why this is so.

In talmudic times, in order to insulate Jews from contact with idolatrous practices, certain laws were established to restrict social intercourse between Jews and idolatrous Gentiles. Many of these prohibitions extended into the Middle Ages and beyond. Paramount amongst them was the prohibition upon Jews to use or to benefit from wine produced or handled by Gentiles.

The original prohibition regarding wine is found in the Mishnah, "The following things belonging to idol worshippers are forbidden and the prohibition extends to any benefit that may be derived from them: wine. . . ."[1] This ruling led to a prohibition against Jewish use of wine used specifically for sacramental use by Gentiles (*yeyn nesekh*) and to a more general prohibition against Jewish use of wine produced or handled by Gentiles, whether for sacramental use or for nonsacramental use (*setam yeinam*).[2]

While medieval halakhic authorities modified various other laws which encouraged social segregation between Jews and Gentiles, such as eating bread produced by Gentiles, they made no such modifications regarding use of Gentile wine. The ban on Gentile wine remained stringent because, besides being a medium for social intercourse, wine was also an article of sacred use in Christian worship. Even when the interdiction was relaxed with regard to other alcoholic beverages, the prohibition against use of Gentile wine remained in effect. In general, no practical distinction was made during the Middle Ages between Gentile wine manufactured for sacramental or nonsacramental use.[3] It was only in Judah Loew's generation that a relaxation of this prohibition against Gentile wine began to occur.

Especially in Polish towns bordering on Hungary and in Moravia wine trading was a common Jewish occupation. In many cases Jews found themselves in the position of having to take Gentile wine in lieu of cash payment for a debt. Consequently, contemporary rabbinic authorities bent the law to respond to the new economic reality.[4] This relaxation of the law was based upon a distinction between Christians and idol worshippers. While the two were not always considered mutually exclusive in the past, sixteenth-century halakhic authorities emphasized the claim that the original talmudic text forbidding use of wine referred specifically to idol-worshipping Gentiles of past eras, and not to contemporary Gentile Christians. These rabbis made a distinction between the idolatrous Gentiles who inhabited Palestine in talmudic times and the nonidolatrous Gentiles of their own times. Though such a distinction had been made by earlier authorities, it was only in the sixteenth century that it was applied to easing the prohibition on Jewish use of Gentile wine. Furthermore, they argued, the talmudic prohibition against wine was originally instituted as a wedge against an intensity of social intercourse which would eventuate in intermarriage between Jew and Gentile. Since, they claimed, contemporary social conditions were not conducive to intermarriage, the prohibition against wine should be relaxed.[5]

Moses Isserles, a sixteenth-century Polish halakhic authority, had a very liberal view on the subject of Jewish use of Gentile wine. With specific reference to the Jewish community of Moravia, Isserles claims that though it is not in accordance with the letter of the law to do so, he nevertheless does not prohibit use of Gentile wine by Jews. Isserles notes that the prohibition is little observed in any case and, therefore, "it is good to find some reason to be lenient in this matter for locales in which it is laxly practiced."[6] Unlike other authorities who permitted use of nonsacramental wine, but who retained the prohibition on sacramental wine, Isserles made no distinction between use of sacramental and nonsacramental Gentile wine. Furthermore, Isserles's position on Gentile wine developed out of what appears to be his assumption that economic factors ought to play a major role when adjudicating specific issues in Jewish law.

When Isserles's view permitting Jewish use of Gentile wine was made public is uncertain. However, as Isserles died in 1572, when Loew was still in Moravia, it is likely that Isserles's position was well known to Moravian Jewry during Judah Loew's tenure of office as Chief Rabbi of Moravia. Loew's sharp condemnation of those who violate the prohibition of Jewish use of Gentile wine was undoubtedly a direct response to what he considered the legally unfounded liberality of Isserles and others on this matter.

During his tenure of office as Chief Rabbi of Moravia, Judah Loew authored a prayer, subsequently recited in Moravian synagogues, invoking God's blessings upon those who observe the prohibition against using Gentile wine.[7] In a record of statutes of the Jewish community of Moravia, edited into its final form in 1650, the following appears:

> It is a statute of early scholars and a decree of the Great Gaon, Our Master, Rabbi Loew of Prague, may the memory of the righteous be for a blessing, that the matter of use of Gentile wine–both sacramental and nonsacramental–by Jews remains unchanged. The strength of this statute is now as it was earlier. Whosoever drinks such wine puts himself under a ban of excommunication. He becomes ineligible to participate in any religious occasion. He may not come before the Holy Ark [in the synagogue to lead the congregation in prayer or to recite blessings over the Torah], for the course of the year, especially not on the New Year or the Day of Atonement.[8]

While there is no evidence that Rabbi Loew pronounced this ban on Moravian Jewry while he was in Moravia, a text of such a ban is found in the published form of his sermon *On the Commandments*. In this sermon, delivered at Posnań soon after his arrival from Prague in 1592, Loew notes the almost universal disregard of the ban on Gentile wine. He admonishes Bohemian Jewry for their laxity and for not setting a better example for their Moravian neighbors. He bemoans that Italian Jewry all but totally disregarded the practice to the extent that ignorance of the prohibition, rather than intentional violation of the law, had led to a lack of observance. He berates German Jewry for their failure even to be embarrassed at its flagrant rejection of the ways of its pious ancestors (*ḥasidei ashkenaz*).[9] It is primarily to Moravian Jewry, however, that Loew directs his remarks.

Rabbi Loew's efforts to discourage laxity on Jewish use of Gentile wine during his tenure in office as Chief Rabbi of Moravia were apparently ineffectual. In a blistering diatribe, he berates Moravian Jewry in general, and its rabbinic leadership in particular. Solemnly but decisively, Loew places Moravian Jewry, specifically the Moravian rabbinate, under a ban of excommunication. Possibly with Isserles's lenient position in mind, Loew states:

> It seems that in many communities, large and small, the wine prohibition is not heeded; indeed, people flaunt its observance as though they were unequivocally permitted to use it [the wine]. It is not sufficient for those who call themselves "rabbis" that they do not protest this violation. They must also [violate it themselves] by associating with those who break the law.[10]

Though Isserles was a leading Polish halakhic authority, his position on Jewish use of Gentile wine appears to have been more influential in Moravia than in his own land. Isserles's position was apparently not typical of Polish rabbinical leadership. The Polish rabbinate had not sanctioned Jewish use of Gentile wine. Rabbi Loew's Polish contemporaries, Joel Sirkes and Meir of Lublin, were allies in Loew's attempt to strengthen observance of this prohibition. Like Loew, Sirkes issued a ban against those who drank or used Gentile wine.[11]

Unlike those who simply leveled a ban against those who transgressed the law, Loew offered a detailed justification of his position. In analyzing his defense of this prohibition, the reason for Loew's obsession with this issue will become evident.

For Judah Loew, Jewish law represented the crystallization of theological assumptions. The commandments were "divine" and true in themselves. They represented an earthly manifestation of ultimate reality. The natural could not abrogate the supernatural. The commandments in general and the wine prohibition in particular had to remain in effect. Finding a natural, logical, economic, or historical "reason for observance" and then dispensing with a given religious practice because the "reason" is presently obsolete is an exercise in futility. Any rationale found cannot be *the* reason, i.e., God's reason. Rabbi Loew's opposition to those who would attempt to rationalize their opposition to the letter of the law is grounded in his theology of the nature of the Torah, the nature of the commandments and in his belief in the futility (which he often identified with exponents of the Jewish philosophical tradition), of attempting to justify rationally the suprarational.[12] The issue of Jewish use of Gentile wine could not be determined, therefore, by an appeal to transient economic or social factors. Being of suprarational origin, the prohibition could not legitimately be rationalized away.

Rabbi Loew's opposition to those who would relax the law not only relates to his views regarding the nature of the Torah and the commandments. It is also the logical corollary of his theory of opposites, which we have seen is basic to this thought. For Loew, the wine prohibition reflects a metaphysical as well as a social reality, i.e., the fundamental incompatibility of the nature of the Jew and the nature of the Gentile, specifically the Christian Gentile.

For Loew, it will be remembered, the Jew and the Christian are contradictory opposites: metaphysically, socially, and physically. All that relates to the Jew represents one variety of entity. All that relates to the Christian represents its opposite. Social distinctions between the two reflect metaphysical distinctions between the two. Therefore, for Rabbi Loew, Jewish use of Gentile wine is not simply a minor infraction of the law, but a distortion of fundamental metaphysical realities.

Gentile wine was of one essence and Jewish wine of another, opposite essence. Just as Jew and Gentile are mutually exclusive, so must be Jewish and Gentile wine. By using Gentile wine, the Jew thereby identifies with his contradictory opposite. Only destruction and defilement could ensue.

For Rabbi Loew, the halakhic question of Jewish use of Gentile wine strikes at the heart of the essence of Jewish existence, indeed, at the essence of reality itself. Loew's discussion of this issue demonstrates the integrated relationship of his mystical theology, his cultural isolationism, his process of halakhic decision, and his social criticism.[13]

In Loew's view, the people of Israel are the terrestrial manifestation of the celestial Israel, identified with the sefirotic realm, specifically with the *sefirah* called *Tiferet* or with the last of the *sefirot,* the *Shekhinah.* The Gentile, in this scheme, is understood to be the terrestrial manifestation of Israel's contradictory opposite, the "other side" (*sitra aḥra*), the embodiment of the forces of evil. The two elements must remain separate and apart, otherwise obliteration or defilement would be Israel's fate.

According to Rabbi Loew, this metaphysical, mystical reality expresses itself in social and cultural terms. For Loew, following the

Jewish mystical tradition, what happens "below" in the social, natural realm has repercussions "above" in the spiritual, metaphysical realm. Jewish cultural isolation from the Gentiles is therefore the social corollary of a metaphysical reality. Unless cultural isolation is maintained "below," repercussions on all levels of existence would occur.

Though Rabbi Loew never quotes the Zohar on the issue of Gentile wine per se, he does allude to it once. His entire approach to the issue echoes the position taken by the Zohar in the following citation:

Rabbi Isaac began his discourse with the verse–"which ate the fat of their sacrifices and drank the wine of their offerings" [Deut. 32:38]. [He continued] Happy are Israel in that they are holy and the Holy One, blessed be He, wishes to sanctify them. All eternal life they inherit derives from the World to Come [i.e., the *sefirah* of *Binah*–Divine Understanding], because it represents life both above and below. It is the place from which the "treasured wine" originates. It is the source of sanctity and life. The wine of Israel [on earth] is used because of the wine of the other Israel [i.e., the counterpart of the people of Israel in the realm of the *sefirot,* namely, *Tiferet* or the *Shekhinah*].

The supernal Israel derives life therefrom [from *Binah*] and therefore it is called the "Tree of Life." It is a tree from the place called "Life" and consequently from it comes life. Therefore, one blesses the Holy One with wine. The wine of Israel below is comparable to this [wine]. The idolater, however, is impure [i.e. derives from the realm of impurity, the "other side"] and whosoever associates with him becomes impure. When he touches the wine of Israel, that wine becomes impure and prohibited [for a Jew to drink or use]; all the more so is wine he makes [prohibited]. This is true not only in this case [of wine, that sanctity relates to Israel and impurity relates to the Gentiles, but such is true in all cases for Israel relates to the sefirotic realm and the Gentiles relate to the "other side"]. For everything that Israel does below sets a pattern for that which happens above, especially with regard to wine which holds a very high rank, like "treasured wine."

Hence Israel drinks the wine of Israel, made properly in sanctity, as does the supernal Israel. He who drinks is strengthened and whosoever recites a blessing over such wine is exalted in holiness. They do not imbibe wine made in impurity by the impure for the spirit of impurity rests upon it. Whosoever drinks such wine thereby pollutes his spirit and makes himself impure. He is not of the side of Israel and he is disqualified from an existence in the World to Come. For the World to Come is the realm of the "treasured wine." Therefore, to be sacred, Israel must observe this above all. For such links them with the World to Come. It is for this reason that with wine, above all, is the Holy One sanctified. [14]

Rabbi Loew believed that the social and cultural isolation of the Jew is a necessary corollary of the metaphysical uniqueness of Jewish existence. Consequently, he asserted, religious laws, such as the wine prohibition, which safeguard this isolation, cannot be abrogated. They must be retained. [15] For Rabbi Loew, Jewish use of Gentile wine represents the attempt to combine, to identify, to join two contradictory opposites. All that can result from such activity is the pollution of the sacred, the violation of Israel. [16] Elsewhere, with specific reference to the wine issue, Loew notes that the cultural isolation of Israel is the only guarantee of its survival as a people. Loew opposes those who believe Jewish survival is guaranteed by increasing social and cultural interchange with the Gentiles. Only through cultural and social isolation expressed by Jews wearing distinct clothing, speaking a distinct language, eating special foods, and drinking only certain wines will Jewish cultural integrity be assured. [17]

Though Rabbi Loew discusses the question of Gentile wine in a number of his works with one degree of intensity or another, he devotes an appendix to his *Gevurot Ha-Shem* to a focused discussion of the issue. In this text Judah Loew states his basic position that the prohibition of Gentile wine was to separate Jew from Gentile in order to reflect the intrinsic metaphysical differences between them. Such being the case, the claims made by contemporary scholars that the prohibition ought to be eased for one reason or another, cannot be seriously considered. First of all, insists Loew, according to talmudic law, the rabbinic decree establishing the prohibition of Gentile wine was one of eighteen rabbinic decrees which may not be changed by post-talmudic authority. Secondly, he continues, the assumption that intermarriage is not a possibility is not a correct one. The wine prohibition is a useful hedge against social intercourse and consequently against intermarriage. To open avenues for social intercourse is to open the possibility of intermarriage.

For Rabbi Loew, contemporary rationales for dispensing with the wine prohibition have no validity. Not only do its detractors fail to justify easing the stricture, but they also fail to comprehend the actual basis for the prohibition, namely, the metaphysical distinction between Jew and Gentile. [18]

The observance of this prohibition, continues Loew, is of height-ened significance for Israel in the Diaspora. When national inde-pendence prevailed, the prohibition was not necessary. With the Babylonian exile, it became necessary. In later times it became crucial to ensure Israel's essential integrity. Without it, Israel's essence would have been compromised, its uniqueness surren-dered, its assimilation assured.[19] Loew therefore claims that the ban against non-Jewish wine must be retained since it symbolizes the necessity of safeguarding the spiritual essence of the people of Israel from penetration by the intrinsically demonic Gentile essence.[20]

Though Jew and Gentile share common external characteristics, inwardly they differ. These distinct inward traits are hidden from appearance. It is for this reason, amongst others, that the prohibi-tion aimed at distinguishing Jew from Gentile relates to wine, which, through ingestion, also becomes internalized. Wine, which enters the body, represents the distinct inward essences of Jew and Gentile.

As has been mentioned above, Rabbi Loew, following the tradi-tion of the mystics, finds great significance in numbers. It is not surprising therefore that he comments on the numerical equivalent (*gematria*) of the Hebrew word for wine (*yayin*) toward the conclu-sion of his discussion. For Loew it is not coincidental that the number "seventy" represents wine, which signifies the super-natural essence of Israel. The number "seventy" is a multiple of ten and seven, both of which signify holiness or completion. Secondly, according to the biblical narrative, the people of Israel began with the seventy individuals who journeyed to Egypt with Jacob (Deut. 10:22; see also Exod. 1:5). Israel, therefore, is linked to the number "seventy." Finally, the number "seventy" has further significance as it equals the numerical equivalent of the Hebrew word for "mystery" (*sod*). The mystery is internal, hidden, not apparent. Similarly, the essence of the people of Israel is not apparent, but hidden.

Rabbi Loew concludes this statement on Gentile wine with a diatribe against those of his rabbinic colleagues who fail to enforce the prohibition against Gentile wine and who permit imbibing Gentile wine. For Loew, the Moravian rabbinate, for example (against whom Loew directs his ban of excommunication), is not simply guilty of mistaken legal decision, but is culpable for denying the supernatural nature of the commandments. It is responsible for compromising the intrinsic sanctity of Jewish existence, and of helping to subvert the natural and the supernatural order. Thus, on the basis of the preceding discussion it may be concluded that Rabbi Loew's halakhic conclusion flows from his theological premises and that his social dissent is grounded in his metaphysical assumptions.

Conversion

A second halakhic issue which concerned Judah Loew was religious conversion to Judaism. Unlike the wine issue, Loew's reflection upon this problem seems more theoretical than practical. While violation of the wine prohibition was widespread in his day, conversion to Judaism at that time seems to have been virtually nonexistent.[21]

As in the issue of Jewish use of Gentile wine, Rabbi Loew's theological assumptions concerning the physical and metaphysical differences between Jew and Gentile influenced his halakhic position with regard to religious conversion.

Being a traditionalist he had to take into account the long-standing halakhic possibility of conversion, developed and sanctioned by earlier authorities. However, his position concerning the essential incompatibility of Jewish and Gentile natures on the physical, social, and metaphysical levels of existence would seem to eliminate the possibility of conversion to Judaism, both theoretically and practically.

Judah Loew's statements on conversion are scattered throughout his work. It is necessary therefore to reconstruct a comprehensive and a comprehensible position from sometimes contradictory and sometimes ambiguous sources. Loew's failure to articulate a clear position on this subject has led a number of contemporary scholars to reach very different conclusions concerning his position on conversion.[22]

In formulating Rabbi Loew's attitude toward religious conversion to Judaism, it would be useful to identify the premises upon which his position rests. First of all, Loew assumes that each people has an essence uniquely peculiar to itself. This essence, or "form," expresses itself in the specific people's particular language, dress, food, and geographical situation (i.e., homeland).[23] Second, Loew claims that since it is impossible for an individual entity, such as a person, to change his essence, consequently it is impossible for one who is a member of a given people, characterized by a specific essence, to relinquish voluntarily or involuntarily that essence and become a member of another people. In other words, one cannot convert from one people to another. One cannot alter one's essence by an act of choice.[21] Third, Loew asserts that while the distinction between individual Gentile peoples is sharp and clear, a greater distinction may be drawn between the Gentile peoples as a whole and the people of Israel. Though the Gentile peoples are individuated, one from the other, they occupy the same level of existence, while the people of Israel, in relation to the Gentile peoples as a whole, occupies a separate class, a different dimension of existence altogether. From these assumptions, Loew's refusal to admit the possibility of conversion from Judaism logically flows.

For Rabbi Loew, as for many sixteenth-century Jewish scholars, the problem of Jews who had converted to Catholicism at the end of the fifteenth century in Spain wanting to return to Judaism after having left Spain appears to have been a constant issue. Loew refuses to close the door back into Judaism for those wishing to reenter. For Loew, the Jew can never cease being a Jew. The apostate need not be readmitted because he never left.[25]

While Judah Loew's conclusion concerning the impossibility of conversion from Judaism is consistent with his premises, his affirmation of the possibility of conversion to Judaism conflicts with his premises. However, Loew seems to have been aware of this conflict and he dealt with this inconsistency in a number of ways. In one text Loew claims that the very fact that an individual wants to convert to Judaism demonstrates an a priori, innate disposition toward Judaism. The individual is not, therefore, really a convert. He is an individual whose potentiality to be a Jew is realized by the process of conversion. No change of essence is involved. The Jewish essence was always there. Through the formal act of conversion the implicit becomes explicit. The formerly recessive Jewish quality now becomes dominant. In Loew's words:

> Do not ask . . . How can a proselyte accept the Torah? He has an inadequate spiritual disposition. There is no difficulty at all. The fact that he is a candidate for conversion demonstrates that he must share a disposition with all Jews, and, once he converts, he is absorbed into the people of Israel and acquires [all] its characteristics.[26]

On a number of other occasions, Judah Loew suggests what appears to be his final position on conversion. He claims that since the convert to Judaism acquires additional sanctity, conversion is desirable from the perspective of the convert. However, since conversion adds members to the Jewish people, who according to Loew, are already "complete" and "perfect," such an addition may only prove harmful to the Jewish people.[27] Thus, Loew's position seems to be that conversion to Judaism is beneficial to the convert but harmful to the people of Israel.

In a discussion of Jethro, Moses' father-in-law, described in rabbinic literature as a convert to Judaism, Rabbi Loew expresses himself most comprehensively on the issue. He writes:

> Conversion [to Judaism] means amalgamation to and joining with the people of Israel. [This possibility of conversion demonstrates] the exalted nature of [the people of] Israel. For a Gentile cannot choose to become a member of another people. For example, if he was one of the "seven nations" [who inhabited Canaan] and he wanted to become a member of another people, he would be unable to do so. If he was a Moabite and wanted to become an Edomite, he could not do so. However, while it is possible for a Gentile to become a Jew, a Jew even if he apostasizes remains a Jew. He cannot change his essence. This is because Israel is distinct from other peoples, in a class by itself. It is more exalted and more holy than the other peoples. Therefore, it may be joined. As [the Talmud puts it], one may ascend in sanctity but not descend. Thus a Gentile who wishes to convert may do so and may [thereby] acquire additional sanctity. He who converts thereby demonstrates that he wishes to cleave to a more exalted plane [of existence] and therefore is compared [by the Talmud] to a newborn child.[28]

Thus for Rabbi Loew conversion to Judaism is possible. It enhances the convert spiritually. He attains an exalted level of sanctity peculiar to Israel. He is physically changed through the circumcision rite.[29] He is metaphysically changed by virtue of having been endowed with a new soul. He is compared to a newborn child because, like a newborn child, he possesses a new soul and a "new" body.[30] He is now considered a member of the people of Israel.[31] Conversion does not represent transition from one condition to another. Rather, it represents the generation of a new entity altogether. Conversion, then, is good for the convert. He attains complete humanity. He achieves an exalted level of sanctity. He becomes a new individual. Rabbi Loew does not construe conversion, however advantageous for the convert, to be beneficial to the people of Israel. He expresses this attitude in a number of places throughout his work where he has occasion to comment upon the quixotic talmudic statement, "Rabbi Helbo said: Converts [to Judaism] are as troublesome to [the people of Israel] as a *sappaḥat*."[32]

The term *sappaḥat* may be translated as "itch," "scab," "rash."[33] Rabbi Helbo employs a verse in Isaiah (14:1) as his proof text, "For the Lord will pardon Jacob and will again choose Israel. He will settle them in their own soil. The *ger* ['resident alien' in biblical Hebrew or 'convert' in rabbinic Hebrew] shall join them and shall cleave to the House of Jacob." In this verse the word *nisphu*—"join" or "cleave"—expresses Rabbi Helbo's pun or perhaps his explanation. It is unclear what his meaning actually is. It is uncertain whether he means converts are a threat to Israel or simply an addition to Israel.[34]

The lack of clarity in Rabbi Helbo's statement evoked diverse explanations of its meaning. Some interpreted him to be in opposition to conversion. Others, who interpreted him to be in favor of conversion, suggested that his only meaning was that converts add to, augment, swell the people of Israel. Already in the Talmud, his statement was taken by a later authority to mean that Rabbi Helbo opposed conversion.[35] A number of medieval European rabbinic authorities, however, took Rabbi Helbo to favor proselytization. They ascribed no derogatory meaning to his use of the term *sappaḥat*. In fact, according to one medieval authority, Rabbi Helbo's intention was actually to laud converts. He wished to extol the convert's strict adherence to Jewish religious law in contrast to the lax observance of those who were Jews by birth rather than by choice.[36]

Rabbi Loew, on a number of occasions, quotes Rabbi Helbo's dictum and translates *sappaḥat* as "addition." Since, according to Loew, the people of Israel represents completion and perfection, an addition is actually a subtraction; "more is less." By attaching himself to the complete people, the convert mars the completion, the perfection, the essence of Israel. Just as a scab adds something to the healthy man and therefore detracts from his health, so does the convert detract from the completeness of Israel by becoming an unneeded supplement to Israel. Any addition to that which is complete violates its form, its nature. In Loew's words, "Conversions to Judaism make additions and changes in the people of Israel. Strange transformations occur in Israel [because of conversions] just as the *sappaḥat* causes a person such changes."[37]

It has been suggested that Rabbi Helbo was theoretically in favor of accepting converts to Judaism but that the social and political dangers inherent in the Jewish community's accepting proselytes encouraged him to caution against such action.[38] One may assume that Rabbi Loew's position on conversion emerges from a similar situation. His personal observation may have been that the Jewish community is inevitably caused to suffer for accepting converts. Such, for example, was the case in Cracow in 1540 when some Polish Jews were charged with having been active in proselytization.[39]

Though Rabbi Loew did not take a stand on conversion so tolerant and open as some of the medieval authorities noted above, he did not adopt the adamant stance against proselytization taken by some of his contemporaries, specifically Solomon Luria. In comparison to Luria's position, Rabbi Loew emerges as a moderate. Reflecting on Rabbi Helbo's meaning, Luria wrote:

> Now we are in a country not our own, like slaves beneath the hands of their owners. Should one of Israel accept him [i.e., a proselyte] he is a rebel and is responsible for his own death. . . . Hence I hereby give warning that anyone who is a participant in such acceptance today, when the Gentile kingdom is stringent in its attitude, let his blood be on his own head, whether he himself engages in proselytization, or whether he merely knows of such; so may there be survival and stability for the seed of Israel among the peoples all the days of our Exile, throughout our exalted communities, without aliens joining us. And this is a matter demanding the greatest possible caution.[40]

Unlike Loew, Luria in effect eliminates the possibility of conversion to Judaism. When seen against its contemporary backdrop, Loew's position emerges as one of moderation rather than intransigence. One may conclude from the preceding discussion that Judah Loew's position on conversion represents his attempt to articulate a theological issue in a halakhic medium while retaining his awareness of contemporary social conditions.

10

Man and Cosmos:
The Quest for Perfection

Judah Loew's Anthropocentric Stance

Judah Loew's thought is anthropocentric.[1] For Loew, man is the center of all, the composite of all. Everything exists for man, and everything that exists is reflected in man. Man is the "form" of the terrestrial world. Without him, the world is formless and void, devoid of purpose and meaning.[2] Man is the knot of existence. He has the power to unite the upper and the lower worlds.[3] Upper, lower, and intermediate dimensions of existence all coalesce within him.[4] Look within man and discover all levels of reality, the natural and the supernatural, the finite and the infinite. Therefore, for man, whose existence embodies reality, self-knowledge leads to knowledge of reality.[5].

In developing his notion of the centrality of man, Loew drew from the anthropocentric views of his predecessors in the history of Jewish thought. Though anthropocentricity is a theme to be found in Western philosophy and Christian theology which preceded Loew, it cannot be assumed that he drew his ideas directly from any of these non-Jewish sources. Rabbi Loew's ideas seem rooted in the history of Jewish thought, especially in Jewish mystical speculation.

Though never formulated in any systematic way, biblical and rabbinic literature contain the notion of the centrality of man in the scheme of creation.[6] While in relationship to God man is "dust and ashes," in relation to the world he is master of creation (Gen. 1:28). Of all creation, only man is claimed by the Bible to have been created in the "image of God" (Gen. 1:27). Man is "a little lower than the divine" (Ps. 8:3).

Rabbinic literature perpetuated the theme of the centrality of man. The Mishnah, for example, states that in certain situations "everyone must say: For my sake the world was created" (Sanh. 4:5). The *Avot According to Rabbi Nathan* already contains a statement of the idea of man as microcosm: "Whatever God created in His world, He created in man."[7] This anthropocentric motif, found in biblical and rabbinic literature, was restated and amplified in medieval Jewish philosophy.[8] The first great medieval Jewish philosopher, Saadya Gaon (b. 882) reads the biblical creation story as a proof text for the centrality of man in creation. He writes that man must have "unquestionably been the intended purpose of creation. . . . Man is the axle of the world and its foundation." Saadya concludes:

> When, therefore, I considered these principles and the inferences to which they were conducive, I realized that the superiority ascribed to man was not due to some false notion that struck our minds or to any inclination on our part toward favoring man, nor was it self-preference or conceit or boastfulness that induced us to arrogate this superiority unto ourselves. On the contrary, it was nothing but unadulterated truth and plain veracity.[9]

A later figure in the history of medieval Jewish philosophy, Joseph Ibn Zaddik (d. 1149) wrote *The Microcosm (Ha-Olam Ha-Katan).* In this work, the author claims that man is the world in miniature because he has represented within him all the elements of existence. The body resembles the corporeal world and the rational soul resembles the spiritual world.

Joseph Albo (d. 1444), often considered the last great figure in the history of medieval Jewish philosophy, also expresses an anthropocentric position. In a chapter which reads like a paraphrasing of Saadya, Albo writes:

> This section makes clear that the human species is the choicest of all the lower existences, and that man is the main purpose of the creation of the lower world. . . . As soon as man made his appearance, creation was complete. . . . Man is thus the end of creation. . . . All the sublunar existences are subject to him and exist for his sake.[10]

In his *Neve Shalom,* Abraham Shalom (d. 1492) reiterates the microcosm motif. Shalom writes, "Man alone of the animals was created in complete perfection in respect of his soul, and therefore he is called a microcosm."[11] While it cannot be established with any certainty that Rabbi Loew utilized Saadya's or Ibn Zaddik's works, it can be established that Loew both read and quoted from Shalom's and Albo's work.

It cannot be assumed that Rabbi Loew derived his anthropocentric stance primarily or solely from the medieval Jewish philosophical tradition. His anthropocentricity more closely echoes that of the Jewish mystical tradition in general, the Zohar in particular. [12] In fact, Loew joins his contemporary, the mystic Meir Ibn Gabbai, in a virulent attack on the leading representative of the medieval philosophical tradition, Maimonides, for the latter's denial of the anthropocentric stance.

In Meir Ibn Gabbai's *Avodat Ha-Kodesh* (1568), which has been called "perhaps the finest account of kabbalistic speculation before the resurgence of the kabbalah in Safed," the author takes issue with Maimonides' denial of human centrality in the order of creation. [13] Loew, who read Ibn Gabbai's work, adopts a similar stance against Maimonides' apparent position on this issue.

Though Maimonides (1135-1204) was not directly familiar with Ibn Zaddik's *Microcosm,* he was apparently aware of the thrust of his work. Maimonides knew Saadya's work and studied the microcosm motif in earlier Jewish, Arabic, and Greek (in Arabic translation) philosophical sources. [14] In his *Guide of the Perplexed,* Maimonides expresses his rejection of the variety of extreme anthropocentricity which he encountered in the writings of many of his predecessors in the history of philosophy. While he does admit that man is "the noblest thing that is composed of the elements," Maimonides rejects any notion of man as microcosm, of man as the purpose of existence; indeed, he denies the possibility of man comprehending the purpose of that which exists above the sublunar sphere of existence. [15] In opposition to the anthropocentric stance, Maimonides claims, "All the existent individuals of the human species and, all the more, those of the other species of the animals are things of no value at all in comparison with the whole that exists and endures." [16] Elsewhere he continues, "It should not be believed that all the beings exist for the sake of the existence of man. On the contrary, all the other beings too have been intended for their own sakes and not for the sake of something else." [17]

Ibn Gabbai identifies Maimonides' position with that of the "philosophers." According to Ibn Gabbai, the views of the philosophers and of Maimonides on the stature of man in the universe are incorrect and are in opposition to the teachings of the Torah. Ibn Gabbai chastises Maimonides for adopting the views of the Greek philosophers in favor of the views of Jewish tradition. In Ibn Gabbai's words, Maimonides "in expressing this position tears down the fortress of Torah and diminishes as well as repudiates the image of God [in man]."[18]

Loew's position in this matter is almost identical to that of Ibn Gabbai. One may assume that Loew modeled his opposition to Maimonides' antianthropocentric stance after that of Ibn Gabbai. In Rabbi Loew's view, those (i.e., the philosophers, especially Maimonides) who belittle the importance of man in the scheme of creation are "diametrically opposed to the teachings of our faith." Furthermore, Loew asserts:

> We have discussed this matter many times. It is the aim of the philosophers to relegate man to the nadir of the earth. This is the opposite of what the sages of Israel have taught. They placed the righteous man at the pinnacle of creation, even above the angels. The philosophers have cast man into hell while the sages of Israel have extolled the righteous man to the most exalted heights.[19]

For Judah Loew, man is not only the *raison d'être* of "this world." He is not the microcosm of only one world; he is not *one* world in miniature, but *three*. For according to Loew, reality consists of three worlds, or three dimensions of existence: the supernatural, the intermediate, and the natural; the "World to Come" (*olam ha-ba*), the "intermediary world" (*olam ha-emza'i*), and "this world" (*olam ha-zeh*).[20] And man represents and embodies all three worlds, all three dimensions of reality. In his words:

> It is fitting that all three worlds should be found in man for he incorporates them all. It is both proper and essential for such to be the case. Within him one finds that which distinguishes each of the three worlds one from the other.[21]

Without man, the three dimensions of existence would be in a state of irreconcilable disunity. However, in man and through man, they coalesce into the unity their Creator intended for them.

Man is God's agent. He is needed to forge unity amongst the three dimensions of existence. He holds reality together. The perfection of man, therefore, represents cosmic reparation and not only human perfection.[22] The perfection of the various aspects of man implies the perfection of the various dimensions of existence. Rabbi Loew also claims that the perfection of each man implies the perfection of all men, for each man contains an element of all men.

For an individual not to seek perfection implies that all men will be somewhat bereft of perfection, disenfranchised from fulfillment.[23] As there can be no agency in striving for perfection, no proxy for human fulfillment, the individual commands both awesome power as well as immense responsibility.[24] A decision by one man not to endeavor to attain perfection retards the perfection of all men, while it simultaneously exacerbates disharmony in the cosmos.

Man's perfection is essential for the realization of the cosmos. All existence relies upon his deeds. If not for man, "the world would be disunited, divided. But such a state is impossible for existence. Stemming from God who is one, His creation should be one. Therefore, it is through man, who is composed of the three worlds, that they can become one. Were such not the case, reality would disintegrate."[25] Elsewhere, Loew notes, "When man is flawed and despoiled, the three worlds become flawed. Man is the knot of existence. When the knot is snapped, everything becomes dissolved. For these three worlds are bound and unified by means of man."[26] This position, which assumes the cosmic significance of human deeds and which correlates the fate of reality with the destiny of man, is clearly drawn from Jewish mystical tradition. The assumption that what man does below affects all, even the divine, is deeply rooted in Jewish mysticism.

According to Judah Loew, man both reflects and embodies the three dimensions of reality. The three aspects of man, intellect (*seikhel*), soul (*nefesh*), and body (*guf*), correspond to the three worlds: celestial, intermediary, and terrestrial.[27] Therefore, to understand Judah Loew's notion of man, one must consider the three aspects of existence and their representations in man.

Form and Matter

The human body, like the material world, is composed of matter, but according to Loew, the nature of matter is not monolithic. Each kind of entity, each level of material existence, each link in the chain of being manifests a distinct quality of matter. Simple, base matter–the four elements–occupies the lowest rung. Above it are minerals, then plants, then animals and finally human matter.[28] Human matter, too, is manifest in a variety of qualities.[29] The quality of human matter before Adam's sin was of a higher degree than after the Fall.[30] The quality of matter of which the body of the Jew is comprised is of a more refined nature than that of the

Gentile.[31] The quality of former generations of Jews, specifically scholars, surpasses that which obtains in later generations. Whereas Adam before his sin was dominated by the intellect (*seikhel*), man after sin is dominated by the body.[32] Whereas in former generations scholars' intellects dominated their bodies, in later generations their bodies dominate and consequently weaken their intellects.[33]

The goal of the human being must be the purification of his body, of his matter, in order for it to coexist with the soul (*nefesh*). Perfection of the body means making the physical compatible with the spiritual. It implies refining the material aspect of man, the body, to the greatest possible degree. It means perfecting matter to the degree that its innate qualities allow.[34] Each material entity may only attain a predetermined degree of perfection conditioned by its material nature and its disposition.

The quality of matter represented by an individual entity is determined by the form associated with it. Form confers identity upon the existents to which it is attached.[35] Matter in itself has virtually no essence of its own. The inherent qualities of matter are change, passivity, and potentiality.[36] Matter is always in potential, awaiting form to provide it with character, essence, and purpose. Matter can be only passive. In itself it affects nothing. It is only the privation of form, of essence, of purpose.[37] As such, matter without form is not even to be considered a viable aspect of the lowest world. It represents that which is not, rather than that which is. Loew associates raw matter with death, which is the privation of life.[38] The soul, the form of man, leaves the body, allowing it to revert once more to formless matter. He identifies hell, which represents the privation of existence, with matter divorced from form.[39] Matter without form stands outside of the order of reality. It only represents that which is not, that which has no essence.

According to Loew, all real existence is characterized by matter associated with form. Some entities' matter have the predisposition to dominate their form; in others, form dominates matter, though it is "stamped into matter." In a third kind of entity, there is form stamped upon matter; however, that form also has a form which is of a more refined variety. This "form of a form" is not directly related to matter. Rabbi Loew identifies each of these relationships which form may have to matter with each of the three "worlds," the three levels of existence.[40] He also identifies them with the three aspects of man. The first variety, where matter may dominate form, Loew compares to the material, natural world. He also relates it to the human body. The second variety, where form is implanted within matter, with form predominating, he relates to the "intermediary world." Loew also identifies this relationship with that which obtains between the body and the soul (*nefesh*). The third relationship, where a noncorporeal form serves as the form of the form implanted within matter, while it itself is unrelated to matter, he identifies with the highest world, the spiritual realm, the supernatural. He also identifies this form with the human intellect, the spiritual aspect of man, the *seikhel*. The first level of human perfection, therefore, is when one transcends the "this world," the material world. One should attempt to refine one's matter, one's body, so that its form, the soul, may dominate. The first task, therefore, in attaining human perfection, is to neutralize the tendency of the body to dominate the soul. For Loew, the human body and the natural world cannot attain perfection in and of themselves. Their perfection may only be achieved through the perfection of their form.

When the material world is perfected, its form dominates its matter. It then becomes transformed into the "intermediary world" where form predominates over matter.[41] Similarly, the perfection of man qua man is not achieved in perfection of the body but in the subjugation of the body to its form, the soul, and the final domination of the intellect over all. The paradigmatic person, representing perfection of soul, i.e., the form of the material world, is the businessman. He is necessary, but not sufficient.[42] The scholar, representing perfection of the intellect, is both necessary and sufficient. He is man qua man.

Perfection of the Body

Judah Loew did not have a very sympathetic view of the material world or of the human body. "Material existence is not to be considered existence."[43] The body is the source of evil, sin, corruption. By its nature, the body, like the material world, must be flawed, imperfect.[44] One must therefore attempt to perfect the body's form, the soul, and to prevent the body from dominating the soul. One must purify one's body so that it may coexist with one's soul. The human being should seek to strengthen the soul by minimizing the potentially corrupting influence of the body.[45] Thus, perfection of the body is not an end in itself, but a means to perfection of the soul. Man's task is to restore the soul to its dominant role over the body. This view of the relationship of the body to the soul compelled Loew's adoption of a rather ascetic attitude. Since man's physical nature may retard the development of his spiritual qualities and impede his eventual communion with God, Loew encouraged restriction of the gratification of one's physical needs. Physically man is little better than the animals; holiness means separation from the corporeal. To obtain a modicum of sanctity, one must relinquish the material and choose the spiritual.[46]

Though Rabbi Loew does adopt an ascetic stance, he does not go to the extremes of the medieval philosophers. The human body is not considered evil in itself, nor are any of its natural functions, such as sex. The body is only potentially evil. It becomes evil and destructive when not subservient to the spiritual ends of human existence. Thus, for Loew, the body, human matter, is potentially a blessing or a curse. It can help elevate man or it can degrade him. While perfection of the body does not signify human fulfillment, while the body is a shield between God and man, preventing the attainment of *devekut,* the body does provide the material foundation for man's spiritual existence. As the material world serves to express the spiritual God, so may the human body serve to elicit the spiritual dimensions of human existence. Just as the body needs the soul to give it form and purpose, the soul needs the body to serve as the instrument by means of which it may attain perfection. Though the soul emanates from the divine realm, it requires a physical home in order to develop, to mature, to be transformed from raw potentiality to completion, toward perfection.

Perfection of the body is the "root and *foundation*" for perfection of the soul, for the realization of man's form. For this reason, Abraham is referred to as the "foundation of the world" by rabbinic literature. Abraham represents perfection of the body.[47] Having achieved that level, he was ready for the higher levels of perfection and consequently was given the commandment of circumcision, for circumcision represents the realization of bodily perfection and the beginning of the perfection of human form. Circumcision testifies to the spiritual implications of physical existence.[48]

Loew interprets human sexuality along similar lines. In itself sex is not evil. Sex may be disgraceful when abused, but not when normally and properly used. Following the mystics, Loew believed that the human sex act is ordained by God and is not an obstruction of man in search of God. Human sexuality is paradigmatic of the interplay of male and female forces which characterizes all of existence. As such, the most physical of human activities has metaphysical implications.

Sex, when used in consonance with the laws of the Torah, is not–as the "philosophers" and the "physicians" have claimed–an embarrassment, an abomination, a disgrace, but a natural act which raises the human body toward God. "Do not say," insists Loew, "that this kind of sex [i.e., human sex] is like that of other animals. Such is not the case. A man and a woman draw their sexual potentialities from the divine."[49] Loew echoes the views of his predecessors in the history of Jewish mysticism that since sex was created by God, it cannot be essentially evil.[50] He adopts the view that sexuality is a necessary good and not a necessary evil, as the "philosophers" had asserted. Marriage is necessary for human perfection. Man and woman are incomplete without one another. Sexual intercourse with one's spouse is an opportunity for sanctification. Woman without man is matter without form. Man without woman is vagabond form. Without a woman, man will be led to attach himself to an entity composed of a base quality of matter. Woman is man's proper variety of matter. In marriage and in the marital act, man and woman achieve a level of human perfection. Physical completion, signified by marriage and concretized in sex, opens the path to metaphysical perfection.[51]

For Rabbi Loew, the physical is good, not in itself, but when its use becomes a prelude to the metaphysical. Man's task, therefore, is to purify matter in order that it may coexist with form. The true attainment of human perfection begins when polar opposites are in proper unison with form dominating matter. The paradigm of this relationship is male and female, supplementing and completing one another. Attainment of this relationship means the cohesion of matter with form, the body with the soul, "this world" with the "intermediate world."

When the human body is used for spiritual ends, when the body is subservient to the soul, man realizes his having been created in the divine image. In holding this view, Rabbi Loew reflects the position of the Zohar which perceives allusions to the metaphysical in the physical, reflections of the *sefirot* in the human body.[52]

According to Loew, man qua man (which for him means the Jew) does not achieve perfection and completion in the material world. The corporeal, the natural, the "this wordly" are the province of the Gentile. For the Jew, perfection means realization of soul and intellect. Perfection occurs in the realization of the perfection of the "intermediate" and "supernatural" worlds. For the Gentile, on the other hand, perfection is attainable only in "this world." For the Gentile, perfection of the body *is* perfection.

According to Loew, physical perfection in the natural realm is both the purpose and the limit of Gentile existence.[53] A Gentile's perfection is a Pyrrhic victory since material perfection signifies no real perfection at all but only privation.[54] Like matter without form, the perfection of matter indicates privation, hell, and the demonic.

According to Loew, the body of the Jew consists of a more refined variety of matter than that of the Gentile.[55] Furthermore, the form which attends the matter of the Jew is also of a higher, i.e., more spiritual, nature than that of the Gentile. While the Gentile does have a soul (*nefesh*) which is the form of his body, it is not so spiritual as that granted the Jew. The *seikhel,* the divine intellect, the soul of the soul, is all but absent in Gentiles.[56] The Jew therefore is predisposed to the spiritual, the supernatural, the divine, while the Gentile is predisposed to the corporeal, the material, the natural.[57] The Gentile soul is encrusted with matter. The Jewish soul is all but independent of corrupting matter.[58] The Gentile soul therefore is overcome by matter, while the Jewish soul erodes the influence of matter.[59] Loew claims that while all men are created in the divine image, the Gentile's soul, which is dominated by matter, obscures his divine image. In the Jewish soul, the divine image is dominant and it may therefore attain its realization. For the Gentile, form is secondary, matter primary. For the Jew, matter is secondary, form is primary.[60]

The Gentile attachment to the material world, to the body, is an expression of the essence of the Gentile nature. The Jewish attachment to the spiritual world is an expression of the nature of the Jew. Rabbi Loew utilizes these assumptions to explain the historical fact of Jewish social, political, and economic degradation and of Gentile power and control of the natural, political, and economic spheres of human existence. Loew's "racism" is not a pretext for engendering hate but rather an essential aspect of his theodicy. For Loew, as for almost all classical Jewish thinkers, the contrast between the theological assumption of Israel's divine election harshly contrasted with Israel's historical fate. In itself a problem which strikes at the very heart of Jewish existence, the issue was continuously exacerbated by the pressures of Christian polemicizers who argued that the Jews' degraded state of existence is proof positive of their rejection by God, of the termination of their divine election. Thus, Loew's position regarding the essentially different natures of Jew and Gentile is polemical as well as theological.

Judah Loew insists that one should not be surprised at the power of the Gentile in "this world." It is, after all, his realm. His total existence is attached to the material, economic, historical dimension of existence. The Gentiles' power is proper as is Israel's lack of power. Israel receives no reward and commands no physical power. Israel's realm is the supernatural dimension. Its perfection is realized *there* and not in "this world." Gentile power, argues Rabbi Loew, is not a demonstration of superiority over the Jew. The Gentiles' assumption that power and physical might and numerical superiority demonstrates their innate eminence is an illusion. Their domination only demonstrates their greater attachment to the material, the natural, the "this worldly" and their alienation from the essentially supernatural, transcendent quality of reality. The subjugation of the Jews in history demonstrates their election not their rejection. Physical domination by the Gentiles only demonstrates their alienation from the divine, from the spiritual, from the essence of human existence. Alienated existence is represented by Gentile existence. Gentile existence symbolizes the sovereignty of matter over form. It is a corrupted variety of existence. Perfection of the lowest level of existence in the lowest of the three worlds, epitomizes Gentile existence and manifests an illusory perfection. Though the Jew is metaphysically superior to the Gentile, this does not mean that the Jew is automatically in a state of perfection. Because the constitution of the Jew embodies greater spiritual potentialities than that of the Gentile, additional strenuous effort is required for the Jew to attain the level of human perfection befitting his exalted status. The Jew has much further to go than the Gentile to attain the variety of perfection peculiar to his nature.[61]

Perfection of the Soul

The human soul, according to Judah Loew, shares a number of qualities with the animals and is identified with a number of bodily functions.[62] The soul is the vital force of the body and is physically located in the heart.[63] All bodily functions depend upon the heart and therefore upon the soul in order to function. The soul also controls various organs directly, especially those connected with movement, cognition, and emotion.[64] By refining the physical aspects of the soul, those facets of man which he shares with the animals become transformed. His matter, his body acquires a more refined quality. His will, his volition becomes peculiarly human as it is elevated from the control of his impulses, his physical needs, his corporeal nature. Once the spiritual aspect of the soul is no longer recessive, the human will, now identified with the intellectual, supernatural aspect of man, dominates. Man thereby becomes distinguished from the animals and from the qualities of the material world.[65]

Just as the body serves as the vehicle for prefection of the soul, so may the "evil inclination" pave the way toward perfection.[66] Animals have no evil inclination. They are therefore incapable of moral discernment. Angels also have no evil inclination. They too are incapable of moral decision. Both animal and angel must follow their natures. But because the human soul possesses the evil inclination, man has moral choice. He may opt for imperfection or for perfection. The evil inclination permits him that choice. Only by virtue of the evil inclination can the human being strive for perfection.[67]

For Rabbi Loew, as for his rabbinic predecessors, the evil inclination is not evil in itself.[68] It only becomes evil when it is misused. Paradoxically, the aspect of the soul most related to privation and matter–the evil inclination–provides man with the possibility of transcending privation and matter. The aspect of man which may lead to sin and to the enslavement of the body may free man from sin and from the corrupting influence of the body.[69] Ironically, the flaw in human nature–the evil inclination–necessitates the remedy required for human perfection–the Torah. The angels, who have no flaws, require no remedy for those flaws. However, in overcoming his flaws, by realizing his will, by identifying with the Torah, man transcends the angels.[70] The angels are God's slaves; they have no choice but to obey. Their obedience therefore is not meritorious. Man, however, is the child of God. His obedience is by choice. By that choice, by means of sacred deeds, man may transcend not only the animals, but the angels as well.[71] The Torah is only for man and not for the angels. The World to Come is for the perfected man, while the angels are imprisoned by their static natures in the "intermediate world." Only man, neither the angels nor the animals, is created in the divine image.[72] That image is free will; freedom is what man most essentially shares with God. Thus, for Rabbi Loew, perfection of the soul may be secured by means of man's freely choosing to observe the commandments of the Torah. To ensure the triumph of the supernatural over the natural, spiritual tools are required; these tools are the commandments of the Torah.[73]

Loew differentiates among natural law (or morality), the commandments of the Torah, and the essence of the Torah. For Loew, these three entities correspond to the three worlds and to the three aspects of man. Natural law corresponds to the material world, to the body. It may be identified with the perfected Gentile who represents the perfection of the body and the perfection of the material aspect of the natural world. The commandments of the Torah, on the other hand, are the physical, outward manifestations of the essence of the Torah.[74] They therefore embody both a physical and a spiritual element. They are the "body" of which the spiritual essence of the Torah is the form. As such, they correspond to the soul and to the intermediary world, which embraces both a physical and a spiritual, a natural and a supernatural component. Observance of the commandments is the key to attaining perfection of the soul.[75] Since the commandments and the Torah are exclusively the province of the Jewish people, only they have the potentiality to attain human perfection.

The Soul Is a Seed

Judah Loew compares the human soul to a seed implanted in the earth. The seed represents potentiality. The commandments are the essential element in propelling the seed of man, the human soul, toward actuality. Observance of the commandments ensures that the soul, representing pure potentiality, once placed into the body, will flourish and attain its perfection. As branches and flowers of a tree betray the quality of its root, the human body, by its deeds, portrays the quality of the soul it contains. Man is like a tree which may choose whether or not to bring forth its fruit.

For Rabbi Loew, the human soul is implanted within man in a state of raw potential so that man, through proper deeds, may nurture it and bring it to actuality and perfection. In the process, the soul may either retain or lose its original purity; it may become corrupted or perfected. The body is the vessel in which the fructification or the putrefaction of the human soul may occur.[76] By means of the commandments man may opt to perfect rather than to pollute, to improve rather than to infect, to complete rather than to corrode. At life's end, man may return more than that which he received at life's beginning. He may return more than he was granted.

Perfection of the Intellect

Judah Loew identifies the Torah, which is the form of the commandments, with the supernatural realm and with the human intellect.[77] Study of the Torah, education, becomes a means of attaining the highest level of perfection. Knowledge of the Torah, study of the Torah, accomplishes the perfection of the intellectual aspect of man which is man's final perfection. Only knowledge of the Torah allows one to know the essence of things. Only by means of the Torah is human perfection actually secured, is perfection of the "form of the form" of man actually attained. Observance of its commandments leads one toward the essence of the Torah, toward permanence, toward the World to Come. Observance of the commandments is a necessary but not sufficient prerequisite for attaining complete human perfection. Knowledge of the Torah, an intellectual component, is required.

Knowledge of the Torah's inner, true meaning implies perfection of the intellect. By means of the Torah, man secures eternity, man acquires static, permanent perfection.[78] By means of the Torah, a supernatural entity, which, like all supernatural entities, transcends space, time, and the other qualities of the always-changing material world, man achieves permanence.[79] He enters the supernatural realm, the World to Come, by means of the Torah, which is equivalent to the World to Come.

One should not confuse Loew's notion of perfection of the intellect with the notion of intellectual perfection advocated by various individuals in the history of medieval Jewish philosophy, Maimonides in particular. Loew's understanding of human perfection differs from the position of the philosophers on a number of counts.[80]

By considering the Torah the sole means of attaining perfection, Loew echoes the views of Joseph Albo and of Hasdai Crescas in their attacks on the position that they attributed to Maimonides, which holds philosophical speculation to be a way toward human perfection. For Loew only the Torah, and neither philosophy nor science, is the way to perfection. A corollary of this assumption is Loew's claim that since the Torah is the exclusive means to perfection and since the Torah is the monopoly of the Jews, only Jews may be candidates for human perfection. Secondly, Loew again joins Albo and also Ibn Gabbai in attacking the philosophers for making immortality conditional upon intellectual attainment. If the intellect (as opposed to the soul) and thought alone (to the

exclusion of the deed) are the sole means to perfection and consequently to immortality, the masses of Jews would be excluded at
the outset from immortality. Furthermore, once one equates
human perfection with intellectual perfection, thoughts rather
than deeds *and* thoughts are all that is required to acquire
immortality. Rabbi Loew holds that this position denigrates the
importance of religious observance and gives credence to the
possibility of immortality coexisting with immorality. Finally, in
Loew's view, the philosophical notion of intellectual perfection,
was predicated upon two other incorrect assumptions. First, it
incorrectly assumed that a part of man–the intellect–is all of man
and consequently that perfection of the intellect alone means the
perfection of man. Secondly, the philosophical notion of human
perfection assumed the existence of an entity known as the
"active intellect." For the philosophers the adhesion of the
"active intellect" (*seikhel ha-po'el*) to the human intellect (*seikhel
ha-enoshi*) signifies the attainment of intellectual perfection which
is human perfection, For Loew, however, the idea of the "active
intellect" is simply a philosopher's fantasy. For Loew, only by
means of the spiritual Torah can material man open a door to the
divine. He may begin to pierce the shield of matter separating
himself from God. During life he may only penetrate to a small
degree. True penetration and removal of the veil may be accomplished only in death. Thus, life is but an opportunity to ensure
one's survival after death. To strive for human perfection during
life is to help ensure oneself permanence in an afterlife. In "this
world," however, man is always on the way toward perfection; he
never attains perfection.[81] In Loew's words:

> Man was not created in his final perfection. This is the
> meaning of the verse "Man was born to toil"[Job 5:7], i.e., he
> is born and exists in order to toil toward the actualization of
> his perfection. However, he can never attain actualized exis-
> tence. Man may always work to actualize his potential and this
> is his final perfection. . . Yet, even when he acquires some
> actualization, he still remains in potential, ever ready to attain
> additional actualization.[82]

Though the human intellect may be identified with the Torah
while the intellect inhabits the body, such an identification is only
partially accurate. Confined by the body, the intellect perceives
only a shadow of the essence of the Torah. It comprehends only a
fraction, not of.the essential Torah, but of the Torah as it appears

to man in the natural realm. As long as man's intellect is affected by matter it cannot claim to be a pure, refined variety of intellect. As long as man relates to matter, the essence of the Torah remains elusive.[83] The embodied perfected human intellect may apprehend the Torah in its apparent form. It may not, however, relate to the Torah in its essential form.

In "this world," the commandments, which are related to physical deeds, serve as the intermediary between the natural man and the supernatural essence of the Torah. They serve as the garb of the essential Torah. In the World to Come, when man will shed this physical garb, the Torah too will be manifest to man without its wordly accoutrements. In the World to Come, man will perceive the essential meaning of the Torah, divested of its narratives and its commandments. The static Torah, embodying absolute truth, will become available only in the World to Come. The vestments of the Torah, required by the imperfections of the natural realm for man to be able to relate to it at all, will be shed. Only the essence will be retained. The accidental will dissolve; the essential will persist.[84]

The essential, spiritual Torah, knowledge of which is vouchsafed for the World to Come, is the actual Torah given at Sinai. According to Loew, the first set of tablets brought down from Sinai by Moses represented the essential Torah. However, when Moses saw that they were too spiritual for "this world," he understood they had to be shattered and replaced by a second set befitting the natural realm. In "this world," we perceive only the Torah represented by the second set of tablets. In the World to Come, we are promised a perception of the meaning of the essential Torah, represented by the first set of tablets.[85]

For Judah Loew the natural world in itself is penultimate. It is but an opportunity, a preparation, for the World to Come. Since "this world" represents privation, while only the World to Come represents true existence and immortality, man's final perfection lies not in this world but in the World to Come.[86] Perception of truth is vouchsafed not in our world, but in the World to Come.[87] However, the entire endeavor to achieve human perfection reaches its climax not simply by means of entrance into the World to Come. Even perfection of the intellect in the World to Come is only a means to a higher end. The goal of human perfection during life is not human perfection but the realization of man's unique ability and awesome responsibility to repair the shattered universe, to unite the fragmented cosmos.[88] But even this goal is penultimate to *devekut* ("cleaving to God"), to repairing the breach between God and man.

Devekut surpasses perfection of the intellect.[89] In *devekut* man is reconciled with God. To aspire to human perfection is to strive to attain that which never was. To strive for *devekut* is to aspire for the reunification of that which once was. In human perfection man seeks to overcome his alienation from his own essence. In *devekut* man attempts to surmount his alienation from God, who is the essence of reality. If he were only a humanist, Judah Loew might be satisfied to aspire for human perfection. However, Rabbi Loew was a mystic. Therefore, the path to human perfection can only be a means to mystical communion with God, for *devekut*. Striving for human perfection is a prelude, not a destination. To aspire for human perfection is to search for the path which leads to God. At the end of the path is God. The time of arrival is eternity The place of arrival is the World to Come.

In his discussion of *devekut,* Judah Loew the mystic clearly emerges. Loew's understanding of *devekut* is the subject of the chapter which follows.

11

Beyond Human Perfection: "Cleaving" to God

Jewish mysticism begins with the realization that a gap separates God and man. The Jewish mystic is one who strives to bridge that gap. For the Jewish mystic, therefore, the quest for human perfection, for personal fulfillment, is penultimate to achieving *devekut,* communion with the divine.

Before examining Judah Loew's understanding of *devekut,* an attempt will be made to sketch the development of major aspects of the idea of *devekut* in sources which most probably influenced him. While by no means exhaustive, this review will provide an historical and conceptual foundation upon which to reconstruct and to evaluate Rabbi Loew's understanding of *devekut.*

The term *devekut* does not appear in the Hebrew Bible; however, forms of its declined root–*d-v-k*–do appear many times in Scripture. The root *d-v-k* means "to cleave"; *devekut* means "cleaving." The Bible uses variants of *d-v-k* to characterize a variety of physical relationships. For example, one's bones cleave to one's flesh;[1] one's tongue cleaves to the roof of one's mouth;[2] man cleaves to woman.[3] Variants of the term are also often used to signify the nature of the relationship of man to God and of the people of Israel to God.[4]

Because of the physical and even erotic connotations of *d-v-k* in the biblical text, some rabbinic authorities found the use of this term a source of embarrassment when employed to describe the relationship between man and God. They attempted, therefore, to interpret such references in a figurative way. A number of examples follow:

"To cleave to Him" [Deut. 4:4]. How is it possible for a human being to ascend to Heaven and cleave to fire? For as it is written–

"The Lord your God is a consuming fire" [4:24]. It is further written: "His throne was fiery flames" [Dan. 7:9]. Therefore, [the verse can not be taken literally and indicates that] one ought to *cleave* to the scholars and to their disciples. I [God] consider such [action] comparable to one's ascending to Heaven. . . . Do you wish to apprehend Him who spoke and thereby created the world?–Study *agaddah,* for in so doing you will apprehend Him who spoke and thereby created the world, and you will *cleave* to His ways.[5]

"Walk after none but the Lord your God, revere none but Him; observe His commandments alone; heed only His orders; worship none but Him and cleave to Him" [Deut. 5:13]. Rabbi Hama b. Rabbi Hanina interpreted the verse as follows: Is it possible for a human being to walk after the *Shekhinah* [God]? For has it not been said–"For the Lord your God is a consuming fire" [Deut. 4:24]? But the meaning is to walk after [i.e., to emulate] the attributes of the Holy One, blessed be He. As He clothes the naked . . . as He visits the sick . . . as He comforts mourners . . . [so ought you do likewise].[6]

"You who did *cleave* to the Lord your God are alive, everyone of you this day" [Deut. 4:4]. How is it possible to *cleave* to God concerning whom it is written, "The Lord your God is a consuming fire" [Deut. 4:24]? But [the meaning of the verse is this:] One who marries his daughter to a scholar or aids in financially supporting scholars or benefits scholars from his estate, is regarded by Scripture as if he had *cleaved* to the divine. Similarly you read "To love the Lord and [to hearken to His voice] and to *cleave* to Him" [Deut. 30:20]. How is it possible for a human being to *cleave* to the divine? But [what is meant is:] Any one who marries his daughter to a scholar, or carries on trade for the benefit of scholars, or benefits scholars from his estate is regarded by Scripture as if he had *cleaved* to the divine.[7]

On the basis of the attitude expressed in the latter text, it has been asserted that the rabbinic mind only perceived *devekut* as indirect communion with God, that it understood biblical references to man's "cleaving" to God only in a figurative way. Maimonides is claimed to have been the initiator in the history of Jewish religious thought of the notion that *devekut,* meaning a direct relationship between God and man, is attainable by man.[8] The evidence, however, indicates otherwise. Biblical references to man's cleaving to God were taken literally by some of the rabbis. They assumed that man can enter into direct communion with the divine. They were not embarrassed by the physical connotations of the term "cleaving," nor were they abashed by its erotic implications. Some examples follow:

"Your eyes have seen what the Lord did in Baal-peor. For all the men who were joined to [the idol] Baal-peor, the Lord your God has destroyed them from your midst. But you that did *cleave* to the Lord your God are alive, every one of you this day" [Deut. 4:3-4]. [The Talmud records an anonymous *baraitha* which comments on the above verses:] "That were joined to Baal-peor"–i.e., [loosely] like a bracelet on the hands of a woman; "but you that did cleave to the Lord your God"–[were] actually attached [*devukim mammash*]. According to Rab, this means that Israel cleaves to God as one sticky date cleaves to another.[9]

Another text quotes Rabbi Meir as follows:

We can draw the following inference: If God gave eternal existence to the oxen which were attached to the work of the tabernacle by man, how much more so will He bestow eternal life on Israel who *cleave* to the Eternal, as it is written, "But you that did *cleave* to the Lord your God are alive, every one of you this day" [Deut. 4:4]?[10]

Whereas some rabbinic texts cited above utilized the analogy of God with fire to dismiss the possibility of a literal interpretation of biblical references to cleaving to God, at least one late rabbinic source utilizes the analogy of God with fire to support a literal interpretation of such references. This bold text reads as follows:

In this world Israel cleaves to the Holy One, blessed be He, as it is said: "You that cleave unto God" [Deut. 4:4]. However, in the time-to-come they will become like [God]. For as the Holy One, blessed be He, is a consuming fire, as it is written–"The Lord your God is a consuming fire" [Deut. 4:24],so shall they be a consuming fire as it is written: "The light of Israel shall be for a fire, and his Holy One for a flame" [Isa. 10:17].[11]

Though some rabbinic authorities sought to neutralize, to circumvent, and to ignore the erotic connotations of "cleaving" when utilized to describe the relationship between God and man, others did not do so.

The narrative in the book of Genesis preserves a tale of the passionate love of a man for a woman. In a fit of passion, Shekhem son of Hamor, the Hivite prince, rapes Jacob's only daughter, Dinah. Crazed with love, lust, and passion, Shekhem is prepared to pay any price to have Dinah as his wife. After the rape, his psychological state is described as follows: "His soul did *cleave* unto Dinah the daughter of Jacob and he loved the maiden and spoke tenderly to the damsel" [Gen. 34:3]. Commenting on this episode, Rabbi Simeon ben Lakish is quoted as saying:

> Hamor spoke with them, saying "My son Shekhem longs for your daughter" [Gen. 34:8]. Rabbi Simeon b. Lakish said: The Holy One, blessed be He, manifested His love to Israel with three expressions of love: *cleaving*, desiring, delighting in. *Cleaving*, as it says: "But you that did *cleave* to the Lord your God" [Deut. 4:4]. . . Here we learn then from the passage dealing with this wretch [Shekhem]; (i.e., we learn that these three expressions connote love from their use in the present biblical passage). *Cleaving* from "His soul did *cleave*" [Gen. 34:3]; desiring from "the soul of my son desires your daughter" [Gen. 34:8]; delighting in from "he had delight in Jacob's daughter." [12]

Similarly, a second source quotes Rabbi Abahu as saying: [13]

> We learn the meaning of God's unexplained, spontaneous love for Israel from this filthy wretch [Shekhem]. For about Shekhem it is written–"His soul *cleaved* to Dinah" and about Israel it is written, "You that *cleave* to God" [Deut. 4:4].

From the immediately preceding citations it should be apparent that direct communion with God is not originally a medieval notion, as has been assumed, but is already clearly identifiable in talmudic and midrashic sources. [14]

While in biblical and rabbinic literature the means of attaining *devekut* are not clear, they may be assumed to be the cult, prayer, study, and general observance of the commandments. Love of God coupled with fear or awe of God were considered the attitudes which engendered *devekut*. [15] With the initiation and development of the Jewish philosophical tradition in the Middle Ages, an additional dimension was added to descriptions of *devekut*. Intellectual contemplation of God became an essential characteristic of *devekut*. While love of God is still assumed to be the prelude to *devekut*, it is now construed to be an intellectual rather than an emotional love. The love of the philosophers, unlike the love described in some of the rabbinic statements noted above, is characterized not by an abundance of passion, but by the absence of passion. The intellect dominates and suppresses passion. Intellectual enlightenment is now considered the essential characteristic of *devekut*.

Most significant in this regard are Maimonides' reflections on the
nature of *devekut*. Not only do they have intrinsic interest, but they
are relevant to an understanding of the development of the notion
of *devekut* in subsequent Jewish mystical literature and eventually
in the writings of Rabbi Loew.

In his legal works, written for the masses, Maimonides generally
reiterates the rabbinic tradition, noted above, which limits *devekut*
to indirect relationship with God.[16] However, in his philosophical
treatise, addressed to the intellectual elite, Maimonides considers
the possibility of direct communion with the divine by means of
intellectual contemplation.

For Maimonides, the quintessence of human perfection is intellectual perfection. To attain intellectual perfection is the purpose
and essential characterization of man qua man. It is the guarantor
of permanence beyond the present life, endurance of the essential
quality of man–the rational faculty of the soul–beyond the grave.
Intellectual perfection qualifies the aspect of man most like God–
the intellect–for relationship with God. For Maimonides, this
relationship is *devekut*.

For Maimonides, the intellect is man's gateway to God. Love of
God means intellectual apprehension of God. The intensity of that
love is determined by the intensity of that apprehension. The
reward for and the consequence of that apprehension, of that love,
is the attainment of *devekut*. For Maimonides, *devekut* is a direct,
immediate experience. It is characterized by the forging of a bond
between God and the part of man most like God. It is an experience
which may be attained only by the select few. The masses must be
content with an indirect variety of *devekut*. As they cannot cleave
directly to God, they must cleave to those who can cleave directly
to God, i.e., to the scholars, to those who can attain the high level of
intellectual perfection which culminates in direct cleaving to the
divine.

For Maimonides, direct *devekut* is not attainable during life.
Only when the impediment to clear apprehension–the body–is
shed can the intellect truly express the intensity of its love of the
divine by means of its intellectual apprehension of the divine. Thus,
for Maimonides, *devekut* is achieved by the few, through the
mind.[17]

Maimonides' portrayal of *devekut* was augmented by some of
the Jewish mystics of Spain (especially Gerona) and of France
(especially Provence) who flourished before the composition of
the Zohar (i.e., before the 1280s).[18] As for Maimonides, so for

Isaac the Blind (d. ca. 1235) of Narbonne (France) and his students, who flourished across the Pyrenees in Gerona, prayer and observance of the commandments are not the ends of the religious life, but merely means to attaining *devekut*.[19] *Devekut* itself is characterized by the cleaving of human thought to God's thought.[20]

Moses ben Nahman (ca. 1194-1240) was the leading Jewish legal and religious authority of his time in Spain. He identified himself with the mystics and prepared the way for the infusion of Jewish mysticism into the lifeblood of Spanish Jewry. Nahmanides, too, held that intellectual contemplation leads to *devekut*. In one place Nahmanides characterizes *devekut* as a state wherein one "leaves all matters of this world as if one has no body, in order to direct all one's thoughts only to one's Creator . . . for one's soul to cleave to the Name."[21]

Though Nahmanides holds that *devekut* may be attained during one's lifetime, he in effect considers *devekut* as the attainment of the afterlife in this life. In his commentary to Deuteronomy (11:22), Nahmanides defines *devekut* as a state of mind in which:

> One constantly remembers God and his love, one thinks only of Him . . . to the point that when [one] speaks with someone else, his heart is not with them at all but is still before God. It may be true of those who attain this rank that their soul is granted immortality even in their lifetime, for they become a dwelling place for the Divine.[22]

This statement is reminiscent of statements found in Maimonides' *Guide of the Perplexed* as is Nahmanides' claim that *devekut* engendered by intellectual apprehension of God assures one divine providence.[23]

While the mystics adopted Maimonides' notion of *devekut* as the goal of religious existence and as an experience to be attained essentially by means of intellectual contemplation, they augmented the Maimonidean position with two interrelated elements which will become relevant for an understanding of Rabbi Loew's presentation of *devekut*.

Some of the mystics insisted that *devekut* represents not only a cleaving to God, but a union with God. For the mystics, *devekut* means remerging with the Source from which one originally emerged.[24] Related to the notion of *devekut* as reunion is the second element introduced by the mystics—the *sefirot*. Return to

God means reuniting elements of man–intellect, will–with the *sefirot* from which they originally derived. Intellectual contemplation leads the human intellect back to its source–the *sefirah* corresponding to the divine intellect. Effacement of one's will to achieve absolute subservience to the divine will leads human volition back to its source–the *sefirah* corresponding to the divine will.[25]

The reunion of the human soul with its sefirotic root was compared by the mystics to the reabsorption of a ray of light or a drop of water by the source of its effulgence. Thus, for some of the mystics who flourished immediately before the Zohar, *devekut* signified not only being with God, but being *within* God, reunion with God.[26]

In the Zohar, love and fear of God are the primary means to *devekut* with God, i.e., with the *sefirot*; specifically, to the *Shekhinah* (the lowest *sefirah*).[27] (Cleaving to the *Shekhinah* is sometimes portrayed by means of erotic imagery.)[28] Furthermore, the Zohar claims that there is an antithesis to *devekut* with God, namely, *devekut* with the forces of evil (*sitra aḥra*: literally, "other side"). Thus, one has a choice between cleaving to God or cleaving to the demonic.

According to the Zohar, this *devekut* with God is attained primarily not by means of mystical contemplation but by the individual Jew's expression of his awe and love for God through performance of the commandments. Hence, for the Zohar, *devekut* is not characterized by intellectual contemplation or ecstatic trances or *unio mystica,* but is an opportunity for ultimate religious experience attainable by everyone.[29]

Medieval Jewish mysticism in Spain, represented by the mystics of Gerona on the one hand and by the Zohar on the other, offers two alternative notions of *devekut.* The mystics of Gerona considered *devekut* to be attainable by only a few, at rare intervals and by means only made available to few. For them, *devekut* was extreme attainment, ultimate fulfillment for the mystical elite, but not for the "uninitiated" masses. The Zohar, however, considered *devekut* readily attainable to all at all times, by means of observance of the commandments of the Torah. It has been claimed that with the rise and development of Eastern European Hasidism in the eighteenth century both approaches–the esoteric and the popular–coalesced. *Devekut* was now construed as the beginning as well as the end of religious experience. On one level, it was attainable by the few, through esoteric means, while on a lower level it was attainable by all through affirming monotheistic faith and by observing the commandments.[30] A careful analysis of Loew's descriptions of *devekut* indicates that already in the sixteenth century, he attempted to combine the two views of *devekut* developed by the Spanish mystics. Furthermore, it appears that a number of characteristics of the Hasidic understanding of *devekut,* usually considered to have been initiated by Hasidism, are already present in Loew's writings; it is quite likely that he influenced Hasidic reflections on this matter. Like the Hasidim, Rabbi Loew understood *devekut* to be both the first and the final rungs of religious experience. It would seem, therefore, that he considered there to be at least two levels of *devekut,* one attainable by faith and observance and the other attainable by a more concerted kind of effort. While these varieties of *devekut* are not clearly differentiated in his work, an attempt will be made to identify them from a consideration of the many occasions Loew has to discuss *devekut* in his writings.

It has been generally assumed that the founder of Hasidism, Israel Baal Shem Tov, introduced a novel element into the previous representations of the notion of *devekut* when he claimed that a variety of *devekut* could be attained by means of simply observing the commandments. It has been claimed that he radically altered the previous understanding of *devekut* when he asserted it to be attainable by means of faith. However, as has already been noted, early rabbinic literature and the central document in Jewish mysticism, the Zohar, already considered observance of the commandments a viable means, available to all, for directly attaining *devekut.* This notion, as will be discussed below, was reiterated by Rabbi Loew. Similarly, the notion of identifying faith with *devekut* is not an innovation of the Baal Shem Tov, as it is stated by Loew a number of times.[31] While the Sabbateans apparently were influenced by Loew's view that Messianic redemption depends upon faith, the Hasidim seem to have been influenced by his identification of *devekut* with faith.[32] According to Rabbi Loew, "By means of faith, man attains *devekut* with God. For the essence of faith is nothing else but *devekut* with God. He believes in Him and cleaves to God with his faith."[33] Both Loew and early Hasidic literature presented their identification of faith and *devekut* as a comment upon the verse: "The righteous shall live by his faith" (Hab. 2:4), and both undoubtedly did so with a well-known talmudic text in mind.

According to talmudic tradition, the Torah contains 613 commandments. The Mishnah reads, "Rabbi Akashia says: The Holy One, blessed be He, desired to make Israel worthy, therefore He gave them the Torah [to study] and many commandments [to perform]." The talmudic discussion deals with the question of *how many* commandments. It quotes Rabbi Simlai as saying: "Six hundred and thirteen commandments were communicated to Moses, three hundred and sixty-five negative precepts, corresponding to the number of solar days [in the year], and two hundred and forty eight positive precepts, corresponding to the number of the members of man's body." A discussion then ensues describing a progressive attempt to "reduce" the commandments to their underlying principles. David is reported to have reduced them to eleven principles, Isaiah to six, Micah to three, Isaiah again to two. Finally, the text reads, "It is Habakkuk who came and based all [the commandments] on one [principle], as it is said–But the righteous shall live by his faith."[34]

Rabbi Loew had this talmudic text in mind when identifying faith and *devekut*. This is clear since in three of the four texts in which he makes this identification Loew quotes that very talmudic source and presents his remarks as a direct commentary upon its meaning. It would seem that Rabbi Loew, utilizing this talmudic source as his proof text, considered faith to be the epitome of all the commandments and therefore most directly identifiable with *devekut*. As faith, the principle upon which the commandments are based, is a way to attain *devekut*, so are each and all of the other commandments of the Torah.

As a material being, man cannot hope to attain communion with the divine. However, by means of the commandments of the Torah, which embody a supernatural essence, man may transcend the natural and identify with the supernatural. The commandments elevate man, they prime him for *devekut*. In Rabbi Loew's words, "Man, who possesses the divine soul, is nevertheless bounded by matter. But through *cleaving* to the supernatural, divine commandments, and by performing them, he *cleaves* to God and liberates his soul from the natural [dimension]."[35] While the preliminary purpose of observance of the commandments is to help man attain human perfection, their ultimate significance lies in their ability to serve as a catalyst for *devekut*.[36] All "six hundred and thirteen commandments are to perfect man in all *until* man achieves *devekut* with God."[37] The final goal of observing the commandments is not human perfection. Human perfection is penultimate to *devekut*. Rabbi Loew writes, "By means of the commandments the soul may *cleave* and attach itself to God. . . . The final perfection of man is *devekut* with God."[38]

While observance of any of the commandments aids one in attaining *devekut,* Loew, in the course of his writings, identified certain of the commandments as being especially efficacious.

Being composed of matter, the body is a stumbling block to attaining human perfection; it is also an impediment to achieving *devekut.* Therefore, observance of those commandments which aid in neutralizing the material element in man while strengthening the spiritual element is especially discussed with reference to *devekut.* For example, observance of the physical restrictions of eating, sex, etc., required by the laws relevant to the Day of Atonement, aid the individual's flight from the material to the spiritual, so that he may attain *devekut.*[39] Repentance, on the Day of Atonement or at other times, helps one become free of matter and attain *devekut.*[40] Similarly, cultivation of certain moral values such as humility, which Loew identified with "complete separation from the material" engenders *devekut.*[41] Likewise, divine afflictions (*yisurin*), weaken the body, the material aspect of man, consequently precipitating *devekut.*[42]

Like a number of his predecessors in Jewish thought, Judah Loew linked the microcosm motif with the mystical notion of the sanctuary.[43] Man is the universe in miniature and the sanctuary in miniature.[44] Like the sanctuary, man is able to establish *devekut* between the natural and the supernatural realms.[45] One of the ways by which man may achieve his own *devekut* with the divine is by identifying himself with the physical place of the sanctuary and the activities taking place within it. The Temple in Jerusalem was the best way to *devekut;* it had to be replaced, however, by the less efficacious synagogue. But even in the synagogue, man may achieve *devekut.*[46] Similarly, though sacrifice at the Temple would be the best means of attaining *devekut,* at present prayer must suffice to replace sacrifice.[47] In identifying prayer as a means to *devekut,* Loew reiterates former traditions.[48] His insistence that the degree of *devekut* increases with the degree of intention (*kavanah*) also has precedents in Jewish mystical thought.[49] His claim that prayer as *devekut* is tantamount to achieving individually, psychologically, that which messianic redemption achieves nationally, historically, is proto-Hasidic and may have directly influenced what has been termed "the neutralization of messianism in early Hasidism."[50]

Besides commandments relating to repentance and the sanctuary, Loew also specifically notes the peculiar significance of the Sabbath in attaining *devekut.* He writes:

> One should know the Sabbath represents the *devekut* which obtains between Israel and God. ... The attachment and *cleaving* of Israel to God represented by the Sabbath differs from that engendered by the other commandments. For the Sabbath represents Creation. ... If Israel would observe its first Sabbath, it would become attached to God through Creation and that which is related to the Creation is eternal and unchanging.[51]

The commandments in general, and certain commandments in particular, help guide the individual toward *devekut.* However, the *devekut* attainable by means of the observance of the commandments and the cultivation of the moral virtues is only a partial variety of *devekut.* [52] All of the commandments are but preparation for "complete *devekut.*"[53]

Though Rabbi Loew accepted the position represented in the Zohar which promised *devekut* for those who observed the commandments, he also held there to be a second variety of *devekut* which could not be attained simply by means of faith and religious observance. This variety, to be sure, was available to all, but in reality attained by few.

To attain the more "complete" variety of *devekut* one had to transform one's potential spirituality into actuality. Observance of the commandments was the necessary though not sufficient means of accomplishing this goal.[54] The commandments, themselves related to the material world, could provide for the ascendancy of the spiritual aspect of man over the material aspect. However, some additional effort was needed to provide for the cleaving of the spiritual aspect of man to the divine. For man to cleave to God, he had to become like God. The commandments, themselves embodying a material element, could not provide this more intense level of *devekut.* Something more than simple observance was required.

For Loew, *devekut* meant the reconciliation of opposites, specifically God and man. Consequently, it should not be surprising to find him insisting that love of God is an essential means to *devekut* beyond simple observance. Love obtains between opposites, even between distant opposites seeking reconciliation. The object of one's love helps one become complete, perfected. Man's love of God promises him perfection and guides him toward *devekut.*

Loew describes love of God as a means to "complete *devekut.*" Like the mystics of Gerona, he considers *devekut* to be the attainment of the *unio mystica,* often claimed to be uncharacteristic of

Jewish mysticism. According to Rabbi Loew, love of God differs from all other varieties of love. In other varieties of love, the subject generates his love toward the object of his love. In love of God, however, man loves God with the love that originally derived from God. Since God is the source of all, the root of all existence, He is the source of all love, including that by which He is loved by man. Second, love of God differs from all other human varieties of love in that only in love of God may one reach a state of *complete cleaving* in which the self is obliterated, totally submerged in the object of love. Other varieties of love are a pilgrimage to new situations. In love of God, however, one returns to one's original position. A previous unity, disjointed by creation, severed by sin, is regained. The human soul and the human intellect, the supernatural aspects of man, refined of their matter through observance of the commandments are now ready, by means of love of God, to return man home to his heavenly source. The preparation having been undertaken, the preliminaries having been fulfilled, partial *devekut* having been attained, the path to complete *devekut,* paved by human love of God, is now open. In Judah Loew's words:

> The love man has for God is not his own but derives from God. It comes from God and man returns it to Him. . . . Love of God is more fitting than love of anything else. For in every kind of love which obtains between two lovers, though they may cleave one to the other, nevertheless, each retains his individuality. However, in the love of man for God, man completely returns his spirit and his soul to Him to the extent that man loses his individuality and completely cleaves to Him, as it is written, "to love the Lord your God and to cleave to Him." This is complete love.[55].

Thus, while Judah Loew does not accept the erotic analogies of his predecessors when discussing *devekut,* he does reiterate the rabbinic notion of literal "cleaving" and does accept the view of the Spanish kabbalists that the *unio mystica* may be attained.

Another notion asserted by Rabbi Loew, similar to that of the Spanish mystics, is that effacement of one's will and the attachment to the divine will engenders *devekut.* Loew considered man's free renunciation of his independent existence as an act of love for God. By recognizing himself as an effect of God, rather than as a cause in himself, man asserts his love for God and finds his way back to God.[56] Love of God engenders *devekut* since it helps reunite the parts of man most like God with God, i.e., the soul and the intellect.

The patriarchs attained *devekut* by means of love of God, each on his own level. Abraham did so through the intellect. Isaac did so through the soul. Jacob, who represents the synthesis of his father and grandfather, did so through both the soul and the intellect. Jacob is the paradigm for his decendants. One may achieve complete *devekut* by realizing the potential inherent in the human soul and in the human intellect. One way in which this may be done is by love of God.[57] In portraying love of God as a means to attaining *devekut,* Rabbi Loew in effect rejects the position held by previous kabbalists that awe (*yirah*) was a more effective means of attaining *devekut.*[58] Awe of God is essentially inferior to love of God.[59] Loew adopts a position found in the Zohar which holds awe to be inferior to love, but which nevertheless considers awe a necessary prerequisite to love of God. In expressing awe, one prepares for love by negating one's own being in relationship to God. In awe one "makes oneself as if one is not [*ayin*] in relation to God."[60]

Because man's love of God is a variety of love between two irreconcilable opposites, rather than between two polar opposites, as is the case of human love between man and woman, it may not be attained directly, but may best be attained through an intermediary. In Rabbi Loew's view, that intermediary is the Torah.[61] Such being the case, knowledge of the Torah, acquired through study of the Torah, engenders love of God and consequently *devekut.* Education is the means to communion with the divine. In Loew's words: "Love of God is *devekut* with God. In love, the lover cleaves to the beloved and this is impossible except by means of the study of the Torah out of love which is *devekut.*"[62] Elsewhere, he writes that "love of God is *devekut* with God. It is impossible for such to obtain except through study of the Torah which is *devekut* with Him."[63]

The Torah's essential kinship with the human soul and the human intellect assures the possibility of *devekut.*[64] By means of the Torah, man's material nature is purged; his spiritual nature is amplified. Through the Torah man asserts his spiritual essence and in so doing he is no longer the irreconcilable opposite of God. Rather, by asserting his kinship with the Torah, man affirms his essential kinship with the divine. He is therefore ready for reconciliation with God. He is prepared for reattachment to God. Now he may return to his source. He is a candidate for *devekut.*

According to Judah Loew, before birth one's soul contains all the knowledge of the Torah. However, when the soul is infused within the body, one forgets the whole Torah. Through observance of the commandments and study of the Torah, one may reacquire during life his forfeited knowledge.[65] The human soul's reconciliation with the Torah prepares the way for reconciliation with God. Since in its original state the soul is associated with the Torah, its return to that state and its reconciliation with God can only be achieved through the Torah. According to Loew, the relationship of God to the Torah may be compared to that of a father to his daughter.[66] Elsewhere, he compares the human soul to the daughter and God to the father. By means of one daughter, the Torah, the other daughter, the soul, is reconciled to her father.[67]

As two daughters may have the same father, so do both the human soul and the Torah derive from the identical source–the sefirotic realm. Rabbi Loew often describes both the Torah and the human soul as well as the human intellect by means of an analogy with a tree with its roots above.[68] This analogy is frequently used by the kabbalists to describe the *sefirot.* By means of the Torah one may become reunited with one's root, one's source, i.e., with the *sefirot,* which are God as He manifests Himself.

What emerges from Rabbi Loew's identification of the spiritual aspects of man with the Torah and with the sefirotic realm is his claim that there is a divine element within man awaiting purification in order that it may be reunited with its source. Human perfection, therefore, ultimately entails not the perfection of man, but the perfection of God. To express his notion, Loew has occasion to utilize the kabbalistic analogy of the human soul to a spark of God. In Loew's words, "Within him [i.e., man] dwells the soul which is a spark of God."[69] The "exalted spark" which man receives is even more than that which the angels receive.[70] It is man's task to purify this element within himself and eventually to return it to God.[71]

By utilizing the analogy of the human soul as a spark of divinity, Rabbi Loew once more expresses his indebtedness to his predecessors in the Jewish mystical tradition. While it is true that Philo of Alexandria had already posited the notion of a divine element within man, it is most unlikely that Loew knew of Philo's view or that, if he did, he utilized it.[72] As has been mentioned above, the late midrash, *Pesikta Rabbati,* already contains the notion that *devekut* entails man's becoming like God.[73] Though Rabbi Loew was probably aware of this source, he does not utilize it in formulating his view. It would appear that Loew's direct source was the Spanish kabbalists.

According to the Zohar, the human soul, or at least the highest part of it, the *neshamah* (as opposed to the *nefesh*), derives from the world of the *sefirot*.[74] It is significant that on most occasions in which Loew identifies the human soul with the sefirotic realm, he also uses the term *neshamah*. It is also interesting to note that the Zohar often identifies the human soul as being derived from the specific *sefirot* of "knowledge" (*hokhmah*) and "understanding" (*binah*), which are also the *sefirot* from which, according to the Zohar, the essential Torah is said to have derived.[75] According to one text in the Zohar, the *neshamah* is a spark of the *sefirah* of "understanding."[76] That the soul derives from these "higher" emanations also appears in the commentaries of Nahmanides and his student Bahya Ibn Asher to the Torah.[77] These two commentaries were undoubtedly utilized by Rabbi Loew.

The idea of the divine spark within man was most clearly stated by Elijah de Vidas, a disciple of Moses Cordovero in his *Reshit Hokhmah*. Though Rabbi Loew is known to have been aware of Cordovero's work, there is no evidence that he was aware of de Vidas's work. However, it is likely that Loew did know of de Vidas's work, which was published for the first time at Venice in 1579. Like de Vidas, Loew rejects the position that awe and not love leads one toward *devekut*.[78]

That Rabbi Loew was at least aware of the writings of de Vidas's teacher, Moses Cordovero, we know from a statement of Loew's own disciple, Shabbtai Sheftel Ha-Levi Horowitz (ca. 1565-1619) of Prague.[79] Horowitz provides this bibliographical datum in his famous kabbalistic book, *Shefa Tal*. It is in this work that the notion of the divine spark within man reaches an additional step in its development. Though later adopted by Hasidic thought, this notion was harshly attacked soon after its appearance in Horowitz's work, as an heretical, polytheistic, and pantheistic doctrine. Horowitz writes, "It is known that the souls of the people of Israel are a portion of God from above" (*helek elohah mi-ma'al*). Horowitz continues, noting the human soul is a portion and a spark separated from the great light which is God. Though in another work, Horowitz notes that de Vidas was one of the sources which inspired this view, it may be that Horowitz's teacher, Rabbi Loew, may also have contributed to Horowitz's expression of the position that the human soul is a spark of the divine, meaning a *part* of God.

While the notion of the human soul as a part of God was often quoted in early Hasidic literature, it reaches a sophisticated level of expression in the writings of the Hasidic master Shneur Zalman of

Liady, the founder of the Ḥabad or Lubavitch School of Hasidic thought.[80] It should be noted that this school was very influenced by the teachings of Judah Loew and that its founder was apparently a direct descendant of his. Prominent in Ḥabad is the notion of "annihilation of the self" (*bittul ha-yesh*).[81] According to this notion, the attainment of *devekut* is characterized by the dissolution of the ego into God, the annihilation of the self while in communion with the divine. The human soul which derives from the Godhead seeks to return to its source and remerge with the divine.[82] As was noted above, a similar view is taken by Rabbi Loew in his discussion of love as a means to *devekut*. In "complete *devekut*," encouraged by love of God, "man completely returns his spirit and his soul to Him to the extent where man loses his individuality and completely cleaves to Him, as it is written, 'to love the Lord your God and to cleave to him.'"[83]

From what has been said thus far, one may conclude that Judah Loew claimed that *devekut* may be attained on two levels. On one level, *devekut* may be considered a variety of "normal mysticism" acquired by means of simple faith in God and observance of the commandments of the Torah.[84] On another level, *devekut* may be obtained only by means of strenuous effort, going above and beyond the "letter of the law." On this second level, *devekut* is considered an intense mystical experience. The first kind of *devekut* might be attained by all; however, the second level, "complete *devekut*," is restricted to very few. Those few are individuals who embody the rare combination of mystic, saint, and scholar.

As was noted above, Loew considered the Torah to be the intermediary between God and man. He especially viewed study of the Torah as a means of attaining *devekut*. For Rabbi Loew, knowledge of the Torah, which originally derived from God, was the way back to God; scholarship was the path to communion with the divine. The scholar, therefore, was a candidate for the higher level of *devekut*.[85] The greater the scholar, the less matter dominated his intellect, the more accurately he apprehended the truths behind appearance. For Loew, only study of the Torah, the repository of revealed truth, might accomplish this goal. Study of other disciplines were incapable of helping one attain this end.[86]

For those unable to excel in knowledge of the Torah, the attainment of the lower level of *devekut* must suffice. Such individuals could, however, capture a reflection of the higher *devekut*. By heeding scholars, by supporting their scholarship, those unable to experience the higher *devekut* directly might do so indirectly. By suggesting this possibility, Loew expands a position, noted above, which was asserted by the rabbis and reiterated in Maimonides' legal code.[87] Just as the intense study of the Torah serves as the catalyst for *devekut* for the scholar, so does the scholar serve as the intermediary for the individual to relate to the Torah and to God. The scholar who is totally dedicated to the Torah eventually embodies the Torah; he becomes the Torah incarnate–"The scholar is himself the Torah."[88] Therefore, as the scholar's attachment to the Torah is his way to the higher *devekut*, attachment of others to the scholar is their way to vicarious attainment of the higher *devekut*.[89]

For Rabbi Loew, the scholar who has attained *devekut* is as different from other men as the intellect is different from the body.[90] "The scholar, in that he has attained *devekut* with God, differs from other men."[91] As the intellect should rule the body, the scholar should rule other men.[92] Only the scholar, through his knowledge of the Torah, has apprehended the truth behind appearance. Only he can lead the people toward human perfection, toward *devekut*.

The scholar is to the community what the brain is to the body.[93] He is the community's motivating and guiding force. Through education, he leads the community back to the Torah and consequently back to God.[94] It is his task to nurture the intellect of the people from potentiality to actuality. The great scholar must be the great teacher. The scholar, as leader, must serve as the heart as well as the head of his community. As the heart vitalizes the body, so must the scholar vitalize his community.[95] The scholar represents "creation in its perfection." Having attained a degree of reconciliation with God, he must now lead the unreconciled to God.[96]

Though one must be a scholar to attain *devekut*, one must also be a saint (*zaddik*).[97] The saint is he who has attained *devekut*.[98] He therefore may serve as an intermediary to God for those who have not attained *devekut*.[99] Like the scholar, the *zaddik* is essentially different from other men. He is God's way to man. The *zaddik* is the instrument of God.[100] He is also the people's way to God. The *zaddik* secures redemption for his generation.[101] One way in which he does this is by his absorption of the suffering for sins committed by others.[102] He not only experiences vicarious suffering like the "red heifer" of biblical times, but his suffering also effects vicarious atonement for the sins of others.[103] In this notion of the *zaddik* as the intermediary, one encounters foreshadowings of the role of the *zaddik* as it developed in Eastern European Hasidism. It is possible that Rabbi Loew may have influenced the development of the idea of the *zaddik* in Hasidism.[104]

For Judah Loew, the saint and the scholar are mutually inclusive. The saint must be wise and learned as well as pious.[105] He must teach not only awe of Heaven and morality, but the traditional wisdom as well.[106] *Devekut* is attained by the saint-scholar, whose task it is to lead the people, through study and piety, to God. The spiritual and intellectual attainments of the saint-scholar are not simply for his own personal fulfillment. They are the basis for community education and social reform.

Just as Rabbi Loew asserted human perfection to be a perpetually elusive goal rather than an obtainable possibility in this world, so did he claim *devekut* on the highest level to be unattainable during life.[107] One's activities during life may prepare one for perfection and the higher *devekut* in the World to Come, after life. This world is preparation for the real world, the true dimension of existence, the World to Come.[108] "This world" was created for the World to Come.[109] "This world" is accidental, while the World to Come is essential. One's function during life is to prepare oneself for eternity in the World to Come.[110]

Since full love of God, complete knowledge of the essence of the Torah, absolute effacement of the human will, total withdrawal from the material is unattainable in this world, they may only be acquired in the afterlife, in the World to Come. Life is inexorably a void which separates man from God.[111] Though this void may be partially bridged in this world, only in the World to Come may the gap be actually closed. In effect, the *devekut* one attains during life is more a path than a bond. To strive for *devekut* during life is to assure that the path back to God in the afterlife is open. The purpose of life is to strive for reconciliation with God in the afterlife.

Rabbi Loew reiterates the position of Maimonides and others that only with death does true *devekut* occur. Even the scholar, even the saint who achieves some level of *devekut* in "this world," is vouchsafed only a glimpse of what will be his in the World to Come.[112]

Though individuals cannot attain complete *devekut* until the World to Come, Rabbi Loew does claim the possibility of "true and complete" *devekut* in "this world" for the people of Israel as a whole.[113] This collective *devekut,* this ending of alienation between God and man in "this world," occurs with the dawning of the Messianic Era. It is to Judah Loew's understanding of the nature of the Messianic Era that we next turn our attention.

12

Messianic Redemption

According to Judah Loew, the world is not eternal. Creation and history have both a beginning and an ending. Creation is manifest in space while history proceeds in time. Space and time are essentially the same.[1] They are characteristics of the present world; they are accidental and apparent, rather than essential and eternal. Apparently echoing a motif found in twelfth-century Jewish mysticism, Rabbi Loew claims that all of creation will eventually become divested of its material garb and will remerge with the divine, supernatural realm.[2] Creation is an act of estrangement and alienation; the effect must eventually rejoin its Cause.[3] Loew identifies this reunification of effect and cause, of creation and God, with the World to Come, with the totally spiritual and supernatural dimension of existence. Before the contradictory opposites—God and creation—unite, an intermediary stage is required; that stage is the Messianic Era. In a sense, the Messianic Era represents on the historical plane that which perfection of the soul represents for the individual. Just as perfection of the soul means the removal of flaws thwarting that perfection and the performance of certain deeds to ensure that attainment, so does realization of the Messianic Era require the removal of the flaws of nature and history and the performance of certain deeds within nature and history to guarantee attainment of that goal. Thus, messianic redemption is not an end in itself, but is the necessary means to the World to Come when the final remerging between God and creation will occur. Just as the Messianic Age will eventually metamorphose into the World to Come, so must historical times eventually transmute into the Messianic Age.

For Rabbi Loew, human history is a series of estrangements from God and reconciliations with God, culminating in messianic redemption, the final reconciliatory event. This dialectical arrangement is ultimately rooted in the mystery of God and is beyond rational explanation. However, the discovery of this dialectic is vouchsafed to man and does provide a framework for making sense out of history, for finding purpose in what is apparently chaos, for explaining the fate of the people of Israel in the world, and for providing Israel in the present with hope for future redemption.

For Judah Loew, alienation and reconciliation with God form part of a pattern of cosmic law. In historical times, alienation from God articulates itself in the "exile" of Israel. Reconciliation with God expresses itself in the "redemption" of Israel. This dialectic, embedded in the cosmic and in the historical order, requires redemption to follow exile. The present exile should therefore engender hope rather than despair. Implicit in the present exile is the future redemption. Indeed, the present exile is the final depression in the dialectic of history. Whereas previous exiles precipitated only partial redemptions, the present exile, being the final exile, holds the promise of complete redemption.[4]

Just as creation begins with alienation and estrangement from God, so human history must commence not with man *with* God, but with man estranged *from* God. For Rabbi Loew therefore, human history begins not with Adam but with Abraham. Created by God himself, Adam is never completely estranged from God. Despite his sin, Adam remains essentially attached to God. His life is not characterized by the dialectic of existence which is initiated with alienation and which culminates with resolution and reconciliation. Adam is not typical; therefore, he cannot serve as the archetype for man.

In Rabbi Loew's reading of the biblical narrative, Abraham emerges as the archetype for man, as the typical man, as the first man. Abraham's life parallels the ebb and flow of existence. Born in Ur of the Chaldeans, far from God, his life begins with alienation, with "exile." By an act of divine grace, he is redeemed from his state of estrangement; he is extricated from his "exile." He is redeemed from Ur of the Chaldeans and is led by God to another land, a Promised Land.[5]

While many earlier sources attempted to find a rationale for the divine choice, Judah Loew rejected such an endeavor. Loew inveighed against those who would ground Abraham's election in Abraham's merit. The sudden, immediate account of Abraham's election in the biblical narrative is purposely not preceded by an account of his merits which occasioned God's selection. To try to fabricate such merit and thereby to justify the divine decision on rational grounds would be a distortion of the event. Unlike Noah, who is characterized as "righteous," and who therefore merits redemption from the Flood sent by God to annihilate the world, no hint of Abraham's acquired worth is posited by the biblical text. The reason is because Abraham, unlike Noah, was not chosen for his merit. Abraham was chosen in an inexplicable act of divine grace.[6] As was previously noted, Rabbi Loew held that election for merit is a conditional election. Election based upon merit persists only as long as the merit is maintained. Election by merit is conditional and, consequently, impermanent. The future election of Israel, implicit in the election of Abraham, is permanent and cannot therefore be determined by merit. The election of Abraham and later of Israel, is rooted in the suprarational divine will. Election rooted in grace is permanent and essential. It is not conditional, accidental, or terminal.[7] In this dialectical understanding of history, Israel's election had to be preceded by a period of estrangement from God. As Abraham's election was preceded by exile, so must be Israel's election. Abraham's experience was to become the prototype for the history of his descendants.[8]

While divine grace could account for election, it could not account for exile. Being eternal, election is essential, while exile is accidental. Rooted in divine grace, election remains unaffected by human sin. Rooted in divine election, redemption is the essential thesis while exile is the accidental antithesis of the historical dialectic.[9] Consequently, the dialectic stops with the messianic redemption. Being accidental and temporal, the exile must eventually pass from existence. As exile cannot be rooted in divine grace, but rather in human sin, Loew had to account for Egyptian bondage by identifying the particular sin which engendered that condition. As the first mention of bondage is found in the biblical narratives concerning Abraham, Loew seeks the source of Israelite bondage in Abraham's sins.

In attempting to identify Abraham's specific sin which engendered the Egyptian bondage, Rabbi Loew first considers three suggestions made by others, only to reject them.[10] Nahmanides, in his *Commentary on the Torah,* had suggested that Abraham's descendants were punished with bondage in Egypt because of Abraham's sin in Egypt. Once, when famine struck Canaan, Abraham visited Egypt. On that occasion, he presented his wife, Sarah, as his sister so that Pharaoh would not kill him in order to be able to marry Sarah, who was of legendary beauty. For endangering his wife to save his own life, claims Nahmanides, Abraham's descendants were punished.[11] Rabbi Loew rejects this suggestion on the grounds that, if Abraham knew that such was the punishment for this specific sin, he would not have repeated this action when he later journeyed to Gerar, nor would his son, Isaac, have later repeated the identical ruse with his own wife, Rebecca. Secondly, he rejects the suggestion that the Egyptian bondage of the people of Israel was a punishment for the sale of Joseph into Egyptian bondage by his brothers. Loew identifies this position as that of "a few latter" authorities and rejects it in harsh terms. To relate the Egyptian bondage to the sale of Joseph is to construct a fantasy unrelated to the biblical text. The Egyptian bondage is stated in the Abraham narrative, long before the sale of Joseph occurs. According to Rabbi Loew, the sale of Joseph was part of the punishment. It was the beginning of Egyptian bondage. It cannot therefore be considered the sin for which the bondage is the punishment. A third approach argues that Egyptian bondage was not the result of sin at all. It was part of God's attempt to allow Israel to accrue merit by their withstanding "afflictions of love." This explanation is rejected on the grounds that, if such were the case, the affliction of a single generation would have sufficed. Yet, four generations dwelled in Egyptian bondage. How then can one argue that God sought to accrue merit for members of the first generation, who died in Egypt? Loew dispenses with these three possibilities in order to offer his own explanation. His argument is a rather liberal interpretation of a talmudic text.[12]

According to Judah Loew, Abraham's sin was lack of faith in God. For example, if Abraham had had complete faith, he would not have required a sign from God when God promised him an heir who would inherit the land of Canaan.[13] Implicit within this suggestion that lack of faith engenders exile is the claim that affirmation of faith aids in reconciliation with God. The redemption from Egypt could only occur because the people affirmed faith in God in spite of difficult circumstances and despite experience rationally dictating otherwise.[14] The final Messianic redemption will also be characterized by an affirmation of faith.[15] While a failure of faith is both a necessary *and* a sufficient cause for punishment in exile, an affirmation of faith is a necessary but not a sufficient cause for redemption. Divine grace is the only sufficient cause of redemption.

Judah Loew draws a close comparison between Israel's redemption from Egypt and Abraham's extrication from Ur. He compares

Abraham, born in Ur, estranged from God, to Israel's gestation in Egypt. As the Chaldeans were the opposite of what Abraham was to come to be, so were the Egyptians Israel's opposite. As Abraham was chosen not for merit but because of divine grace, so was Israel's selection primarily because of grace and not merit. As Abraham left the place of his birth and journeyed to the Land of Israel, from exile to redemption, so did the people of Israel leave Egypt and journey toward the land promised to Abraham. Both Abraham and Israel emerge dialectically out of their respective opposites. Abraham represents "the beginning of the world," a new entity in Creation, while Israel denotes the completion of creation. [16]

Abraham is promised the Land of Israel. However, by asking God for a demonstration of the validity of that promise, Abraham's descendants are punished with exile from that land, with bondage in Egypt. Though the people of Israel are redeemed from Egypt in order to inherit the land promised Abraham, the generation which experienced redemption never reaches the land but wanders in the desert, in exile, as punishment for their sin. For Rabbi Loew, the fate of the desert generation is paradigmatic of Israel throughout its history. Most of the history of Israel is characterized by exile, by being on the way to the Promised Land. Only in messianic times will the wandering cease and will redemption endure.

According to Rabbi Loew, the sin which engendered the exile of the desert generation was the failure of the people of Israel to realize its destiny, to actualize its essence. The Exodus from Egypt and the theophany at Sinai were part of a process of redemption which was to culminate with the entrance into the Land of Israel. The last step in the process was interrupted, however, by the "sin of the spies." Not the sin of the golden calf, but the sin of the spies, prevented the fulfillment of the redemptive process for the generation liberated from Egypt.

The spies, sent by Moses to reconnoiter the Promised Land, returned with a report which dissuaded the people from fulfilling their destiny of possessing the land. According to the biblical narrative, the report of the spies stimulated dissension amongst the people, encouraging the people to desire a return to exile in Egypt (Num. 13, 14). Loew interprets the sin of the spies as an attempt to fragment the people of Israel, to stifle their progression toward realizing their destiny, to return them to exile, once more to alienate them from God. The specific sin of the spies which caused the reassertion of exile and alienation was the misuse of language, slander, *leshon ha-ra.* [17]

Though condemned to exile, the desert generation gives birth to a new generation whose destiny it will be to enter the Land. Implicit within the desert exile is the beginning of a process which culminates in the introduction of a new redemptive force into creation–the Temple. Like Abraham's redemption from Ur and Israel's redemption from Egypt, the construction of the Temple, which marked the culmination of Israel's conquest of Canaan, signified the introduction of a novel element into the world. A new path to God opened up, a new route to human perfection was provided; a new gateway to *devekut* was disclosed. The Temple represented an end to alienation from God and a means of reconciliation with God.[18]

According to Rabbi Loew, the Temple came into existence "by virtue of the Torah."[19] The function of the Temple is to help reinstitute the *devekut* which obtained between God and Israel at Sinai, at the zenith of human reconciliation with the divine. The Temple, therefore, supplements the Torah in effecting a restored relationship with God. Like the Torah, the Temple serves as an intermediary (*emza'i*) between the divine and the human. Like the Torah, the Temple is a synthesis of natural and supernatural elements.[20] Like the Torah, the Temple represents the completion of creation which, though accomplished at Sinai, was partially undone by the sins of the desert generation.

The Temple is for the world what the Torah is for man. The Temple is the heart of creation. As the human heart sustains the body, the Temple sustains the world. As the human heart is situated in the center of the body, the Temple is situated at the center of the world.[21] The Temple is the conduit between the natural and the supernatural realm. Its condition epitomizes the state of God's relationship to the world. By means of the Temple, "this world is connected to and is put into order by the higher world from which it derives sustenance." While the Temple stands and functions, the divine and the human are reconciled. However, while the Temple lies in ruins, man and the world remain alienated from God.[22]

Like man, the Temple represents the purpose of creation, the intermediary between God and the world, the coalescence of the three dimensions of existence. It should not be surprising therefore that Loew, following rabbinic and medieval precedent, relates the Temple to man. Following rabbinic precedent, he considers the spot of man's creation to have been the exact place later destined for the Temple.[23] Following medieval precedent, he relates man as microcosm to the Temple as macrocosm. Man is a "miniature Temple."[24]

According to Rabbi Loew, construction of the Temple was made possible by the introduction of a second element, which signified the completion of the settlement of Canaan, namely, the establishment of the Davidic kingship.

As the form of his people, the Davidic king must bring his people together and unite them. While essentially apart from the people as form is to matter, as the center of a circle is to its circumference, the king must help his people fulfill its unique purpose.[25] In constructing the Temple, the Davidic king fulfilled his primary function as king. The Temple unifies the people and helps them attain perfection. The Temple provides a remedy for the disunity and imperfection engendered by the sins of the desert generation.

The reconciliation accomplished by the construction of the Temple was eventually nullified by the destruction of the Temple. Once more, as the result of sin, exile became the reality of Jewish existence. This time, the place of exile was Babylonia.

Because of the significance he attaches to the Temple, Rabbi Loew understood the destruction of the Temple to be an event of metaphysical as well as of historical consequence. As the intermediary between the supernatural and natural realms, the Temple represents the relationship between God and man. The destruction of the Temple therefore signifies the severance of man from God. Furthermore, with the destruction of the Temple, which serves as the conduit sustaining the natural world, the world cannot properly function. Creation can no longer be considered perfect or complete. A means to attaining human perfection is eliminated. The accidental replaces the essential; exile and alienation replace redemption and perfection.[26]

Rabbi Loew follows precedent by identifying the three cardinal sins defined by the Talmud as being the cause of the destruction of the Temple. Only the three most heinous sins could engender such a metaphysical and physical catastrophe. According to the Talmud, these three sins are illicit sexual activity (i.e., adultery or incest), murder, and idolatry. Loew relates these three sins to the three aspects of man: body, soul, and intellect. As the Temple reflects the structure of man and as the Temple ensures the attainment of human perfection represented by perfection of body, soul, and intellect, so must the committing of these three sins result in the destruction of the Temple, the nullification of a path toward perfection.[27]

With the destruction of the Temple, Judah Loew's dialectical history proceeds. A new epoch begins. Another exile commences. Implicit in the new exile is the promised redemption. The destruction of the Temple causes a new possibility to join creation in order to enable it to fulfill its destiny. With the Temple's destruction, messianic redemption becomes a possibility.[28]

Unlike previous redemptions, messianic redemption will occur at the end of time. It will be a final redemption. With it the world reaches the fulfillment of the divine plan. With it the historical dialectic comes to an end.

A long and dark epoch of history begins with the destruction of the First Temple and the subsequent exile in Babylonia. Loew follows the standard interpretation of the Book of Daniel (Dan. 7) which sees this era as being divided into four parts. Daniel's vision of four beasts is interpreted to mean that the world will be ruled by the sequential domination of four powers. Loew identifies the first of these kingdoms with Babylonia. He perceives history from the Babylonian exile until messianic redemption as a long, dark night replete with progressive oppression by each of the four successive kingdoms. Though he does not consistently identify these four kingdoms with the same historical entities, Rabbi Loew generally identifies the first kingdom with Babylonia, the second with Persia, the third with Greece, and the fourth with Rome.[29] Christendom is considered to be a continuation of Rome; the Holy Roman Empire is presumed to be a continuation of the Roman Empire. Loew specifically rejects the suggestion, current in medieval Jewish literature, which identified Ishamel or Islam with the fourth and final kingdom.[30] In a typical gesture of toleration toward Islam, Loew specifically discounts Ishmael as one of the four kingdoms which are ultimately destined to be annihilated at the end of their term of domination. Being of the stock of Abraham, Ishmael is the complementary opposite of Israel. But Edom–Christendom, a contradictory opposite of Israel–is destined for annihilation.[31] Loew's decision not to consider Ishmael the fourth Kingdom may have been an expression of his sympathy for the Turks in their struggle with Christendom.[32]

The history of Israel from the destruction of the Temple by the Babylonians until messianic redemption is one great movement of the dialectic of exile and redemption. Within this great historical swoop, the process of exile and redemption continues. Acts of alienation and reconciliation regularly occur. The first takes place in Persia.

According to the biblical narrative, a plan is hatched to annihilate Israel in ancient Persia. The king's counselor, Haman, devises this plan. Following earlier sources, Loew identifies Haman with

Amalek, the archenemy and contradictory opposite of Israel. The clash between Mordecai (often identified with Moses) and Haman (the reputed descendant of Amalek) results in Haman's destruction. Loew considers this event to be a preview of the messianic event which will conclude history in that the total annihilation of Israel's contradictory opposite will foreshadow the final redemption.

Judah Loew continually stresses the anomalous nature of the redemption narrated by the Book of Esther. Unlike other redemptions, the people are not freed from exile, but remain in exile. The miracle wrought by God is "hidden." In the biblical text no divinely engineered miracles are mentioned; indeed, God's name never even appears in the Book of Esther. The redemption seems to be the result of human effort and not of divine providence. The redemption is secretive and incomplete, but is miraculous nonetheless. The people are saved from annihilation by God elusively operative within history.[33] Thus, even within the dark tunnel of history, there are glimpses of light, preparing the way for final redemption.

In the period preceding oppression by the third kingdom, Israel is restored to its land and the Temple is rebuilt. A penultimate restoration takes place. Loew is quick to note, however, that the rebuilt Temple, the Second Temple, does not restore that which was destroyed with the First Temple. Following talmudic precedent (Yom. 9b), he maintains that the divine "Presence" dwelt only in the First Temple. The physical structure of the Temple may have been replaced, but not its metaphysical function. According to Loew, the Second Temple serves an essentially sociological function. It helps to unify the people.[34]

Judah Loew compares the kinds of oppression visited upon Israel by the first three kingdoms to the three aspects of man. The Babylonian exile, which represents the first watch of that long night which is the exile, is characterized by physical oppression. The Babylonians oppressed the body. The Persians, as recorded in the Esther narrative, wanted to exterminate the people. Murder corresponds to the soul. The Greeks, the third kingdom, wished to suppress the intellect. They therefore attacked the wisdom of Israel, the Torah, and sought to replace it with their own thinking. While the first two kingdoms wished only physical domination, the Greeks wished to subdue Israel spiritually.[35]

By attacking the Torah the Greeks hit at the vitals of Jewish existence. They struck at the supernatural basis of Judaism. This necessitated a supernatural response. That response was the miracle of the festival of Hanukah, symbolized by the miracle of the oil, sufficient in quantity to burn one day, but burning eight days instead. The miracle of redemption, celebrated on Hanukah, is not the military victory of the Maccabees over the Greeks, but the miracle of the oil. A military victory only indicates the superiority of one physical force over another. True redemption, however, is grounded in spiritual victory over physical power.[36]

For Judah Loew, the miracle of Hanukah occurred because the people of Israel would not submit to the assimilationist aims of spiritual and cultural oppression. They maintained their adherence to the Torah and to their unique cultural and intellectual heritage. The Greeks offered an alternative to the Torah. The wisdom of the Greeks, however, represented a variety of knowledge and culture antithetical to that embodied by the Torah. The miracle of Hanukah, the redemption of the Festival of Lights, represents God's miraculous intervention as reward for the people's resistance to assimilation with Gentile culture.[37]

Though restored from the contamination of the Greeks, the Temple is eventually destroyed by the fourth kingdom. This fourth kingdom, the empire of Rome, is identified with Christendom in medieval Jewish sources as well as by Loew. This final kingdom represents the combination of all three previous kingdoms. It oppresses the entire person: body, soul, and intellect.[38] It is the longest term of exile. The domination by Rome, which begins with the destruction of the Second Temple, concludes only with messianic redemption.

Following talmudic precedent, Rabbi Loew maintains that the sin of baseless hatred (*sinat ḥinam*) caused the destruction of the Second Temple. While the First Temple was destroyed because the people committed the three cardinal sins, baseless hatred is tantamount to committing the three cardinal sins together. Expressed through slander (*leshon ha-ra*), baseless hate sows dissension and disunity amongst the people. It repeats the "sin of the spies." Those who are guilty of committing it, therefore, deserve the identical punishment visited upon the spies' generation–exile.[39]

Judah Loew believed that the domination of the fourth kingdom was to be the last scene in the drama of history. When the fourth kingdom fell, the Messianic Era would commence. Unlike a number of his contemporaries, Loew did not believe his time to be the Messianic Era. He did believe, however, that his generation was closer to the time of redemption than any since the destruction of the First Temple. As domination by the fourth kingdom had already persisted for many centuries, messianic redemption, while not an immediate expectation, could not be very far off. The unfortunate, contemporary plight of the Jewish people, therefore, was not a disaster, but an opportunity; not a time of despair, but one of expectation. The resolution of history in messianic redemption is assured, not only by faith, but by the very structure of creation.

According to Loew, messianic redemption cannot occur until the dialectic of history has reached its fast-approaching chronological point of resolution.[40] With an act of divine grace the Messianic Era may commence. But divine intervention is only one aspect of messianic redemption. There is also a human element in messianic redemption. Human activity must repair the breach between God and man. Man must establish the prerequisite conditions for messianic redemption. Divine grace is the abscissa while human action is the axis of messianic redemption.[41]

Israel's plight in the world, Israel's state of exile, is paradigmatic of the distorted condition of the natural world. For the natural world to reach perfection, Israel must first attain perfection in the world. For this to occur, the people of Israel must first eliminate the causes of imperfection, of exile. For example, if slander and disunity caused the destruction of the Temple and the exile, every effort must be made to eliminate slander and to forge unity within the community of Israel. All available means to perfection must be utilized and not discarded. Without the Temple, study of the Torah and observance of its commandments remain the primary means for securing perfection. The Torah is the means to reconciliation with God. It is the "Temple of the Exile." To achieve the perfection of the people of Israel in the world, the Torah must realize the totality of its potentiality as the intermediary between God and man, as the primary means of attaining human perfection. Loew considered the Torah given to Israel to be the "form of the world" as well as the form of Israel.[42] For the world to achieve perfection, Israel must do so. For Israel to do so, the Torah's role must be actualized. Thus, Israel's relationship to the Torah is a primary determinant for the redemption of the world. For Loew, therefore, the reformation of Jewish education and the restoration of proper religious observance are necessary requirements for messianic redemption. Once Israel has prepared the world for redemption, divine grace can intercede and complete the process. Israel's efforts are the premise of which divine redeeming grace is the conclusion. The seed of redemption, implanted within history, must be ripened; human effort must be spent to harvest that seed.

Judah Loew believed his generation to be living in the dusk of the reign of the fourth kingdom, when the chronological prerequisites for messianic redemption had almost been attained. He therefore stresses the critical and urgent need to correlate contemporary Jewish existence with its destined role in the messianic drama. Loew's harsh critique of the quality of contemporary Jewish life and his strategy for reform and restoration are the logical and theological consequences of his philosophy of history and his views on Jewish messianism. In the following chapter an attempt will be made to reconstruct Judah Loew's critique of contemporary Jewish existence and to describe his blueprint for Jewish life as he believed it should be; to portray the flaws he perceived in contemporary Jewish existence and to discuss his remedies for them; and to set forth Loew's social philosophy, which is, in effect, his plan for preparing the way for messianic redemption. The remainder of the present chapter, however, will sketch his characterization of the Messiah and of the Messianic Age.

For Judah Loew, the messianic potential comes into existence with the destruction of the First Temple. The task of the Messiah is to restore the link between God and man which was severed with the Temple's destruction. For Loew, however, the messianic advent is not simply restorative. It represents a new dimension of existence, a novel element within creation.[43]

The Messianic Age simultaneously represents the perfection of the natural dimension and the initiation of a new variety of existence. Though messianic existence is definitely of "this world," it nevertheless represents the transformation of the present world to such a total extent that it is *as if* a new creation has occurred.[44] In the Messianic Age, the perfection of the natural world will radically alter its previous nature. Matter will acquire a new, refined quality.[45] It will be of an ephemeral quality, not unlike that of the celestial beings who dwell in the "intermediate world." The spiritual elements of the natural world will become amplified to the nth degree. The natural world will realize all its inherent supernatural qualities. Just as the Messianic Age is itself an intermediary stage between "this world" and the World to Come, so is an intermediary, transitional stage required between historical times and the Messianic Age. This intermediary stage is known as the "birthpangs of the Messiah." In Rabbi Loew's words:

Before the Messiah can become manifest, the weeding out of being in the world must occur, for every new being is the ruin of the being which preceded it and only then with the end of the old can the new being begin. . . . It seems that there will be a ruin of the old being in the world that changes different things; and just as there will be change from the ruin of the old being, so will there be a difference in the world because of the new which has entered into it. And every ruin is change, so every being is change in the world–and this is called the birthpangs of the Messiah. . . . Thus when the new reality is actualized, the age of the Messiah will be realized, the actualization of the new being–and that will be truly different. In this manner, the pangs of the Messiah will appear, just as with a woman in labor, because of the new being, the creation entering the world.[46]

Though anticipation of the "birthpangs of the Messiah" appears in Jewish messianism from the talmudic era, through the Middle Ages, Loew suggests a new understanding of this ancient idea. He reiterates the catastrophic dimension of this intermediary stage described in the Talmud and amplified to fantastic proportions in the Geonic era. However, unlike those earlier sources, he offers no detailed scenario of the occasion. Unlike earlier sources which perceive that stage as an unleashing of demonic fury, Loew sees it as a necessary step in the process of redemption and consequently attaches no dysteleological or demonic dimension to it.[47] Unlike Saadya, who understands the period of transition to be required only as a means of causing recalcitrant Israel to repent, Judah Loew considers it a necessary period of transition, required by the structure of the historical dialectic. For Saadya, the transitionary catastrophe is optional; it is linked to the resolve of the people to repent.[48] For Loew, the transitional period is irrelevant to human deeds; it is not optional. Loew's assumption is that only after the human role in the messianic drama has been fulfilled can the birthpangs commence. Unlike Maimonides, who stresses the continuity between historical times and messianic times and who dismisses the importance attached to the intermediary era by the traditions which preceded him, Loew insists upon the essential differentiation between historical and messianic times and therefore does attach a very special significance to the transitional period between them.[49] Unlike his more immediate predecessor in the history of Jewish thought, Don Isaac Abravanel, and unlike many contemporary Jewish thinkers and Reformation theologians, Loew did not consider his own times to be the "birthpangs of the

Messiah." Unlike Abravanel, Judah Loew did not anticipate the immediate "knocking on the door."[50] Loew believed he was living in historical times and that before thoughts of imminent messianic redemption could be seriously entertained, a massive effort to reform Jewish life was first required.

Judah Loew's position was not atypical considering the tradition within Judaism from which he emerged. While Abravanel's trilogy on messianism represents the summation of the Sefardic traditions on the subject, Loew's book on messianism represents the summation of the Ashkenazic tradition. As Sefardic messianism was always charged with militant millenarial excitement, it is not surprising to find great messianic fervor after the Spanish expulsion amongst the Sefardic community. This fervor clearly appears in the writings of Abravanel and in the millenarian activity of the Safed kabbalists. As Ashkenazic messianism generally manifested an antimillenarial tone, as messianic speculation was severely limited amongst Ashkenazic Jewry, it is not surprising to find Rabbi Loew's sharp disavowal that his era was the beginning of the messianic era. Abravanel's calculations, which led him to believe the Messianic Age was soon to begin are as typical of Sefardic messianism as Loew's admonition against "calculating the end" is typical of Ashkenazic messianism.[51] Abravanel's militant messianism calling for war and revenge against specific historical and political enemies of Israel is typically Sefardic, while Loew's failure to identify contemporary political or military events with the messianic advent, his quiescence, his insistence that piety, observance, and study and not militancy were the path to messianic redemption are peculiarly Ashkenazic. Thus, Loew's portrayal of the "birthpangs of the Messiah" is unique while his antimillenarial attitude and his refusal to recognize his own times as the "birthpangs of the Messiah" are what must be expected from the author of the summation of Ashkenazic messianism as it developed from the talmudic era throughout the Middle Ages down to his own day.[52]

According to Judah Loew, following both talmudic and medieval precedent, a major feature of the intermediary period will be the catastrophic war of "Gog and Magog." Unlike his Geonic predecessors, Loew does not offer a detailed description of the war of Gog and Magog.[53] He represents it as a point in the transitionary process. Though at this point the Messiah has already come, his reign too must undergo a process of realization. The time of Gog and Magog is at the commencement of the Messianic Age. The demise of Gog and Magog is a necessary step in the establishment of the Messiah's reign. The purpose of this war is to eliminate all remnants of flaws in the natural order in preparation for the introduction of the new order of existence under absolute messianic rule. In this war the nations of the world, representing conflict and multiplicity, will oppose God, the Messiah, and Israel, which represent the unity peculiar to the realized Messianic Era. The nations of the world, personified as Gog and Magog, will oppose the people of Israel as in the days of Joshua. They will gather together to oppose God as they did at the Tower of Babel. As a result of the war, the power of the nations will be neutralized. In the course of the war, however, the Messiah ben Joseph will be slain. Before God and the Messiah ben David can triumph, the Messiah ben Joseph will be killed and his essence will cease to exist.[54]

The Messiah ben Joseph, the penultimate Messiah, mentioned in talmudic and midrashic literature, and discussed in great detail throughout apocalyptic midrashim dating from the Geonic period, is given an almost nondescript role in Judah Loew's account of the messianic drama.[55] Rabbi Loew follows the lead of some earlier sources and identifies him with the northern kingdom of Israel as opposed to the Davidic Messiah, who represents the southern kingdom of Judah. Unlike others, Loew does not identify his appearance with the reappearance of the Ten Lost Tribes of Israel. Unlike Abravanel, Loew did not expect the Ten Tribes to return to wage a war of revenge against the armies of Christendom.[56] Judah Loew only refers to the Messiah ben Joseph as a symbol of the unity of the tribes of Israel. As the heart is the symbol of the unity of the body, so is the Messiah ben Joseph the symbol of the unity of Israel in anticipation of the final establishment of messianic rule.

The Messiah ben Joseph plays no active role in completing the process of redemption, according to Loew. He does not lead an army to war against Gog and Magog as he is described as doing in numerous apocalyptic midrashim and in other medieval sources. Nor does Loew describe him as the epitome of the suffering servant who willingly suffers for the sins of others, despite the many precedents in the literature that do so describe him.[57] Nor does Loew describe him as being resurrected either by the Messiah ben David or by God as many earlier sources do. For Loew, once the Messiah ben Joseph is killed, the element in creation he represents passes out of existence. Furthermore, in keeping with his position that his own times are historical and not messianic times, Loew, unlike other of his contemporaries, fails to identify himself (as Luria appears to have done) or others as the Messiah ben Joseph.[58] It would thus appear that for Judah Loew, the notion of the Messiah ben Joseph, like the notion of the conflict with Gog and Magog, is one which he inherited from his forebears in the history of Jewish messianism. Being a traditionalist, he is drawn to fit these notions, albeit awkwardly, into his portrait of the intermediary stage between fragmented historical times and fulfilled messianic times. The conflict with Gog and Magog and the role of the Messiah ben Joseph, while not neutralized or rationalized away as Maimonides attempted to do, are nevertheless deflated when compared to the form they take in the apocalyptic midrashim which date from the Geonic era. The war between Gog and Magog and the Messiah ben Joseph represent the nullification of the negative factors in the world in preparation for the final realization of the messianic potential. The Messiah ben Joseph, in particular, personifies a preliminary stage in the transitional period representing the military and political security of Israel. This stage, however, is but a prelude to the final step in effecting messianic redemption.

Once Israel's physical security is guaranteed, its metaphysical essence may become truly manifest. Once the natural realm is complete, it is ready for its transformation into a more supernatural dimension. The Messiah ben Joseph cannot therefore be resurrected in Judah Loew's scheme; he must pass out of existence. He represents a step, albeit a necessary step, in the redemptive process. However, once that level has been realized, he must be removed since he becomes obsolete.

Besides the Messiah ben Joseph, Rabbi Loew also includes a second character in his description of the beginnings of the messianic era, namely, Elijah the Prophet. As early as biblical times, Elijah was afforded a role in the messianic advent by Jewish messianic literature.[59] However, just as he diminished the role of the Messiah ben Joseph, so Rabbi Loew diminished that of the Prophet Elijah. Whereas previous sources describe Elijah as performing miracles, making final decisions in Jewish law, announcing the dawning of the messianic redemption, being a redeemer comparable to Moses,[60] serving as High Priest at the restored Temple and co-ruler with the Messiah ben David, Loew ascribes no such roles to Elijah during the period of the messianic advent. Like the Messiah ben Joseph, Elijah is described as fulfilling the rather pedestrian role of helping to unify the people. This role, assigned to Elijah and the Messiah ben Joseph, is logically superfluous since ultimate and complete unity can only be accomplished by the Messiah ben David. Rabbi Loew, however, seems to feel obliged by his traditionalist persuasion to include these two individuals in his description of messianic redemption; nevertheless, he apparently felt it necessary to neutralize their roles in order to accentuate that of the Messiah ben David.

Like much of Jewish messianic literature, Loew compares the first redemption–from Egypt–to the final redemption.[61] He compares the role of Elijah in the final redemption to that of Aaron in the initial redemption. He compares the role of Moses to that of the Messiah ben David. In effect, the final redemption is the conclusion of the process begun with the Exodus.[62] The messianic redemption will accomplish those very tasks originally intended as part of the first redemption: the actualization of creation, the proper functioning of the Torah in the world as the intermediary between God and man, and the people of Israel dwelling in their "natural place"–the Land of Israel.[63] The messianic redemption will conclude that which was begun with the Exodus. The Messiah will complete that which Moses initiated.

Unlike some of his predecessors and contemporaries in the history of Jewish messianism, Judah Loew does not consider Moses to be the final Messiah.[64] He does not anticipate Moses' return to effect final redemption.[65] Nor does he claim that the Messiah and Moses are one and the same person–that the Messiah ben David is the transmigration of the soul of Moses.[66] Nor does he expect Moses to return to share in the process of redemption with the Messiah ben David.[67] Rabbi Loew, however, does draw a close comparison, both explicitly and implicitly, between the first redeemer and the final redeemer.

In apparent opposition to Maimonides' naturalistic description of the nature and function of the Messiah, Rabbi Loew attempted to portray a supernatural Messiah.[68] Judah Loew's account of the Messiah is rooted in the Jewish mystical tradition in general and in the Zohar in particular. The Zohar, for example, portrays the Messiah as an essentially heavenly being whose proper abode is in Heaven.[69] Loew, however, goes beyond the view enunciated in the Zohar and bestows upon the Messiah a number of the supernatural traits he had already identified with Moses.[70]

Like Moses, the Messiah is a supernatural entity.[71] Like Moses, he is to be identified with the intellectual (*sikhli*) dimension of existence. While the Messiah ben Joseph is compared to the heart which is identified with the soul, the Messiah ben David is compared to the brain which is identified with the intellect.[72] Like Moses, he is to Israel what the intellect is to an individual person.

Like Moses, the Messiah ben David is described as "holy of holies" and like Moses, his matter is detached from his form.[73] As Moses' essence preexisted his birth from Creation, so did the Messiah's. As Moses' birth is not to be considered a natural birth and his parents are not to be considered the cause of his birth, such is also true of the Messiah. Like Moses, the Messiah is considered an entity apart from the people of Israel. As Moses is the first king of Israel, the Messiah is the final king of Israel. As king of Israel, the Messiah, like Moses, represents the form of Israel, the unifying force within Israel, the completion of Israel.[74]

For Judah Loew, the messianic king of Israel, unlike all previous kings and redeemers, is the final king and redeemer. Unlike other kings, who conquer with physical power, he will lead by virtue of his wisdom. Other kings, presumably Gentile kings, will consider him their king; he will be King of Kings.[75] Only during the rule of the messianic king will the relationship between man and God be set aright. Only in the Messianic Era will God, the form of all, really be king of all.[76] Unlike all former redemptions, e.g., redemption from Egypt, messianic redemption will be complete and will endure to the end of time.[77] Having realized its perfection, the purely material realm having become transformed into a more refined level of existence, the messianic world having been realized, all will have been prepared for the final dissolution of creation back to the Creator. The messianic world is but a rung by means of which creation is elevated to the World to Come, to the totally supernatural dimension, to God.[78]

For Judah Loew the advent of the Messiah does not represent the abrogation or superseding of the commandments of the Torah of Moses. The commandments, Loew insists (perhaps with a polemical thrust), will be in force in the Messianic Age. The messianic advent signifies the actualization of the observance of the commandments, not their abolition. Actualization of the observance of the commandments is indicative of the completion of the process begun with the Exodus and with the theophany at Sinai. The role of the Messiah is not so much to bring about this conclusion of the historical age but to symbolize that it has been attained. Just as the actualization of the natural world in the Messianic Era is but a prelude to the supernatural world, so the actualization of the Torah in this world is but a prelude to its ultimate return to its completely supernatural form. While the commandments are totally operative in the messianic world, they are abrogated in the World to Come. For in the World to Come, everything, including the Torah, which derives from God, i.e., from the sefirotic realm, reverts back to God.[79] Thus, for Judah Loew, the intrusion of the supernatural entities into "this world," i.e., Moses, Messiah, Torah, Temple, soul, intellect, etc., is for the purpose of guiding creation back to its source – back to the totally spiritual realm, back to the World to Come, back to God.

13

Mystical Theology and Social Reform

Mysticism and Social Action

Judah Loew's theological reflections did not emerge from a historical or social vacuum. His writings reveal something more than his remarkable erudition and his immense intellectual prowess. Being conceptually and textually oriented, his writings often obscure his personal concerns. Rabbi Loew's theological inquiries, exegetical investigations, and legal arguments often serve to camouflage his involvement with contemporary problems. Occasionally, however, the usually constant, reliable stream of discussion is interrupted by an outcry of personal anguish. The calm but steady pulse of his flowing classical Hebrew style now and then erupts into a caustic torrent of social criticism, biting sarcasm, and personal confession. Were these opportunities for penetrating Loew's theoretical formulations in order to uncover the personal and social conditions which engendered them not available, one might rest content with having reconstructed the facts of his life and the content of his theology from the scrambled mosaic of available data about him and from the mass of writings by him. However, these windows to Judah Loew's soul provide his readers with an occasion to discern why he formulated his theological conception of Judaism and of Jewry in the manner in which he did. By peering through these portals, the organic relationship between the labyrinth of Loew's theological constructs and his program for social reform will hopefully become apparent.

By intertwining his mystical theology with his social dissent, Judah Loew follows a pattern characteristic of the Western mystical tradition in general and of the Jewish mystical tradition in particular. Contrary to popular belief, mysticism and social action are more often partners than strangers. The mystic attempts to reform his religious community rather than to flee from it. [1] On the basis of his claim of having attained an authentic understanding of his religious tradition, the mystic challenges the religious institutions of his day. His claim is that they represent only an indirect institutionalization of wisdom which he has apprehended in a direct manner. The radical changes in contemporary patterns of religious life, proposed by the mystic, are not understood by him to be opposed to his tradition. Rather, they are construed as the proper, correct, and authentic interpretations of his religious tradition. Thus, the mystic's assumption that he is simply making explicit what is implicit, that he is merely advocating what the tradition intends for its adherents, is a conservative claim which often yields a radical change in his religious community. What the mystic perceives as a conservative endeavor often engenders revolutionary results. [2] Judah Loew's program for social reform, rooted in his mystical theology, provides a paradigm case of the interaction of mystical speculation and social action. In seeking to correlate present realities with past traditions, Loew stimulated radical reforms in Jewish religious experience.

As was noted in the previous chapter, Judah Loew understood his times to be the final movement in the symphony of history. While he did not perceive his times to be messianic times, he was convinced that the seed of redemption, divinely implanted within history, had ripened and was almost ready for harvest. While Rabbi Loew did not calculate the "end," he did calculate how to bring about the end of history. Because he believed human action, specifically the activity of the people of Israel, to be so very crucial an element in realizing the messianic advent, Loew stressed the critical and urgent need to correlate contemporary Jewish existence with its destined role in the messianic drama.

Judah Loew's spirit was troubled when he surveyed the social and religious state of contemporary Jewry. It was not primarily Gentile oppression which disturbed him, since for Rabbi Loew, the physical subjugation of the people of Israel was characteristic of premessianic, historical times. What unnerved Judah Loew was his co-religionists' failure to respond to the extraordinary challenge of their hour in history. The seeds of redemption were beginning their germination and the reapers were asleep. Loew attempted to awaken his contemporaries to respond to the call of the hour.

Rather than seeking to prepare the world for its fulfillment, rather than help bring history toward its final resolution, the Jewish community was ignoring and even rejecting the means toward securing its own redemption and the redemption of the world. Rabbi Loew perceived contemporary views toward religious observance and contemporary practices in Jewish education to be a rejection of traditionally established means of attaining reconciliation with God and of precipitating the messianic advent. In line with the Jewish mystical tradition, he believed social and religious abuses to have cosmic consequences. The perpetuation of such conditions retard messianic redemption, obstruct reconciliation with God, and prolong the "abnormal" condition of the "exile." Such abuses only extend the term of the physical suppression of the Jewish people. Furthermore, Loew contended, contemporary Jewry not only initiated new abuses to extend the exile and to retard redemption, but it also aggravated some of the very conditions responsible for exile in the first place. Contemporary Jewry failed to accelerate redemption and thereby generated additional deterioration rather than activating dormant amelioration. Rather than seeking to heal the flaws in the natural order, rather than working to repair the tears in the fabric of nature engendered by their ancestors' sins, contemporary Jewry was repeating those sins. Thus, in Loew's view, his generation not only was failing to heal the breach but was deepening the fissure between God and man and lengthening the suppression of Israel in the "exile."

Rabbi Loew countered current abuses and responded to the repetition of what he considered heinous sins by offering a plan for the reformation of Jewish life. Though not clearly or comprehensively outlined in a single work or in a specific continuum of his writings, Loew's plan for reform emerges from the occasional asides in his work when the general composure which dominates his discussion erupts into grating outbursts of social criticism and personal indignation. Since this plan for reform lies imbedded in Loew's work, the present task will be to reconstruct it and to relate it to the categories of his theology outlined above. From the following discussion the conclusion will hopefully emerge that in an age of Reformation, Judah Loew was a social and religious reformer.

Judah Loew's Blueprint for Reformation

For Rabbi Loew, reformation meant restoration. The Torah–its teachings and observance of its commandments–had to be restored to its proper place, its "natural place," as the form of Israel, the means toward attaining human perfection, the catalyst for achieving *devekut* and the instrument by means of which messianic redemption might be realized. To accomplish this task not innovation, but a reaffirmation of classical Judaism as he understood it, was required.

Loew evaluated contemporary Jewish life from the perspective of what he understood authentic Judaism to be. In his view, that which deviated was a threat to the spiritual integrity of Israel and, therefore, had to be combatted. Thus, the theological categories of Loew's mystical theology serve as the basis for his evaluation of Jewish life in his times.

Typical of the late medieval mentality, Loew attempted to correlate the ideal with the real, hope for the future with reality in the present. However, atypical of the late medieval mentality, Loew's aspirations culminated not in flights to a dreamland of bright fantasy, but to concrete social programs. Rather than reject this world and hope for perfection in a future world, Loew sought to change this world, to seek the realization of "this world" which he believed to be the necessary prerequisite for perfection in a future world.

Unlike those late medieval men who, under Christian influence, were convinced of the insurmountable obstacle of human sinfulness, Loew maintained that man may accelerate his own redemption, in this world, by means of affirmative individual action as well as by social action.[3] Judah Loew believed that the ideal could become the real because the historical hour demanded it. Achievement of the ideal means restoration of formerly attained heights. To do what has been done before is both possible and necessary.

Judah Loew's social criticism was primarily directed toward the rabbinical leadership and the educational practices of his day, for he believed poor leadership and low-quality education to be the major causes of contemporary undesirable realities. Though largely unheeded in his own generation, much of Loew's plan for social change in these areas was implemented in the two centuries after his death. For example, the Hasidic movement, which began as an attack upon the rabbinic leadership of the early eighteenth century, virtually duplicated his analysis of rabbinic leadership. The new model for rabbinic leadership which emerged from the Hasidic movement–the *zaddik*– bears remarkable similarity to the model for rabbinic leadership described by Loew. Similarly, the educational reforms he advocated (virtually ignored by his contemporaries) became the basis for changes in Jewish educational theory and practice which dominated much of Jewish education in Eastern Europe during the eighteenth and nineteenth centuries, especially in communities under Hasidic influence.[4] While Loew's plan for reform did not help to bring messianic redemption during his lifetime, his programs did not go unheeded and had a significant social impact during the centuries after his death.

A Crisis of Leadership

Judah Loew's critique of the contemporary rabbinate is rooted in his mystical theology, specifically, in his ideas of human perfection, messianic redemption, and *devekut*. For Loew, the rabbi should function primarily as community leader, scholar-educator, and halakhic authority. As community leader, the relationship of the rabbi to the community ought to be like that of a king to his subjects. Like a king, the rabbi ought to be the "form" of which his community is the "matter." He is to give them purpose and direction. As a king rules his people, so should the rabbi be the ruler of his constituency. Just as the king differs from his subjects, so should the rabbi-leader differ from the members of his community. The leader is the essential part of the community and the complementary opposite of the community. As the heart is essential to the body, the leader is crucial to the people. As the heart vitalizes the body, so must the rabbinic leader vitalize his community.

In relating the role of the king to that of the rabbinic leader, Loew introduces a messianic motif into his prototype for Jewish leadership. In Jewish religious thought, the monarch was a model for leadership reserved for messianic times. Therefore, by ascribing monarchial qualities to the Jewish leader, Loew bestows a messianic quality upon the Jewish religious leader. In so doing, he anticipates the Hasidic model for leadership by almost two centuries.

As leader, the rabbi relates to his community as a king to his people, as a heart to its body.[5] However, as scholar *and* leader, the rabbi relates to his community as the brain relates to the body. For, as was noted above, Rabbi Loew considered the brain as the instrument by which the noncoporeal intellect (*seikhel*) becomes operative in the material world. For Loew, the rabbi-scholar represents the highest degree of human attainment–*devekut*. As such, the scholar must act as the intermediary for the individual members of his community to relate to the Torah and to God.

Besides community leader and scholar-teacher, the rabbi must also be a *zaddik*, a saint. The *zaddik* is one who has attained *devekut*. He therefore may serve as an intermediary to God for those who have not attained *devekut*. The *zaddik* too is a messianic figure in that he helps secure redemption for his generation. Thus, Loew's portrait of the model leader, in name (*zaddik*) and in description, accurately foreshadows the model for rabbinic leadership introduced by the Hasidic movement, possibly under the influence of Loew's writings.

For Rabbi Loew, the saint-scholar is the ideal rabbinic leader. The task of the rabbinic leader is to bring the people to God through study of the Torah and observance of the commandments. Thus, the spiritual and intellectual attainments of the saint-scholar are not simply for his own personal fulfillment. They are the basis for community education and social reform.[6]

As the primary function of the saint-scholar is to lead the people toward messianic fulfillment and *devekut,* it is not suprising that Loew's evaluation of the contemporary rabbinate was caustic and harsh. The contemporary rabbinate was the antithesis of his notion of proper rabbinic leadership. Neither saints nor scholars, they only alienated the people from study and observance. In so doing, they retarded messianic redemption and widened the gap between God and man. Having discussed Loew's notion of proper rabbinic leadership, we now turn to a description of the daily realities with which he was confronted.

In Judah Loew's time rabbis served as religious leaders of Jewish communities (*kehillot*) by virtue of their having been elected to their position by a board of lay leaders within the given community. Applicants for rabbinic positions were required to demonstrate their suitability by producing a document of ordination (*semikhah*) and by manifesting personal traits acceptable to the lay leadership. Often, the local secular authorities played a role in making or in ratifying the appointment. Since the Jewish community was virtually an autonomous entity within the larger community, and the rabbi was a legal as well as a religious authority, the local government had a vested interest in his appointment. It in effect awarded him the power to make decisions within the Jewish community in matters of civil law (e.g., torts, property, contracts) and in some communities even in criminal law. Therefore, the local civil authorities (e.g., the king or the parliament) often took part in the process of rabbinic appointment. Once appointed, the rabbi often derived his income in the form of a set salary from the community. Sometimes his income derived from fees or "gifts" for certain services he performed, e.g., solemnizing marriages, executing writs, etc. Occasionally, his income derived from a monopoly granted him by the community, e.g., the sale of candles or baked goods. In some cases, his income derived from two or more of the above. It was not uncommon in Rabbi Loew's time for individuals to "buy" rabbinic posts from a local community or from its lay board, especially those posts promising lucrative income. It was not rare for pressures–often economic–to be directed at local governments and their officials in order that certain individuals might receive appointments in a specific community. [7]

In a variety of places throughout his writings, Loew expresses his intense dissatisfaction concerning the then current manner in which communities obtained their rabbinic leaders. In his view, the dubious machinations surrounding rabbinic appointments virtually ensured poor leadership for the Jewish community at a crucial juncture in history when proper leadership was a sine qua non. Specifically, Loew was disturbed by the improprieties which sometimes accompanied appointments made because of governmental influence. Therefore, when he served as Chief Rabbi of Moravia, Loew attempted to prevent this abuse. The community statutes of Moravia retain a prayer, attributed to Loew, in honor of those rabbis who secured their positions without government influence. [8] In addition, Loew voiced his displeasure regarding the then current practice of hiring a rabbi on a short-term contract, i.e., three years or less. This practice created a situation in which the rabbi, in order to retain his position, had to accede to the wishes of his laymen. In such a case the rabbi becomes a follower and not a leader. His actions would not be governed by the requirements of his office, but by the whims of his parishioners. Consequently, the halakhic decisions of such a rabbi cannot be considered valid or binding as he is an "interested party" in each issue he adjudicates. [9]

Besides the short-term contract, Rabbi Loew also opposed the then current practice of rabbis receiving gifts for the performance of their services. While, in opposition to Maimonides, Loew defended the propriety of a salaried rabbinate, he perceived abuses endemic to the practice of rabbis receiving gifts. Like the short-term contract, Loew understood the gift as a means by which rabbinic independence and dignity might be surrendered. He cautioned his rabbinic colleagues to restrain themselves "lest laymen come to believe that the essence of scholarship is to enjoy the bounty of others." In Loew's view, short-term rabbinic contracts and the abuse of rabbinic gift-giving "have cast the honor of the Torah to the ground until there is not a scholar to be found amongst this generation." [10]

Though the authority of a given rabbi over a given community was granted by the community, the rabbi's right to accept and to exercise that authority derived from his ordination. In his critique of the contemporary rabbinate, Loew challenged the propriety of many current claims to ordination. In one of his occasional outbursts of personal indignation, Judah Loew condemns the then current proliferation of ordinations. The granting of ordination, he claims, was established to acknowledge publicly unusual academic attainment in talmudic and halakhic studies. At present, however, he laments, ordination is readily granted to many who have only a sparse knowledge of the Talmud and of Jewish law. While ordination was once granted in order to provide a goal towards which an aspiring and talented scholar could aim, it is granted to virtually anyone. Rather than fulfilling its original task of raising academic standards in the Jewish community in general and amongst the rabbinic leadership in particular, the rash of ordinations only serves to lower the standards of Jewish education and scholarship and "to cause the Torah to be forgotten." The low level of learning required for ordination, Loew insists, permits the mantle of rabbinic leadership to be granted to individuals who are academically deficient in their office at the outset. They have not sufficient knowledge to make proper decisions in matters of Jewish law. They have not adequate academic training to administer the educational institutions under their jurisdiction. Consequently, the study of the Torah and proper observance of the commandments can not be furthered in communities where such individuals hold office. Since proper religious education and correct observance are essential for attaining *devekut* and for repairing the natural order in preparation for the messianic advent, the poor quality of contemporary rabbinic leadership, engendered by the low standards required for ordination, has metaphysical as well as social consequences.[11]

For Judah Loew, practices characteristic of the contemporary rabbinate stripped the rabbinate of all potentiality for independent leadership. The leaders have become the followers. The laymen are the masters and the rabbis their servants.[12] Rather than serving as spiritual guides, the rabbis pander to popular demand. They pursue their own professional security and financial gain rather than the religious and intellectual needs of the communities they lead. They cater to the whims of those who decide upon whether to retain their employ, rather than serving the requirements of their posts.[13] Worse than the academically incompetent rabbis who act in this manner are those who have some learning, but who fail to protest against current conditions.[14] It's bad enough, Loew asserts, that ignorant rabbis permit public flaunting of religious prohibitions, such as those against slander and the Jewish use of Gentile wine. What is worse, however, is that rabbinic figures who are not ignorant fail to oppose such blatant abuses.[15]

Judah Loew laments the futility of his own efforts to awaken the community in general and his rabbinic colleagues in particular to the sorry state of affairs. How can one blame the community when its leaders refuse to act or even refuse to heed those (such as Loew) who wish to reform the current deplorable condition of Jewish life?[16] Too impotent to lead and too indolent to act, the rabbis have become hostile to constructive suggestions and defensive concerning their behavior. This situation has produced haughtiness in the rabbinate. They are proud, though they have no merits which would justify such behavior. According to Loew, haughtiness is not simply a moral affront, but an act of metaphysical significance. It represents a disturbance of the natural order.[17] Thus, the poor quality of contemporary rabbinic leadership served further to fragment the already shattered natural order. It prevented the neutralization of the sins which engendered the exile. It obstructed the Torah from playing its proper role as intermediary between God and man. It retarded messianic redemption and widened the breach between God and man.

Throughout his work, Rabbi Loew singles out three specific areas in which contemporary rabbinic leadership has been particularly negligent. Much of the above-noted criticism of the contemporary rabbinate is found in the course of his discussion of these three problems. The three problems are: (1) Jewish use of Gentile wine, (2) Jewish education, and (3) the "Nadler" controversy. The first problem has been discussed above at length.[18] The condition of Jewish education will be discussed below. At present, however, the so-called "Nadler" controversy will be discussed, as it closely relates to Loew's analysis of contemporary rabbinic leadership and is intimately intertwined with his theological reflections concerning messianic redemption.

The "Nadler" Controversy

Throughout Rabbi Loew's lifetime and after his death the "Nadler" controversy continued to cause disunity and social turmoil amongst the Jewish communities of Central and Eastern

Europe. The derisive epithet "Nadler," a term in the middle high-German dialect suggesting the illegitimacy of a man's birth or that of his ancestors, was leveled against many individuals and their families (especially families from the upper strata of Jewish economic and social life).[19] Throughout his rabbinic career, Loew was a vocal opponent of Nadlerism.

In the fall of 1584, Rabbi Loew denounced the Nadler calumny from the pulpit of the Altneuschul synagogue in Prague. In what was probably his first public appearance in Prague, Loew denounced and officially excommunicated those guilty of this public slander.[20] Loew reiterates this ban in striking and uncompromising terms in *Netivot Olam.*[21]

In his treatise on ethico-religious values, *Netivot Olam*, Loew includes a letter from a former student of his, identified simply as Israel of Moravia. In this pleading letter, saturated with extraordinarily exorbitant praise for Rabbi Loew and replete with expressions of desperate hopelessness in the face of heartless and timid rabbinic leadership, Israel appeals to his former teacher as a final hope and as a recognized powerful authority who could undoubtedly stem the abuse of Nadlerism. If Loew would take a public stand against the current rash of Nadlerism in Moravia, Israel asserts, his views would be accepted by Moravian Jewry without question and the problem would vanish.

In a lengthy departure from conceptual and exegetical discourse, Rabbi Loew responds to Israel's plea. Slander, Nadlerism, "evil speech," is not a new problem, Loew contends. It is the resurgence of an old one, which, in past generations, had engendered disastrous results. For example, the sin of slander engendered the exile of the desert generation and of the exile which has stretched from the days of the Second Temple until the present.[22] Though the committing of this sin had subsided for many generations, it resurfaced once more in the Middle Ages (specifically, the thirteenth century). At that time, however, courageous rabbinic leadership suppressed the abuse by a series of communal decrees and a number of bans of excommunication. In the present generation, however, Rabbi Loew asserts, feeble rabbinic leadership refuses to condemn the abuse with the persistent fortitude characteristic of previous generations. By failing to vilify the abuse, present rabbinic leadership only encourages it to grow and to intensify. Because of the abdication of moral responsibility by the current rabbinic leadership, Rabbi Loew laments, the situation has degenerated to the stage at which "youngsters have become accustomed to hurl invectives at each other and to impugn the saints of the land while walking down the streets of their town." They slander the dead as well as the living. They injure reputations without any basis, at whim.[23] In a rare outburst of personal emotion, Loew grieves for the current state of his people, brought on in part by the resurgence of the sin of slander. No one will heed his words concerning this terrible sin. The people fail to realize the gravity of this sin which engenders exile, perpetuates alienation from God, sows disunity amongst Israel, while its leadership refuses to exercise its prerogative to stem the abuse. The generation which was to accelerate messianic redemption has only retarded it. Regression to the sins of the past, rather than acceleration toward future redemption, characterizes the state of his generation. Rabbi Loew writes, "Behold, my spirit is shattered and my heart is pained . . . for an orphaned generation without a leader or a guardian or one to rebuke them for their faults." Though the present generation seems oblivious to its faults, Loew expresses the hope that future generations would heed those few in his generation who attempted to stem the "Nadler" abuse. Perhaps because of this hope, the balance of Loew's discussion of this matter in *Netivot Olam* records the statements of eleven courageous (apparently contemporary) rabbinic leaders who joined him in opposing the "Nadler" calumny.[24] Within a generation after his death, Loew's hope was realized. Affirmative action was taken in Poland and in Lithuania to curb the abuse of Nadlerism. Joel Sirkes, the eminent Polish rabbinical authority, condemned the "Nadler" calumny in his responsa and in the 1620s and 1630s the Jewish Council of Lithuania issued decrees combatting slander.[25] Sirkes, who was well aware of Loew and at least some of his works, may have been influenced by Judah Loew's defiant stance on the "Nadler" question. Another probable influence upon Sirkes in this regard was Solomon Luria. Sirkes was raised at Lublin and records his childhood experiences at Luria's synagogue. It is certain that Luria exerted a profound influence upon Joel Sirkes.[26] Furthermore, Solomon Luria's condemnation of Nadlerism may shed light upon why Loew was so overwhelmingly concerned with the problem.

Solomon Luria discusses the "Nadler" slur both in his magnum opus, *Yam shel Shelomo,* and in a number of his collected responsa.[27] In one responsum, Luria condemns such defamation of character with regard to a specific family–that of Judah Loew.[28] Luria defends Loew and his brothers from what appears to have been an aspersion concerning their legitimacy and that of their forebears. Luria dismisses the claim and notes in passing that he is distantly related to Loew's family. One may conclude, therefore, that Loew's intense interest in combatting slander may have been because of his having been a victim of such slander. The centrality Loew gives to the sin of slander may have been precipated by personal experience. Thus, one may suggest a cohesive bond amongst Loew's mystical theology, his social dissent, and his personal life.[29]

Educational Reform

As was noted above, Judah Loew considered the condition of Jewish education in his generation to be primarily responsible for the spiritual and intellectual nadir to which Jewish life in general and Jewish leadership in particular had sunk in his generation. Since only proper education can ensure both understanding of the contents of the Torah and observance of its commandments, the educational enterprise must be set aright for the Torah to function properly in the human, historical, and natural spheres of existence. The reform of Jewish education is essential to ensure social change. For Loew, a radical reassessment of Jewish education was not merely a social desideratum, not merely a therapeutic reform, but an essential part of a plan for messianic redemption, part of a blueprint for the reconciliation of both man and the world with God. Current educational abuses were not simply indicative of pedagogic corruption, but were the primary cause of metaphysical disruption.[30] It is not surprising, therefore, that Loew provides a harsh but penetrating and comprehensive critique of Jewish education in his own generation. His overwhelming concern with the quality of Jewish education is reflected not only in his writings, but also in his rabbinical activities.

In a rare but telling autobiographical confession Loew relates that he was once guilty of having committed the identical pedagogic abuses he was later to condemn. At first, he notes, he was reticent to rebuke others for what he himself had done. He was reluctant to chastise others for faults he himself had once had. He therefore tried at first to share the results of his personal discoveries with his better students and with his colleagues, the "scholars of the generation," but to no avail. Consequently, he found it necessary to rebuke rather than to cajole, to criticize rather than to seek to persuade. Perhaps future generations would heed what his contemporaries refused to accept.[31]

In another of his works, a second rare autobiographical statement appears. As most of Loew's personal asides, it occurs in the
course of his discussion of a social issue. Here, too, the issue is the
quality of contemporary Jewish education. Judah Loew writes:

> Since I began to think independently [i.e., since I began to
> pursue my own mystical way] and I reflected upon the current
> conduct of scholarship and pedagogy I realized that it [i.e., the
> process of Jewish education] was being handled improperly. This
> is not the way of our sacred ancestors; it is a deviation wanting in
> every value. Therefore, I strengthened myself as a lion, these
> many years, to correct what I have thought to be wrong. But my
> contemporaries disagreed with me, following the rule of the
> majority. Some time ago, I had wished to write to Poland and
> Russia to delineate what needed to be defined, but I did not do
> so, but my strength now is as my vitality was then. Perhaps some
> will take counsel from me. . . . Perhaps I will save one in a
> thousand. . . . Though we have written these things in numerous
> places, we have seen fit to reiterate them [here]. Their value is
> great, their importance is clear and the abuse they receive is
> considerable.[32]

This citation states Rabbi Loew's own awareness of the radical
nature of his views, especially in the area of Jewish education. His
reticence throughout his works to reveal the names of his teachers
may be because of his rejection of their views on educational and
other matters. Loew claims independence of thought, not from
tradition, but from the many and varied abuses which he perceives
to have infected tradition. He calls not for a denial of tradition, but
for an assertion of the authenticity of tradition in the face of what
he considers to be the bastardization and the violation of tradition,
sanctioned only by popular misconceptions and incompetent,
mediocre leadership. Loew wanted nothing less than a reformation
of Judaism, a return of Judaism to its authentic Jewish community
life. This may explain his double rejection as Chief Rabbi of
Prague. This may explain the close proximity of his lengthy and
explicit sermons (from which the above quotation is taken) to his
assumption of his new position in Posnań.
    From the two texts just noted it should be apparent that Judah
Loew's turbulent and controversial rabbinical career was primarily
due to a change of heart, a reevaluation of himself and his community, which he underwent sometime before his works, with their
biting social criticism, began to appear, i.e., before 1578, when *Gur*

Aryeh was published. It may well be that Loew's withdrawal from community leadership in Moravia to retire to private life in Prague may have been the result of his reflections and his self-evaluation.

For Rabbi Loew, therefore, current educational abuses were not simply bad pedagogy, not merely a lack of quality education, but a repudiation of educational theories and techniques rooted in long-established practice.[33] Loew evaluated educational practices not simply out of a hope for what they might be, but out of an awareness of what they once were. From his own perspective, his particular innovations were not innovative at all, but were a return to a proper standard, currently being repudiated. His radical plan for Jewish education, therefore, was reactionary in intention but revolutionary in its implementation. As is the case elsewhere, Loew's social criticism is grounded in the concepts of his mystical theology and in his understanding of what is authentic and what is antithetical to Jewish religious existence.

Loew did not criticize the quantity of contemporary Jewish education, but the quality.[34] In past generations, the Torah was made operative in Jewish life by means of proper methods of study which engendered proper religious observance. Despite persecution, past generations were "people of knowledge and people of deeds"; their knowledge precipitated their observance. The present generation, however, though not severely persecuted, is bereft of knowledge and consequently is bereft of action.[35]

Though Loew does relate "action" to such things as an occupation, the primary referent of physical activity in his writings is observance of the commandments. Thus, study of the Torah and observance of the commandments are intertwined. In Loew's educational philosophy, a close integration of theory and practice is advocated. Observance of the commandments acquires full significance only when practiced on the basis of an understanding of their theoretical significance. It is only when theory and activity, study of the Torah and observance of its commandments are integrated into the individual's personality, can they serve their proper roles as intermediaries between God and man and as vehicles for human perfection.

According to Loew, theoretical study without correlative physical activity contradicts the nature of man as a composite of the physical and the spiritual. Similarly, routine physical activity alone runs counter to human nature as it compromises the rational component in man. Consequently, practice serves as the premise and as the conclusion of the educational process. In doing, one comes to understanding; in understanding, the significance of one's actions gains added meaning.[36]

According to Loew, a major cause of widespread ignorance was that students not only knew little, but they forgot what they had been taught. Loew therefore recommended practice and review as a means of retaining knowledge.[37] For this reason, he condemned long vacations. As they deny the possibility for the retention of that which had already been learned, vacations can only be counterproductive.[38]

For Rabbi Loew, the educational process must be in accord with the "natural order," with human nature, with the psychological nature of the student. Educational practice must adjust to the laws of psychological maturation, in keeping with the fundamental principle that in nature—including human nature—"everything is realized in its proper time."[39]

Loew's claim that education must be based upon principles of psychological progression precipitated his attack upon a number of educational practices popular in his day. In past generations, he maintains, children were taught according to the stages in their psychological development.[40] Today, however, he claims, they are taught subjects for which they are not psychologically or intellectually equipped.[41] For example, he notes, six- and seven-year-olds are being taught Talmud, for which they are certainly not prepared.[42] The difficult dialectics contained in the marginal glosses to the Talmud, known as the *tosafot,* are taught to youths who cannot possibly grasp the complexity of their arguments.[43]

According to Loew, former generations had instituted a curriculum for study which corresponded to the nature of the student as well as to the nature of the subject of study. By rejecting this curriculum, contemporary educators were disturbing the natural order, violating human nature, ignoring psychological progression in the child and repudiating the wisdom of past generations.

According to Loew, past generations followed an identical curricular pattern which his generation had rejected.[44] This curriculum progresses from biblical studies to mishnaic studies, to talmudic (*gemara*) studies and to advanced studies in Jewish law (for the gifted few).[45] In the current generation, however, the student is given a disjointed survey of the Pentateuch and then goes directly into talmudic studies, virtually ignoring the Mishnah. Eventually, the student becomes involved with the *tosafot,* which are beyond his understanding. He then proceeds to the sterile mental gymnastics of the *pilpul,* which in Loew's view is a waste of time as it sharpens one's wits while diminishing one's wisdom.[46]

In the area of curriculum content, Loew's criticism was aimed at reinstating what he believed to be the standard curriculum of past ages. To do so, he had to call for a reestablishment of the primacy of biblical and mishnaic studies and a deemphasis upon tosafistic and pilpulistic studies.

Rabbi Loew not only criticized the place biblical studies had been assigned in the contemporary curriculum. He also took issue with the manner in which it was taught. In an effort to emphasize the study of talmudic dialectics and *tosafot* and *pilpul,* study of Scripture (save the Pentateuch) was virtually eliminated from the curriculum. In fact, scriptural studies were even *forbidden* by some of Loew's contemporaries. For example, Aaron of Posnań, Loew's predecessor as Chief Rabbi of Posnań, delivered a sermon at Posnań in 1559 forbidding the study of philosophy, secular studies, and Scripture.[47] It may be that Loew's insistence upon scriptural study was a direct response to his own experiences as a student in Posnań during his childhood there.

Judah Loew condemned contemporary educators for not teaching parts of Scripture other than the Pentateuch. He also criticized the manner in which the Pentateuch was being taught. Loew opposed the then popular practice of teaching the Pentateuch in conjunction with the weekly portion of the Torah (*parashah* or *sidrah*) read in the synagogue. Such a manner of procedure precluded the possibility of completing the entire portion within a week. Because the onset of the following week would initiate study of the portion assigned to that week, substantial sections of each week's portion were eliminated. Portions read during the holiday period were never studied at all. As a result of this system, the student's knowledge of the Pentateuch was sketchy and disjointed. To remedy this situation, Loew suggested study of the Pentateuch in sequential *order* of the text. This may be done, he claims, if the long vacations are eliminated and if the student waits until the age proper for mishnaic and talmudic studies (ten and fifteen, respectively, following talmudic precedent) rather than launching into more advanced studies before the proper age.[48]

Loew's insistence upon sequential study, rather than haphazard, disjointed study, led him to stress the importance of logical graduation of subject matter in curriculum design. In his view, the subject matter ought to be organized in such a manner so that each unit of study may serve as the basis for the succeeding unit of study. Once one unit has been taught and learned by extensive drill and review, the next unit might be introduced.[49] This notion of programmed study led to the writing of the first textbooks in studies of the Pentateuch and of Hebrew grammar.[50] Unlike many of his contemporaries, Loew stressed the need for a careful study of Hebrew grammar as the basis for scriptural and talmudic studies.[51] It is also significant that Loew's last literary act was an endorsement of Issaschar Eulenberg's textbook *Sefer Be'er Sheva.*

After the student has had a thorough grounding in scriptural studies, reinforced by review and by religious observance, he should proceed to the study of the basis of rabbinic literature, the Mishnah. Like Maimonides some 400 years before, Loew attempted to reestablish the centrality of the Mishnah in Jewish education. By virtually ignoring the Mishnah and stressing the Talmud (*gemara*), students were learning neither the Mishnah nor the Talmud. Without a firm grounding in mishnaic studies, the student cannot attain complete understanding of the Talmud and its commentaries. Nor may he become proficient, therefore, in Jewish legal problems which are grounded in mishnaic texts. It is important to reiterate here that under the influence of Rabbi Loew, societies for the study of the Mishnah spread throughout Central and Eastern Europe in the centuries after his death. The study of the Mishnah by members of these societies was greatly facilitated by the commentary to the Mishnah by Yom Tov Lipmann Heller Ha-Levi, written under Loew's influence.[52]

As was mentioned above, Loew was an ardent opponent of the centrality the *pilpul* had attained in contemporary Jewish education. The position of Chief Rabbi of Prague may have eluded Loew in 1584 because of his criticism of this mode of rabbinic scholarship which had already become so endemic in the educational process.

It has been generally assumed that Rabbi Loew was an uncompromising opponent of all forms of *pilpul*. However, such is not the case. He only rejected *pilpul* when it became an end rather than a means. The method of casuistry and qualification known as *pilpul* is a viable method of textual analysis when it leads to an understanding of the text in question or when it provides clarification of the problem under analysis. However, when mental gymnastics and academic hairsplitting becomes an end in itself, the *pilpul* is worthless. *Pilpul* which clouds issues rather than clarifying them may sharpen the mind but does nothing to increase the store of knowledge. However, *pilpul amiti*–"true *pilpul*"–may help to make useful distinctions, elicit the implicit, increase the substance of knowledge, and serve as the basis for halakhic decision.[53]

Having studied Scripture and Mishnah, the student may proceed to the study of the Talmud (*gemara*), which in Loew's view, is essentially an example of "proper *pilpul*."[54] Once the student has mastered the talmudic dialectic, he is ready to study Jewish legal literature.

Though Loew encouraged the study of Jewish legal literature, he expressed strong reservations concerning study of the various codes of Jewish law. Specifically, Loew suggested limiting the study of the codes only to the most advanced students.[55] This was because of the position he takes concerning what he considered to be the proper role the codes should play in the process of halakhic decision.

According to Loew, the Jewish legal codes were being given too central a role both in the curriculum of rabbinical training and in the process of halakhic decision. He viewed the current abuses in Jewish religious practice as having their root in a practicing rabbinate incapable of making viable and correct halakhic decisions because of sparse knowledge in the area of Jewish law. Loew considered the centrality given the codes in study and practice to be a major contributing factor to the current dearth of capable halakhists amongst the ranks of the contemporary rabbinate.

A major stimulus for Loew's critique of the place of the codes in the curriculum and their role in halakhic decision was the appearance in 1565-66 of a short but decisive code, the *Shulḥan Arukh,* written by a Sefardic mystic and legalist named Joseph Karo. To make this code acceptable for all Jews–Ashkenazic as well as Sefardic–Moses Isserles, a Polish rabbi, added a series of detailed glosses to Karo's code which incorporated Ashkenazic variations of religious observance. Like his brother, Hayyim of Friedberg, who wrote a blistering attack against codification in general and against Isserles in particular, Loew sharply criticized both the codes and those who decide questions of Jewish law based upon the positions found in the codes, especially in the recent *Shulḥan Arukh.*

In satirical tones, Loew maintains that the "set table" (*Shulḥan Arukh*) is bereft of proper food to eat. God's covenant, he claims, is the Torah, and not, as some seem to think, the *Shulḥan Arukh.* Loew expresses his apprehension that the *Shulḥan Arukh* may eventually replace the Talmud as a subject for study and as a primary source for halakhic decisions. Once the *Shulḥan Arukh* becomes part of the curriculum, he suggests, students will read the codes before studying the law in the Talmud. They will make their legal decisions upon the basis of the codes rather than upon the talmudic text. They will be predisposed to reading and understanding the Talmud in accordance with the interpretations assumed by the decisions in the codes. For Loew, halakhah must be found in sources, not in "signs" (*simanim*), i.e., in the paragraphs of the *Shulḥan Arukh*. As the *Shulḥan Arukh* does not record its sources, those making decisions in Jewish law based upon its texts will never know, nor will they believe they need know, the talmudic sources upon which the law is based. The shortcut provided by the codes will circumvent the use and study of the Talmud. Loew therefore opposes the *Shulḥan Arukh* because, unlike earlier codes, it established itself and was being regarded as a basis for halakhic decisions. The earlier codes (e.g., Maimonides' *Mishneh Torah* and Jacob ben Asher's *Arba'ah Turim*) were never intended to be used as a basis for legal decision. They were only intended to provide a summary of the talmudic discussion on a given issue. Had the authors of those codes known that students and rabbis would abandon study of the Talmud and would base legal decisions upon their codes, Loew maintains, they would never have written those codes.

Loew's views concerning the codes, particularly the *Shulḥan Arukh,* are intrinsically related to his critique of the contemporary rabbinate and to his plan for the reformation of Jewish education. If the rabbis did not rely on the codes, he contends, they would have to study the Talmud more carefully. They would be more learned than they are. They would not allow the observance of the commandments to be flaunted. The Torah would serve its proper role. The commandments would be correctly observed and would serve as a means to human perfection. If his curriculum were introduced, Loew insists, halakhic decision would be made as the result of careful study of the particular legal problem, first in the Mishnah, then in related talmudic discussion and then in subsequent halakhic literature. The classical codes (i.e., not the *Shulḥan Arukh*) might then be consulted for their summaries of the talmudic position. Finally, the facts of the specific case would be evaluated and halakhic decision would be reached. Since the method of attaining a proper halakhic decision is closely related to his curriculum design, Loew contends that, until his curriculum is implemented, the legal capabilities of the rabbinate will remain at a low ebb, the quality of halakhic decision will be poor and un-reliable; observance will remain lax. The quality of Jewish existence will progressively atrophy. The quest for human perfection will not be possible; the messianic advent will be retarded.[56]

Unlike many of his Central and Eastern European Jewish contemporaries, Rabbi Loew insisted that mathematics and the natural sciences merit study. His positive attitude toward the natural sciences, particularly astronomy, led a number of nineteenth-century scholars to portray him as a "modern." Under Loew's influence, they noted, his student David Ganz delved into the study of physics, mathematics, and astronomy. Ganz and possibly Judah Loew himself visited the observatory outside Prague, built by Emperor Rudolf, where Kepler and Tycho Brahe did their scientific work.[57] This, they claimed, demonstrates that Loew was not a mystic-obscurantist, but a man of science, a citizen of the modern age of enlightenment. Because of the views of these nineteenth-century scholars and the influence they have had upon subsequent literature concerning Judah Loew, it is necessary to clarify Loew's position on the natural sciences.[58]

Natural Science

For Judah Loew, science assures one only limited knowledge. Science may lead one to truth, but is not itself truth. Concerning the study of science, he writes:

> Though all the science of nature is "Greek" Wisdom, secular knowledge and therefore outside of the Torah, nevertheless, it is permissible to study it since knowledge of it is needed to fix the seasons of the year [and therefore to determine the correct dates for celebrating Jewish religious festivals].[59]

Elsewhere he writes, "The sciences which treat the existence and order of the world are certainly a fitting subject for study. It is absolutely permissible to study them."[60] He continues, "Everything which treats the essence of the world could and should be studied. For all existence was created by God. Through studying the phenomena of creation, one comes to perceive the Creator."[61] Rabbi Loew also notes that Gentiles are very interested in astronomy. He relates that a new astronomer has recently presented a new theory of astronomy. He may be referring here to

Copernicus's heliocentric view.[62] Nevertheless, Loew rejects the Copernican view as it would challenge the anthropocentric foundation of his mystical theology.

Judah Loew considered science a means to an end and not an end in itself. It would be a mistake to assume, as has been done, that he put scientific knowledge on a par with knowledge of the Torah. Scientific knowledge is "natural" wisdom while knowledge of the Torah is "supernatural" wisdom. Scientific knowledge may allow us to understand phenomena; however, only knowledge of the Torah can provide knowledge of noumena, knowledge of the "things in themselves."[63] Thus, for Loew, while natural science is a viable subject of study, it is merely a "ladder with which to ascend to the wisdom of the Torah."[64]

While some nineteenth-century scholars understood Loew's positive position on the study of the natural sciences to be indicative of his modernity, other nineteenth-century scholars perceived his volatile criticism of his contemporary, Azariah dei Rossi, to be indicative of his antiscientific, medieval mentality.[65] By examining Loew's attitude to Azariah dei Rossi, we shall clarify his views concerning natural science. But what is more significant, his methodology for the study of non-halakhic rabbinic literature will be elucidated.

Following a position rooted in the writings of the Gaonim and Maimonides, Azariah dei Rossi claims that, while the views of the talmudic sages are true with regard to theological and halakhic issues, they need not be considered authoritative when they contradict the findings of the natural sciences. One should admit, Azariah insists, that the rabbis were ignoramuses in science, when judged by contemporary standards.[66]

Judah Loew rejected the attempt by dei Rossi and others to reduce all or part of classical Jewish literature to "natural" wisdom, i.e., to science, to conventional ethics, to history. He therefore also opposed Nahmanides' claim that the Torah is a book of conventional ethics. He rejected the attempts of Gersonides and others to offer a natural or scientific explanation of miracles, but assumed that miracles, being essentially supernatural, could not be explained scientifically.[67] Loew rejected Azariah dei Rossi's attempts to refute the accuracy of geographical and medical data recorded in the Talmud on the grounds that the Talmud is not a book of science at all and that by taking rabbinic texts literally and examining them scientifically, dei Rossi only indicated that the "true" inner meaning of the texts eluded him.[68]

According to Loew, scientific study is only valid when it helps reinforce or clarify the views of classical Judaism. It is irrelevant, specious, and dangerous when it opposes those views. In fact, one reason for the study of scientific works is to become aware of the heretical ideas they often represent so as to enable one to refute them. One should study astronomical tracts, for example, not only to learn astronomy, but to become aware of philosophical ideas inimical to faith such as the "eternity of the world." Only once these views are known may they be effectively encountered and challenged.[69]

Judah Loew rejected Azariah dei Rossi's attempt to elucidate rabbinic literature from knowledge garnered from "Gentile works," especially from such works in the field of history, literature, and metaphysics. According to Loew, there is no substance to such works. Therefore, to utilize such writings in order to understand rabbinic literature is a severe affront to the sages of past generations and a denial of the essentially supernatural quality of rabbinic literature. The writings of Azariah dei Rossi are "in opposition to the Torah which is our sacred tradition." As they are replete with dangerous and heretical notions, one ought not read them.[70]

Judah Loew's attack upon dei Rossi was launched for the same reasons that he had attacked another of his contemporaries–Eliezer Ashkenazi. As was noted above, Loew attacked these two individuals because both of them had advocated a critical, historical reevaluation of classical texts and traditional ideas.

Ashkenazi and dei Rossi had met while the former was in Italy. After this visit, dei Rossi praised Ashkenazi in print for the nobility of his humanistic efforts. Dei Rossi even called Ashkenazi "the outstanding authority of his generation." It would seem, therefore, that Rabbi Loew perceived this combined effort to be a threat to tradition. To Loew, who considered classical ideas and traditional texts to be above question, beyond literary or historical analysis, the possibilities represented by Ashkenazi and dei Rossi were unthinkable, and therefore had to be opposed. Since the position represented by Ashkenazi and dei Rossi were the contemporary expressions of an outlook Loew identified with the medieval philosophical tradition, he attacked not only these two individuals, but the whole intellectual tradition from which he understood them to have emerged. In focusing his critique on his contemporaries, he was able, through them, to repudiate positions held by them but originally stated by earlier scholars–e.g., Maimonides–who had attained an aura of respectability and were beyond reproach. In Loew's analysis of the views of dei Rossi concerning the nature of rabbinic literature, he offers a veiled criticism of Maimonides.

Loew rebukes dei Rossi's adaptation of Maimonides' view that some rabbinic texts "have the character of poetical conceits whose meaning is not obscure for someone endowed with understanding. At that time [i.e., the talmudic era] this method was generally known and used by everyone just as the poets used poetical expressions."[71] Loew rejected Maimonides' position in veiled terms, but attacked dei Rossi harshly and openly for his contention that "these usages [in rabbinic literature] are termed metaphor, symbol and allegory by the gentile sages." Thus, following Maimonides, dei Rossi held that, like their views on scientific matters, many of the non-halakhic views of the sages are expressions of personal opinion or of poetic fantasy, and therefore are not above dispute.[72]

Judah Loew categorically denied that any of the utterances of the rabbis "were in the manner of those who speak with linguistic embellishment." He refused to consider any part of rabbinic literature an exercise in literary fantasy. He rejects Azariah dei Rossi's claim that the rabbis utilized literary techniques simply to inspire and to edify the masses. Loew viewed the entire approach exemplified by dei Rossi to be symptomatic of the rationalist bent of those under the influence of philosophical speculation. It is not surprising, therefore, that Loew's rejoinder to dei Rossi (and to Maimonides by implication) reflects an approach to non-halakhic rabbinic literature rooted in the Jewish mystical tradition.

According to Loew, rabbinic literature is often attacked on the grounds that many of its statements are not reasonable. Such a claim, he asserts, is only made by readers uninitiated into specific works which contain the correct interpretations and the "true," "inner" meanings of rabbinic literature. It is significant that both works named by Loew in this regard are decisive elements of Jewish mystical literature, i.e., *Sefer Ha-Bahir* and the Zohar. Thus, the key to a true understanding of rabbinic literature is not critical, "scientific" analysis, but immersion in "books of wisdom," which Loew identifies with Jewish mystical literature. Reasonableness is not a criterion by which to evaluate the meaning of rabbinic literature. In fact, claims Loew, the more a work appears to be "unreasonable," the greater the possibility that it embodies supernal wisdom.[73] While other works may be subjected to analysis in order to establish their validity or the cogency of their arguments, rabbinic literature is valid in and of itself.[74]

According to Loew, much of rabbinic literature is deliberately esoteric. In fact, he argues, the more obscure and esoteric a text, the greater the wisdom it holds.[75] Therefore, knowledge of esoteric wisdom and of esoteric literature–the mystical literature–is essential for a true understanding of rabbinic literature. It may be for this very reason that the kabbalistic element in Loew's writings is most evident in his exposition of non-halakhic talmudic passages in *Hiddushei Aggadot.*[76]

Having examined Judah Loew's views on contemporary social issues, specifically the quality of rabbinic leadership, and the theory, practice, and content of Jewish education, it should be clear that his social criticism, his mystical theology, and his personal concerns, rather than being separate and disjoined, coalesce to form a comprehensive whole. One may not separate Judah Loew the educator from Judah Loew the mystic. One may not disassociate Judah Loew the social reformer from Judah Loew the theologian. One may not disjoin the mystical theology of the Maharal of Prague, nor his social dissent, from the man whose legacy they are.

14

Conclusion

The primary purpose of the preceding study has been to demonstrate that Judah Loew deserves a niche, if not an essential place, in the history of Jewish mystical speculation. A penultimate goal of the above discussion has been to demonstrate the cohesion amongst the events which constitute Judah Loew's biography, the mystical theology contained in his massive writings, and the social conditions which evoked his concern. In order to accomplish these tasks it became necessary to reconstruct his biography from the scattered sources by and about him, to provide a comprehensive sketch of the works by him, to isolate and explicate his positions concerning the major problems in Jewish theology, to identify the essentially mystical foundation of that theology, and to relate the facts of his life and the content of his theological reflections to his views concerning contemporary social and religious issues. Because previous studies of Loew had left these tasks largely undone, it fell to the present work to attempt to complete them.

Nathan Grün's first attempt at a biography of Rabbi Loew, written in the 1880s, proved inadequate. Grün's failure to have read all of Loew's works, his antimystical bias, and the availability of new data since he composed his work made the reconstruction of Loew's biography a desideratum. The failure of more recent studies of Loew to provide a comprehensive biography of their subject, stimulated the present writer to do so (chapter 3). To examine the relationship of the man to his works and the content of those works, a complete bibliography would be needed. Unfortunately, previous studies of Judah Loew had not provided such information. Consequently, it became a requisite task to reconstruct a sorely needed complete bibliography of Rabbi Loew's writings (chapter 4). Having outlined the biography of the man and the scope of his writings, the primary task of demonstrating Loew's mystical proclivities could proceed.

Since most previous studies of Judah Loew ignored his theology, it became necessary to provide a first attempt at a comprehensive study of the major themes of Loew's theology of Judaism. To defend the assertion that Loew's theological concerns were essentially drawn from his interpretation of the Jewish mystical tradition, continual reference has been made above to the possible or probable sources in Jewish religious literature, especially kabbalistic literature, upon which he drew in formulating his ideas (chapters 5-8; 10-12). Finally, the application of Loew's theoretical concerns to legal and social issues was discussed in order to defend the claim that the facts of Loew's life, the concepts of his theology, and his stance on social concerns were inevitably interrelated (chapters 9, 13). Thus, the preceding discussion represents the first attempt at a comprehensive portrait of the life, works, and thought of Judah Loew of Prague. While other studies of Loew have chosen to concentrate upon a single aspect of his thought, while largely ignoring his biography and his bibliography, the present study has chosen to provide a comprehensive sketch of his life, his works, and his major ideas within the context of his essentially mystical world-view.

Previous studies of Judah Loew have attempted to portray him as he was not, i.e., as a proto-modern. Recent studies of Loew, for example, have isolated in his works anticipations of Kant's epistemology, Hegel's dialectic, Pascal's theology, Comenius's pedagogy, Rousseau's politics, Vico's historiography, Bergson's metaphysics, and Einstein's physics. While selections from his writings do bear striking resemblance to many later ideas, Loew's world view radically differed from that of any of the above-named individuals. As has been continually noted above, Judah Loew's world view derived from Jewish religious tradition, specifically from Jewish mystical tradition.

Jewish life and thought in Central and Eastern Europe have been neglected by modern Jewish scholarship. Historians of Jewish mysticism have virtually disregarded the significant contributions of late medieval Jewish European mystics to the development of Jewish mystical speculation. With specific reference to Judah Loew, the comprehensive scope and the mystical content of his writings have generally been ignored. Hopefully, this work has made some amends for the omissions of past scholars. Possibly, the present study will encourage others further to examine Jewish life and thought in Central and Eastern Europe during the end of the medieval period.

Appendix 1

When Was Judah Loew Born?

As has been noted above (chapter 3), the year of Loew's birth cannot be established with any certainty. Suggestions range from 1512 to 1526. The purpose of the present discussion is to evaluate these suggestions.

The *terminus a quo* of 1512 was first suggested by M. Perles in 1718, in a treatise about Loew's family. Perles, a great-grand-nephew of Judah Loew, wrote this treatise at the request of his cousin, Isaiah Katz, who was a direct descendant of Judah Loew. Because Perles wrote his tract a little more than a century after Loew's death, and because Perles apparently relied upon family traditions in composing his work, the accuracy of Perles's claim has been assumed by many scholars. The following scholars accept Perles's claim that Judah Loew was born in 1512: Stein, p. 69; Willman, p. 45; Gottesdiener, p. 288; Bokser, p. 13; Thieberger, p. 13; Neher (1966), p. 10; Dreyfus, p. 11; Gross (1969), p. 17, no. 10; A. Weiss, p.1.

In 1885, in the first and only attempt (until the present one) at a critical biography of Loew, N. Grün challenged Perles's claim that Judah Loew had been born in 1512. Grün assumed that, if he could establish an approximate birthdate later than 1512 for Loew's older brother, Hayyim, he could demonstrate the incorrectness of Perles's suggestion. Noting that Hayyim was a schoolmate of Moses Isserles, and assuming that Isserles was born in 1520, Grün proposed that Hayyim also must have been born before or during 1520. Since Judah Loew was Hayyim's younger brother, Grün concludes that he must have been born in 1520. The following authors accept Grün's position: Muneles (1965), p. 75; Ben Sasson (1970), p. 65, no. 186.

In addition to 1512 and 1520, 1525 has been claimed as the year of Loew's birth; see M. Friedlander, p. 16. Unfortunately, Friedlander provides no data to support his claim.

187

Jerábek, p. 32, claims that Loew could not have been born before 1526. This date, he claims, may be established "on the basis of new evidence." Regretfully, Jerábek never reveals what that evidence might be. The *EJ*, s.v. "Judah Loew Ben Bezalel," apparently following Jerábek, records 1526 as the birthdate.

Jerábek, it must be noted, is not consistent in referring to 1526 as the approximate date of Loew's birth. Apparently in agreement with M. Perles, Jerábek, p. 39, claims that Loew died in 1609 at the age of ninety-seven. This would place Loew's birthdate at 1512. Jerábek also notes, p. 32, that Loew came to Prague in 1573 from Moravia when about fifty years of age. This would place Loew's birth at about 1523. Finally, it ought to be noted that as the basis of his 1526 date, Jerábek cites Grün, p. 7, but Grün placed Loew's birth at about 1520. The 1526 date, p. 32, may simply be a misprint. However, the internal discrepancies in Jerábek's discussion concerning Loew's birthdate remain.

Since Friedlander's and Jerábek's claims are supported neither with documentation nor with argumentation, they cannot be critically evaluated. However, since Grün attempts to ascertain the year of Loew's birth by induction, the data he assumes and the inferences he makes are open to question.

Grün's assumption that Isserles was born in 1520 is problematic. In rebutting Grün, Thieberger notes, p. 12, that establishing the year of Loew's birth from the contemporaneity of Hayyim and Isserles is groundless because "it is generally accepted that Isserles was born about 1510." In his extensive work on Isserles, A. Ziev, pp. 12 and 57, fixes Isserles's birthdate at 1530 and concludes that Hayyim, too, must have been born about then. Therefore, since the year of Isserles's birth cannot be established with any certainty, one cannot utilize claims regarding the alleged year of Isserles's birth to establish the year of Hayyim's birth.

Though the year of Hayyim's birth is far from certain, on the basis of statements in his writings, which apparently eluded Grün and Ziev, one may arrive at a reasonable approximation for the *terminus ad quem* of Hayyim's birthdate. In one autobiographical aside in his writings, Hayyim mentions having been born at Posnań. In another he records a recollection from his childhood in Posnań. In a third written, in 1545, he records having lived in Cracow for twenty years. This would put his arrival in Cracow at 1525. If we assume that Hayyim lived in Posnań as a child and was sent to Cracow to study when still a young lad, a common practice of his time and place, it is reasonable to assume that he was born no later than 1520. See Sherwin (1975), p. 36.

Though Grün overlooked Hayyim's autobiographical asides, which help establish the apparent year of Hayyim's birth, Grün nevertheless correctly estimates 1520 as the approximate year of Hayyim's birth. To conclude that Loew was born in 1520 from the conclusion that Hayyim was born in that year, however, does not necessarily follow for two reasons. First, 1520 is an approximation, rather than a definite birthdate. Second, it is unlikely that two brothers of the identical mother would be born in the same year.

If we assume that Hayyim was born no later than 1520, the unsubstantiated claims of Friedlander that Loew was born in 1525 and of Jerábek that Loew was born in 1526 become reasonable.

At this point an additional factor should be considered: namely, the possible span of age separating Hayyim and Judah Loew. This determination is difficult because of conflicting sources. Perles, supposedly reporting a family tradition, places Judah as the youngest of four sons, the eldest being Hayyim. In a responsum written during Loew's and Hayyim's lifetimes by their distant relative by marriage, Solomon Luria, Judah is placed second in the list of brothers, rather than fourth. Similarly, another contemporary of Loew's, the chronicler David Ganz, lists Judah as the second rather than as the last of the brothers. If these contemporary accounts represent the order of birth, then it may be assumed that Perles's report is inaccurate and that Loew was born directly after Hayyim. See Luria (1969), no. 12, and, Ganz, I, p. 30a. Gottesdiener, p. 267, accepts Perles's view that Loew was the youngest son, while Thieberger, pp. 11-12, lists Loew as the second son. Grün, p. 6, no. 1, notes both possibilities. (Loew's brothers, other than Hayyim, were Sinai and Samson. Sinai dwelt in Prague and accompanied Loew to his meeting with Rudolf. Samson remained in Poland and became Chief Rabbi of Krzemienic.)

If Loew was indeed the second son of Bezalel, and if Hayyim was born no later than 1520, one may conclude that Perles's claim that Loew was born in 1512 is most unlikely. Therefore, rather than place the year of Loew's birth somewhere between 1512 and 1526, one may further narrow the scope of possibilities. If Hayyim was the first of four sons and Loew the second, and if Hayyim was born about 1520, it is reasonable to assume that Judah Loew was born in the early 1520s.

Appendix 2

In What Order Did Loew Write His Works?

As has been noted above (chapter 4), the order of the publication of Loew's works does not represent the order of their composition. The present discussion will attempt to establish the approximate dates that Loew composed his major works. Certain claims in this regard were made above (chapter 4). These must now be defended.

Loew often refers to books published later in his life in those published earlier in his life. In *Gur Aryeh,* first published in 1578, he refers to *Gevurot Ha-Shem,* first published in 1582. In *Gevurot Ha-Shem,* he refers to *Derekh Ha-Ḥayyim,* first published in 1589, and to *Neẓah Yisrael, Tiferet Yisrael* and *Be'er Ha-Golah,* first published in 1600. In his *Sermon for the Sabbath of Penitence,* first published in 1584, he mentions *Be'er Ha-Golah.* In *Derekh Ha-Ḥayyim,* he mentions *Tiferet Yisrael* and *Netivot Olam* (the latter as a "future work"). In the published version of his *Sermon on the Great Sabbath* (1589), he mentions the *Netivot Olam* published in 1595 and *Neẓah Yisrael* published in 1600. From this one may conclude that Loew did not compose his published works in the order of their publication. One may assume that he wrote them, in some cases, long before they finally were published.

The claim that Loew completed *Gur Aryeh* by 1578 is evident, since that is the year it was published. It is reasonable to assume that Loew had completed the manuscript of *Gevurot Ha-Shem* by that date, or was close to completing it, because he refers to *Gevurot Ha-Shem* in *Gur Aryeh* many times; for example: 1:93, 2:10, 11, 23, 26, 28, 42, 54, 56, 62, 69, 99; 3:118; 4:122; 5:123. (See also Kleinberger, p. 15, no. 17.) Thus, *Gevurot Ha-Shem* appears to have been completed well in advance of its 1582 publication date.

That Loew began writing *Derekh Ha-Hayyim* before 1578 is evident from references to it in *Gur Aryeh*. In *Gur Aryeh*, Loew mentions *Derekh Ha-Hayyim* twice, once as if it had already been completed (*GA*, 1:36; 3:114), and once as if it were yet to be completed (*GA*, 1:255). Despite Loew's claim in *Gur Aryeh* that *Derekh Ha-Hayyim* had already been completed, such was not the case. That Loew could not have completed *Derekh Ha-Hayyim* before 1583 is based upon the fact that in *Derekh Ha-Hayyim* (p. 234), Loew refers to Eliezer Ashkenazi's attack upon views expressed in *Gevurot Ha-Shem*. Ashkenazi's attack is to be found in his *Ma'aseh Ha-Shem*, first published in 1583 and again in 1584 (Michael, p. 199; Michael's claim that Ashkenazi completed his work by 1580 is to be doubted unless one assumes that he read *Gevurot Ha-Shem* in manuscript; however, there is no reason to assume such to be the case). Therefore, it is likely that since Ashkenazi's work was published first in 1583, and that Loew refers to it in *Derekh Ha-Hayyim*, he could not have completed *Derekh Ha-Hayyim* before 1583. However, Loew's references to *Derekh Ha-Hayyim* in *Gur Aryeh* and in *Gevurot Ha-Shem* as a completed work, would indicate that by 1582 (the date of the publication of *Gevurot Ha-Shem*) and certainly by 1583, *Derekh Ha-Hayyim* was near completion.

That *Be'er Ha-Golah* was probably completed by 1584 is evident from references to it as a completed work both in *Gevurot Ha-Shem* and in the *Sermon for the Sabbath of Penitence,* published in 1584. Thus, one may assume that *Be'er Ha-Golah*, though first published in 1600, was either in its final form or close to it by 1584.

Though the date of the composition of *Hidushei Aggadot* is unclear, there is reason to believe it was composed by 1585 or 1586. On the manuscript of this work, the scribe notes such things as, "until date so-and-so I have copied thus far." The four dates noted are from the summer of 1585 and from the winter of 1586. See *HA*, 1:8; note Kasher (1958), p. 36. Since Loew makes frequent references in *Hidushei Aggadot* to *Tiferet Yisrael*, it is likely that by 1586 he had completed *Tiferet Yisrael* as well.

Netivot Olam was published in 1595. It is mentioned in none of Loew's works published before 1594 (except as a book yet to be written). In Loew's *Sermon on the Torah*, published in 1593, he has a lengthy discussion on the nature of the Torah. Yet, in the *Sermon on the Torah* he makes no reference to his discussion of this issue in *Netivot Olam*. Consequently, one may assume that *Netivot Olam* was written between 1593 and 1595.

Abbreviations

(Abbreviations for biblical works follow standard usage.)

1. Abbreviations for Judah Loew's Works

BG–*Be'er Ha-Golah*
DH–*Derekh Ha-Ḥayyim*
Eulogy–*Eulogy (Hesped) for Akiva Günzberg*
GA–*Gur Aryeh*
GH–*Gevurot Ha Shem*
HA–*Ḥidushei Aggadot*
NM–*Ner Miẓvah*
NO–*Netivot Olam*
NY–*Neẓaḥ Yisrael*
OH–*Or Ḥadash*
SGS–*Sermon for the Great Sabbath (Derush L'Shabbat Ha-Gadol)*
SOC–*Sermon on the Commandments (Derush Al Ha-Miẓvot)*
SOT–*Sermon on the Torah (Derush Al Ha-Torah)*
SSR–*Sermon for Sabbath of Penitence (Derush L'Shabbat Shuva)*
TY–*Tiferet Yisrael*

2. Abbreviations for Other Works

ARN–*Avot d'Rabbi Natan*
Av. Zar.–*Babylonian Talmud—Tractate Avodah Zara*
BB–*Babylonian Talmud—Tractate Bava Batra*
CM–Maimonides' *Commentary to the Mishnah (Perush La-Mishnah)*
Deut. R.–*Midrash Deuteronomy Rabbah*
EJ–*Encyclopedia Judaica*, Jerusalem 1972
Est. R.–*Midrash Esther Rabbah*
Ethics–Aristotle's *Nicomachean Ethics*

Ex. R.–*Midrash Exodus Rabbah*
Gen. R.–*Midrash Genesis Rabbah*
Git.–*Babylonian Talmud—Tractate Gittin*
Guide–Maimonides' *Guide of the Perplexed*
Ket.–*Babylonian Talmud—Tractate Ketubot*
Kid.–*Babylonian Talmud—Tractate Kiddushin*
Lam. R.–*Midrash Lamentations Rabbah*
PR–*Midrash Pesikta Rabbati*
PRE–*Midrash Pirkei d'Rabbi Eliezer*
SA–J. Karo's *Shulḥan Arukh*
Sanh.–*Babylonian Talmud—Tractate Sanhedrin*
Shab.–*Babylonian Talmud—Tractate Shabbat*
Sif. Deut.–*Sifre on Deuteronomy*
SM–Maimonides' *Sefer Hu-Miẓvot (Book of the Commandments)*
Suk.–*Babylonian Talmud—Tractate Sukkah*
Tan.–*Midrash Tanḥuma*
YD–*Yoreh De'ah*
Yev.–*Babylonian Talmud—Tractate Yevamot*
Yom.–*Babylonian Talmud—Tractate Yoma*
YS–*Midrash Yalkut Shimoni*

Notes

Chapter 1

1. Ira Sud, the rabbi of this tale, related this story to the author.
2. Ganz, 1:31a.
3. *Ha-Magid*, 14:163-64. English translation in Bloch, pp. 186-88. Also see Thieberger, pp. 38-41.
4. Evans, chapters 6 and 7.
5. Kaufman, 3:523. On Bachrach's relationship to Loew, see Bachrach's introduction to his collected responsa, *Ḥavvot Yair*.
6. The following works provide a general account of the legends about Loew: Thieberger, pp. 76-97, 131-176; Gottesdiener, pp. 348-53.
7. D. Ganz, Loew's student, reports two of his own visits to Tycho Brahe's observatory near Prague. Loew had a high regard for astronomy, mathematics, and optics. According to *EJ*, "Judah Loew ben Bezalel," Brahe and Loew did enjoy a social relationship. *EJ* offers no documentation for either claim regarding Loew and Brahe.

   The language of conversation between Loew and Rudolf was probably German; see Kisch (1946), 8:20-21 and Gottesdiener, p 305.
8. Sanh. 20b.
9. A number of these tales was collected by Alois Jirásek in *Old Tales from Bohemia;* see Thieberger, pp. 150-51.
10. There is both a Jewish and a Bohemian version of this tale; see Thieberger, pp. 174-75; note Jerábek, pp. 38-39.
11. Sanh. 65b, 67b.
12. Bin Gorion, p. 752
13. Scholem (1965), pp. 158-205, and Scholem (1974), pp. 351-355.
14. In one of his responsa, Zevi Ashkenazi attributes the golem to his grandfather, Elijah of Chelm; see Z. Ashkenazi, responsa no. 93. This responsum, apparently written in 1709, shows that as of that date Loew had not yet been identified with the golem legend. Ashkenazi was certainly familiar with Loew's life and thought, as is clear from references he makes to Loew in his other responsa, e.g., no. 76.

    In 1727, Meir Perles, a great-grandnephew of Judah Loew, wrote a tract on Loew's life. In this tract, Perles makes no mention of the golem legend. Had the legend been associated with Loew at the time, Perles certainly would have mentioned it. In his biography of Loew, Grün, p. 37, suggests that Perles omitted the story of Rabbi Loew and the golem because everyone knew it. This suggestion is not convincing. Considering Perles does mention the meeting with Rudolf, which was at least equally famous, why would he not also mention the golem legend if it were well known? Grün's suggestion, therefore, must be rejected. It would seem reasonable to assume that the

194

golem legend became identified with Loew sometime after the first quarter of the eighteenth century, though exactly when is uncertain. See also Stein, pp. 69-70, and Lion and Lukas, pp. 48-53.

Loew does mention the term "golem" a number of times in his work, but never in relation to a discussion of an "artificial man." On a number of occasions (*NO*, 2:102 and *HA*, 2:132), he described a deaf person as a "golem." He defines a "golem" as an incomplete entity, as a being who has not reached its potential, as matter incompleted by form (*DH*, p. 240; *OH*, p 53; *HA*, 3:143). It is also significant that in discussing the talmudic sources related to the golem legend, Loew notes that the creation of life is a natural act and therefore not prohibited by Jewish law. Even if it were a disturbance of nature, it would still be permitted because if disturbing nature would qualify an act as forbidden, then petitionary prayer, assumed to be efficacious, would also have to be forbidden and we know it is not; see *BG*, p. 27, where Loew discusses Sanh. 67b.

15. Rosenberg's work claims to be an authentic account of the golem legend of Rabbi Loew of Prague, based upon a manuscript written by Isaac Katz, Loew's son-in-law.

    Rosenberg's work is the first source which connects the blood libel to the golem legend. The fact that the blood libel was no issue in Prague during Rabbi Loew's lifetime as well as many other historical distortions and linguistic considerations, has proven this work to be a product of imagination rather than a historical document. Chayyim Bloch accepted Rosenberg's book as authentic and based his own work largely upon it.

16. Weiner, p 95; also see Scholem (1971), pp. 335-340; note Rosenfeld (1977), pp. 58-75.

17. Brod, esp. chapter 15; Meyrink; Rothberg; Rosenfeld (1934) provides an extensive picture of the influence of the golem legend on German literature; also note Ish Kishor.

18. Borges, p. 80.

Chapter 2

1. On attitudes toward Jewish mysticism in modern Jewish scholarship, see, for example, Scholem (1941), pp. 1-3, 22, and Scholem (1971), pp. 228, 321.

2. Graetz, 9:13. Also see A Weiss, p. 1v.

3. Rapoport's "Introduction," in Lieben, Hebrew section, p. ii. On Rapoport's anti-mystical attitude, see Barzilay (1969), p. 49.

4. Scholem (1974), p. 5. For a similar distinction between mystical theology and practical mysticism, see discussion and sources noted in Ozment, p. 1, no. 1.

5. It will be the primary aim of this work to demonstrate the viability of the claim that Judah Loew was a mystic. This claim is far from being unanimously accepted in recent scholarship relating to Rabbi Loew.

    Gottesdiener, pp. 299-304, was the first modern scholar who neither minimized nor rejected the mystical element in Loew's writings. The first study to claim uncategorically that Loew was indeed a mystic was Bokser's. Thieberger, p. 67, casually identifies Loew with the mystics. Scholem, while he does consider Loew a mystic, never devotes any extensive discussion to his mystical theology. Scholem, however, discusses Loew in connection with the golem legend. The studies by Neher and his two students, Gross and Dreyfus, are sympathetic to the notion of Loew as a mystic. Only Neher, however, strongly argues the case. See A. Neher (1966), e.g., pp. 16, 115, 143; Dreyfus and Gross. Weiss's study of Loew's theory of human nature and morality does identify the mystical element in his writings as they apply to Loew's views on human nature; see A. Weiss, pp. 37-41, 95-96, 122, 182-224, etc. In his study of Loew's exegesis of *agada* Elbaum notes the frequency of Loew's "kabbalistic expositions of rabbinic dicta" in his *HA*. That view would correspond with the present findings. Apparently *HA* was written for a more select and learned audience than Loew's other works and therefore treats kabbalistic motifs more explicitly than elsewhere. It may also be noted that since *HA* was not published until the 1960s, scholars writing before then did not utilize this work, which is crucial in an attempt to explicate and identify mystical motifs in Loew's work. See Elbaum, 22:39, no. 36.

While the above-noted studies are sympathetic to the claim that Loew deserves a place in the history of Jewish mystical speculation, none of them has adequately defended that claim through a careful analysis of the mystical element in Loew's theological writings.

Despite the claims of the above-noted scholars, there are significant dissenters from their view. Katz and others seek to neutralize Bokser's claim that Loew was a kabbalist. Katz writes: "Bokser styles Maharal a qabbalist. The Qabbalah's influence on him, however, expresses itself more as a general trend than in an adaptation of terms and concepts." See J. Katz (1961), *Exclusiveness and Tolerance*, p. 140, no. 1. Katz apparently overlooks the possibility that Loew's failure to adapt kabbalistic terminology is part of his sustained attempt to popularize and to disseminate kabbalistic ideas without the use of technical, cumbersome terminology. Kleinberger likewise pays little attention to Loew's mystical sources. But he also notes that Loew's theology is not a subject of his deliberations; see Kleinberger (1962), p. 70, no. 172. The early study by Mauskopf disregards the mystical element in Loew. Kariv also attempts to demonstrate that Loew was not a mystic. Many other studies that have occasion to mention Rabbi Loew, note his views on education and his interest in science, but are mute on his involvement with mysticism.

Chapter 3

1. M. Perles, p. 18, placed Loew's birth at Worms. Stein, p. 69, and Willman, p. 45, followed Perles's view. Grün, pp. 6-7, placed Loew's birth at Posnań. Most scholars have followed Grün's view; for example: Thieberger, pp. 8-9; Gottesdiener, p. 268; Bokser, p. 18; Neher, 1966, p. 10; Dreyfus, p. 11; Gross (1974), p. 17, no. 10; A. Weiss, p. 1. The claim that Loew was born at Posnań is based upon two documents written during Judah Loew's lifetime. The first is the autobiographical statement by Loew's brother, Hayyim of Friedberg, that he (i.e., Hayyim) was born in Posnań; see Hayyim ben Bezalel, *Vikuah Mayim Hayyim*, "Introduction" and "Klal" 4:3; note, Sherwin (1975), p. 36. The assumption made by Grün and others is that if Loew's brother was born at Posnań, it is likely that Loew was also born there. The second document is a responsum of Solomon Luria. Luria notes that his grandfather, Isaac Klauber, was a relative of Loew's family and that he resided in Posnań at the same time as did Loew and his family (i.e., Loew's father, Bezalel, Loew, and his brothers). See Luria (1969), no. 12.

2. On the question of when Loew was born, see appendix 1.

3. Apparently following Grün, p. 8, Gottesdiener, p. 268, assumes that Bezalel left Worms toward the end of the fifteenth century. Thieberger, p. 10, assumes Bezalel left Worms before his marriage but gives no approximate date Gross (1974), p. 12, no. 10, and p. 17, no 10, agrees with these views. On the immigration of Jews to Poland during the fifteenth century, see Weinryb, pp. 27-32.

4. 1520 being the approximate date of the birth of Loew's brother, Hayyim, who reports the place of his birth as Posnań
5. M. Perles, p. 17.
6. Judah the Elder was Avigdor Kara's maternal uncle. Tradition has it that Avigdor was close to King Wenceslas (Vaclav) IV (1378-1419). Kara was apparently involved in polemics with the Catholics and influenced the thinking of the Hussites. He achieved some fame as a kabbalist. He wrote a number of liturgical pieces, among them an elegy commemorating the pogroms of April 18, 1389, to which he was an eyewitness There is reason to believe he also wrote on Jewish law and composed a commentary to Genesis and Exodus, though no such manuscript has survived. The origin of the unusual name "Kara" is unknown. It might signify expertise in the *kra*, the biblical text, ascribed to him on his tombstone It may designate the Bohemian town of his family's origin. For source material about Kara see the following: Stein, pp. 21, 60, Gottesdiener, p. 264; Jerábek, p. 26; Landshuth, p. 1; Michael, pp. 7-8; Lieben, German section, pp. 1-2, Hebrew section, pp. xliv and p. 1; Markus, pp. 391-408; *EJ*, s.v. "Abigdor Kara"; J. Kaufmann, pp. 10-11. The most comprehensive essay on Kara is Kamelhar.
7. Quoted by Ben Sasson (1970), p. 8.
8. Willman, p. 45, argues that Loew spent his adolescence in Prague. This proposal is apparently based upon his understanding of M. Perles, p. 18. Grün's, p. 5, circumlocution, attempting to demonstrate why Loew could not have spent his adolescence in Prague, is not convincing
9. Only once in his writings does Rabbi Loew even allude to his teachers, but not by their names, namely, in his published *Sermon on the Great Sabbath* delivered at Prague in 1589. Loew's reason for not mentioning his teachers' names may be because of his rejection of their views on education; see, e.g., Bokser, p. 20. There is no evidence to prove or reason to accept the suggestion by Thieberger, p. 10, that Loew's brother Hayyim's teacher, Isaac Sefardi, was also Loew's teacher.

    Hayyim, in the introduction to his *Be'er Mayim Hayyim,* mentions Sefardi as having taught him the Pentateuch with Rashi's commentary. However, there is no reason to assume Sefardi also taught Loew. Hayyim was educated in Cracow while there is no evidence Loew was ever there. It is likely that it was in Cracow that Hayyim studied with Sefardi. Gottesdiener, p 269, apparently following the suggestion of Grün, p. 9, claimed Loew to have been an autodidact on the grounds that such was characteristic of the system of Polish Jewish education of the time This claim cannot be completely affirmed because it does not account for Loew's single allusion to his teachers. The suggestion made by Willman, p. 45, that Loew studied at Prague with Jacob Pollak has already been handily dismissed by Grün, p. 5. M. Perles's, p 18, suggestions as to whom Loew's teachers could have been are chronologically dubious; see Thieberger, p 15. On the identity of Hayyim's teachers, see Sherwin, 1975, pp. 36-37.
10. M. Perles, p 18
11. Ganz, p. 31a. On Ganz and Loew, see Neher (1974).
12. Friedlander, pp. 14-15; Willman, p. 45; Gottesdiener, p. 273.
13. Friedlander, p 15; Stein, p. 69. Note, Baron (1945), 1:338, 2:94, 2:190.
14. Flesch, pp. 50, 267. Gottesdiener, p. 274, no. 9, refers to Flesch, but mistakenly quotes the source as being p. 51. In his *SSR*, delivered at Prague in 1584, Loew discussed this abuse
15. Flesch, pp. 50, 267. See below, chapter 9.
16. Goldschmied, p. 491, and, Rivkind (1942), p. 33, on the order of being called to the Torah. On other prayers introduced by Loew in Moravia, see E. Roth, p. 51, no. 62;

Halperin, p. 59, no. 13 and p. 60, no. 1. See also Kahane, pp 11-12. In E. Roth, p. 20, no. 1a, Loew is credited with permitting a boy to lead a religious service a month before reaching his majority.

17. Halperin, p. 55, no. 5.

18. Schwenger, pp. 321, 328, no. 8. See also Gottesdiener, p. 274, no. 11; Thieberger, pp. 19-20; Bokser, p. 35.

19. NO, 1:83-84.

20. Grün, pp. 14-15; Gottesdiener, p. 277; Muneles, 1965, p. 75; Thieberger, p. 20.

21. Sources for the preceding sketch of the history of Bohemian Jewry during these years, in order of their direct relevance to the issue, are as follows: Ganz, pp. 29b-30a; Steinhartz, 1950; Baron (1969), 14:146-71; Muneles (1965), pp. 15-101; Stein, p. 167; Gottesdiener, p. 278; Stern, pp. 144-45 and 184-85; Thompson, pp. 41-147; Klemperer (1950), pp 38-39. For additional general information, see Bergman; Kolitz; Steinhartz (1927); Kisch (1968), pp. 1-12.

22. Heller, "Introduction." It has been generally assumed that Heller had been Loew's student at the Klaus; see, e.g.: Lieben, Hebrew section, p. liii; Gottesdiener, p. 278; Thieberger, p. 24; Bokser, p. 38. Klemperer, p. 52, rejects this long-standing assumption. Though influenced by Loew, Heller was not his student, claims Klemperer. One indication of this is that Heller never refers to Loew as his teacher. If Loew had been Heller's teacher, Heller would have undoubtedly acknowledged that fact. Klemperer's assumption seems to have been drawn from Azulai, p. 52.

23. Grün, p. 15; Stein, pp. 170-71.

24. Ganz, I, p. 30b; Grun, pp 19-22.

25. Hayot was the stepbrother of Loew's wife.

26 Grun, p 26; Gottesdiener, pp. 284-85; Klemperer (1950), p. 42. On the conflicting views of Loew and Hayot on *pilpul*, see Bachrach, no. 124.

27. For further discussion of Loew's views on *pilpul*, see chapter 13 below.

28. Hayot, "Foreword."

29. Three possibilities as to Loew's whereabouts between 1584 and 1587 present themselves: Prague, Posnań, and Moravia. That he was in Prague during those years is dubious because of Ganz's statement that Loew was director of the Klaus from his arrival in Prague in 1573 for a period of eleven years. Ganz's statement seems to suggest that after 1584, Loew left Prague for some other place. It has been suggested that Ganz hints that Posnań is that other place, for when Ganz reports that in 1592 Loew went to Poland, he adds that it was to become Chief Rabbi of the whole of Greater Poland for the *second time.* See, Ganz. 1, p. 31a. This suggests, it has been claimed, that at some time before 1592 Loew was Chief Rabbi of Posnań and Greater Poland, presumably during the unaccounted four years of 1584-88. See Grün, pp. 22-23; Stein, p. 69; Gottesdiener, p. 287; Thieberger, p. 37. Note J. Perles, p. 373. This suggestion is claimed to be strengthened by the existence of a responsum written by Loew at Posnań in 1584. See Lieben, German section, p. 3.

Though it seems that Loew was indeed in Posnań from 1584 and 1587, the assumption that Loew was in Posnań the latter part of 1587 and in 1588 may be questioned. First of all, there is a book of community statutes from Prossnitz (Moravia) with Judah Loew's signature affixed thereon. This document is dated August 27, 1587. This establishes Loew's presence in Moravia, at least during the summer of 1587. While it is possible that Loew affixed his signature to the document elsewhere than at Prossnitz, such is not likely, since he not only signed the documents but most probably aided in formulating the statutes. It is also unlikely that the community statute books would be signed, validated, and witnessed outside of

Prossnitz. Furthermore, Loew is not therein identified as Chief Rabbi of Posnań, which one might assume he would have been, had he then held that post. It would therefore appear that for at least part of the period in question (1584-88), Loew was in Prossnitz.

The claim made by Leiben that Loew's responsum *(Al Ha-Agunah)* proves his presence in Posnań in 1584 is open to question. See Goldschmied, p. 502, no. 6; Wachstein, pp. 172-79. There is no evidence that it was written in that year. The responsum, printed in Prague in 1597, notes Posnań as the place of its authorship, but the date of its authorship is not stated. It is a response to an issue discussed in a document dated Monday, 21 Tammuz 1583. Possibly referring to this document, Loew notes in the opening lines of his statement that, when the issue came to his attention, several *years* had elapsed since the original disposition of the issue. All this would lend little credence to the claim that Loew's responsum dates from 1584. It would be more reasonable to assume that the responsum dates from the time of his later ministry at Posnań beginning in 1592. Nevertheless, on the basis of Ganz's testimony, it may be assumed that Loew did leave Prague in 1584 to become Chief Rabbi of Posnań.

30. Goldschmied, p. 502, no. 6; Wachstein, pp. 178-79; compare Gottesdiener, p. 286. That Loew returned to Prague in the late summer or early fall of 1587 is not certain. From Ganz's chronicle, we know he served as director of the Klaus for an additional four years some time after his first departure from Prague in 1584. It is generally assumed that these four years account for his whereabouts between 1588 and 1592, for we know that in the spring of 1592 Loew left Prague for Posnań. This would place his rearrival at Prague in 1588. Only if Ganz's dates are considered approximate rather than precise, it may be assumed that Loew returned to Prague in the late summer or early fall of 1587.

31. Gottesdiener, p. 288.

32 Jerábek, p. 34, suggests that already in 1588 the Prague Jewish community offered the post of chief rabbi to Loew. However, there is no documented basis for this conjecture.

33. See above, chapter 1.

34. Stein, p. 69.

35. Grün, pp. 25-26; Klemperer, 1950, p. 36; Jerábek, p. 35. Compare Gottesdiener, pp 309-10; Stein, p. 29.

36. Muneles (1965), p. 86.

37. Lieben, Hebrew section, p. 3.

38. M. Perles, p. 20.

39. On Meisels, see Ganz, I, pp. 31 a-b; Lieben, German section, pp. 15-19; Stein, pp. 62-68.

40 Stein, pp. 42, 71. On Lenzycz, see Bettan; Klemperer (1950), pp. 38-48.

41. M. Perles, p. 20; Lieben, Hebrew section, p. 3. Azulai, pp. 82-83, incorrectly places their resting place at Cracow rather than at Prague.

42. For general genealogical data, see M. Perles, pp. 20-26; Grün, pp. 39-40. On Loew's descendants who served as Chief Rabbi of Frankfurt, see Horovitz, pp. 46-48, 70-81.

43. Schneersohn, 2:181.

Chapter 4

1. The latest edition of Judah Loew's works is *Kol Sifrei Maharal Mi-Prag.* This multi-volume edition contains the following works: (Vol. 1) *Gevurot Ha-Shem;* (Vol. 2) *Derekh Ha-Hayyim;* (Vol. 3) *Hagadah Shel Pesah* (Loew's *Sermon for the Great Sabbath,* a compendium from Loew's works, especially *Gevurot Ha-Shem,* presented in commentary form on the Passover *Hagadah*); (Vol 4) *Be'er Ha-Golah* and *Derashot* (Sermons); (Vol. 5) *Tiferet Yisrael;* (Vol. 6) *Nezah Yisrael;* (Vols. 7 and 8) *Netivot Olam,* (Vols. 9-12) *Hidushei Aggadot.* Not included in this series are the five-volume edition of *Gur Aryeh* and the single volume *Or Hadash - Ner Mizvah* Unless otherwise specified, *all citations throughout this work, especially page references, relate to the above editions.*

2. For general bibliographical data on Loew's works, see Gottesdiener, pp. 279-83, 312-17; Grün, pp. 15, 17, 23; Lieben, German section, pp. 4-6; Stein, p. 70; Thieberger, pp. 31-36.

    O. Muneles lists all the holdings of the Jewish Library of Prague, a part of the State Jewish Museum at Prague. He lists editions of Loew, many of them first editions, held by the library. He generally dates the works a year earlier than other bibliographical sources. See also *Steinschneider,* 2:1620, 6153, and, *Collectio Davidis.* Note, Kohen-Yashar, 7:66-71.

    Unless otherwise noted, bibliographical data regarding specific works noted below are drawn from Friedberg

3   Friedberg, I, *gimmel,* no. 189, p. 192, lists these editions: Prague, 1578, Lwow, 1858, and III, *peh,* no. 292 lists; Warsaw, 1862. Another edition is New York 1965. The New York Public Library possesses another edition, Michalovce, 1938.

4. First published from an Oxford manuscript in 1964, in London, in 3 vols., by S. Schneebalg, a descendant of Hayyim of Friedberg.

5   Chavel, p. 153.

6. Perles, 1969, p. 20.

7. Friedberg, I, *gimmel,* no 60, p. 187, lists these editions: Cracow, 1582; Nowy Dwor, 1796; Lwow, 1850 and 1896; Warsaw, 1873; Lublin, 1876. Muneles, p 18, records 1581-82 as the date of the first edition.

8. Grün, p. 17.

9. *GH,* p. 21.

10. Friedberg, IV, *tav,* no. 1537, pp. 1111-12, lists the following editions of *TY:* Venice, 1599; Slavuta, 1793; Warsaw, 1836; Lwow, 1859; Warsaw, 1871, 1873, 1883, 1886. The title is ostensibly drawn from Ber. 58a; see *TY,* p. 6. T. Dreyfus's work is an analysis of *TY.*

11. Thieberger, p. 33. H.Hoenig, the editor of *HA,* also claims that these other three volumes were actually written; see, *HA,* 3, "Introduction."

12. Neher, 1966, p. 23.

13. A. Weiss, p. 7.

14. *NY,* p. 102; *HA,* 3:209.

15. See editor's introduction to *GH,* no. 1.

16. Friedberg, III, *nun,* no. 638, p. 732, lists the following editions of *NY:* Prague, 1599, Nowy Dwor, 1793; Warsaw, 1838, 1841; Lwow, 1860, 1873, 1886. Gross, 1969, 1974, is an analysis of *NY.* Friedberg, III, *nun,* no. 703, p 734, lists the following edition of *NM.* Warsaw, 1874; and the following editions of *NM* published together with *OH:* Prague, 1600; Warsaw, 1798; Nowy Dwor, 1804; Leipzig, 1859; Warsaw, 1874; see Friedberg, I, *alef,* no. 1115, p. 46.

17. See Est. 8:16; Meg. 16b.
18. *OH*, p. 47.
19. The Hebrew verse in Prov. 6:23 reads, "Ner *mizvah* ve-torah or."
20. Friedberg, I, *dalet*, no. 1124, p. 247, lists these editions of *DH:* Cracow, 1589; Warsaw, 1833, 1877; Lwow, 1857. E. Sarashohn's *Nishmat Ḥayyim* is a commentary to this work. A more recent, more extensive commentary is that of Halevi Pardes.
21. "For the commandment is a lamp [*Kinermizvah*] and the teaching is a light, and reproofs of instruction are–the way of life [*derekh ha-ḥayyim*]." See *DH*, p. 7.
22. Friedberg, III, *nun*, no. 803, p. 738, lists these editions of *NO:* Prague, 1595-96; Nowy Dwor, 1809; Jozefow, 1837; Stettin, 1860; Zhitomir, 1867; Warsaw, 1872, 1884. Library of Congress lists additional Stettin editions, 1865 and 1866. A. Weiss provides a careful analysis of *NO*.
23. "Thus saith the Lord: Stand ye in the ways and see and ask for the old paths [*netivot olam*] where is the good way and walk therein."
24. *BG*, p. 11.
25. Friedberg, I, *het*, no. 108, pp. 116, notes these editions: Prague, 1598; Nowy Dwor, 1804; Warsaw, 1838, 1873, 1928; Zolkiew, 1848; Zhitomir, 1860. Thieberger, p. 35, and others, place the first edition of *BG* at 1600.
26. *BG*, p. 11.
27. Thieberger, p. 29.
28. Friedberg lists the following editions of the following sermons:
    Sabbath of Penitence, I, *dalet*, no. 1044, p. 244: Prague, 1584; Warsaw 1830, 1841.
    Great Sabbath, I, *dalet*, no. 1005, p. 241: Prague, 1589; Warsaw, 1870; Bilgoraj, 1931 The New York Public Library possesses a Warsaw, 1841 edition.
    Torah and Commandments, I, *dalet*, no. 1005, p. 241: Prague, 1593; Warsaw, 1836; Lwow, 1848, 1871, 1873.
    Eulogy, I, *zayin*, no. 190, p. 321: Warsaw 1871; Piotrkov, 1905.
    All five works are reprinted in *Sefer Derashot Maharal Mi-Prag*, 1968.
29. Besides *Ḥidushei Aggadot* noted above, there is also the edition edited by Moses Kasher and Jacob Belcherovich, *Perushei Maharal Mi-Prag*, 4 vols. This edition is printed from a manuscript Oxford no. 917 at the Bodleian Library. Kasher, "Introduction," vol. 1, p. 36, and *HA*, 1:9, notes that the manuscript of the first volume contains statements of the copyist as: "Until date such and such I have gone this far." The dates are from 1585 and 1586. This means the manuscript was written during Loew's lifetime and that it was begun before 1585. According to *HA*, 1:8, the manuscript is an incomplete one with the commentary to certain tractates and certain parts of certain tractates missing.
30. Friedberg, I, *vav*, no. 219, p. 310, lists this edition: Prague, 1595. In *GA*, 5:159-202 the responsum, together with the responsum of Jacob Pollak, is published under the title *Sefer Teshuvot Geonim*. On the title page three previous editions are noted: Prague, 1597; Frankfurt and Hungary (dates not noted). New York Public Library possesses a Frankfurt, 1719 edition. Muneles corroborates the existence of the Frankfurt edition. Muneles, p. 22, places the first edition at 1594.
31. Friedberg, II, *het*, no. 162, p. 347. This text lists these editions: Sulzbach, 1775; Lwow, 1841; Warsaw, 1912. The title page of the 1775 edition has the place of publication as Fürth; actually it was Amsterdam. There is also: Zolkiew, 1841 edition. This represents Loew's commentary to sections of the part of that work called *Yoreh Deah*. A. Weiss, p. 4, claims Loew's novellae to another section of that work–*Even Ha-Ezer*, were published in Jerusalem in 1955.
32. See *She'elot u-Teshuvot Ha-Geonim Batrei, 10*. Joel Sirkes rejected Loew's position; see Sirkes, no. 77. On the *agunah* problem in general and Loew's place in deliberation

upon it, see Kahana, p. 24. Loew's decision to accept the testimony of a single witness
"in his naiveté" is noted by Samuel of Fürth as a basis for precedent in his commentary
Bet Shemuel to Karo's code *Shulḥan Arukh–Even Ha-Ezer*, 17:24. Grün, p. 27, recalls
the *Responsum* in his attempt to establish Loew's whereabouts between 1588-92.
Thieberger, p. 26, mistakenly claims that Loew did not free the *agunah*. See also
Gottesdiener, p. 312, no. 20.

33.   Sirkes, no. 117. The first edition was published for the first time by Solomon ben
      Simon. The first edition was published more than fifty years after Sirkes's death at
      Frankfurt, 1697; see Schochet, pp. 83-86, 229.

34.   *GH*, pp. 270, 304. While in this case Loew is in opposition to standard practice of
      Passover observance, in other cases his views correspond to the standard views. An
      example of the latter is his view that the *ḥaroset* is dipped during the *seder*. In the
      commentary, *Ba'er Heitev*, to Karo's *SA–Orah Ḥayyim*, 475:1, Loew's view is quoted
      to support that of Karo and of others.

35.   *TY*, chapter 67, for Loew's discussion of this matter. His view opposes that of
      Nahmanides and of the *Arba'ah Turim*. See also: *SA–Orah Ḥayyim*, 143:4, Judah
      Ashkenazi's (*Ba'er Heitev*) commentary.

36.   Z. Ashkenazi mentions Loew by name but does not mention the exact source to which
      he is referring. It appears to be *DH*, p. 273 (compare *TY*, p. 52). According to Markus,
      p. 38, Ashkenazi was a descendant of Loew's on his mother's side. This claim is
      possible but doubtful. In his collection of responsa Ashkenazi never refers to Loew as
      his ancestor, which he certainly would have done if such were the case. In a collection
      of his responsa, Ashkenazi quotes a responsum of Loew's great-grandson, whom
      Ashkenazi identifies as a descendant of Rabbi Loew. If Ashkenazi were similarly a
      descendant, it is reasonable to assume he would have also identified himself as a
      descendant of Rabbi Loew.

37.   Z. Ashkenazi, no. 49. The issue concerns the problem of when one is liable to the
      biblical penalty of extirpation (*karet*)

38.   Z. Ashkenazi, no. 76; note Zimmels, pp. 39-41.

39.   Kaufman, 3:302.

40.   Sassoon, 2:943-44.

41.   Assaf, 1:53; also see Gottesdiener, p. 344, and, Grün, p. 39.

42.   Kaufman, 2:302.

43.   Perles (1969), p. 20.

44.   See Muneles (1952), p. 77.

45.   Lwow, 1862. Library of Congress also lists Piotrkov, 1906, and Baltimore, 1947.

46.   On Nathanson's visit to Prague, see N. Levine's Commentary to Perles, 1969, p. 19,
      no. 7. According to Markus, p. 246, Loew began but never completed this ambitious
      project.

47.   Lieben, German section, p. 6.

48.   Rabinowitsch, p. 228.

49.   Kleinberger, 1962, pp. 14-17.

50.   See appendix 2 below for data leading to these conclusions.

51.   Besides the many works which Loew wrote, one might also note that a number of
      works, especially letters, have been incorrectly ascribed to Loew. One example is a
      letter which Loew is alleged to have written to Jacob Ginzberg concerning the creation
      of the golem. See Gershom Scholem (1924), 1:104-106, where the letter is convinc-
      ingly shown to be a forgery.

52.   Thieberger, pp. 30, 33.

53.   E.g., *GH*, chapter 66; *TY*, chapter 57; *NY*, chapter 49; *NM*, p. 24.

54. Kleinberger (1962), p. 17, skeptically notes that this observation would hold true only if Kasher (1958), p. 35, accurately reports that Loew himself corrected the manuscript from which his talmudic commentaries were printed.

55. Thieberger, p. 30.

56. Loew notes, *DH*, pp. 9-10, that "it is the custom in our lands to study chapters of *Avot* from after Passover until the New Year." He expresses an awareness of the custom in "some places" to recite *Avot* from Passover until *Azeret* (i.e., the eighth day of the Feast of Booths).

57. Gottesdiener (1962), p. 319, notes the places of Loew's poetical interludes.

58. For discussions of Loew's sources, see Bokser, pp. 19-20, p. 196, no. 4; Gottesdiener, pp. 269-70; A. Weiss, pp. 20-42.

59. He refers to Moses ben Nahman, Ibn Ezra, Mizrahi, and Kimhi many times in his works, especially in *GA*. In this section, only references to infrequently noted authors will be noted; for example, Samuel ben Meir: *GA*, 1:190; 3:140; *NO*, 2:241; *Hizkuni*: *GA*, 2:78.

60. Al-Fasi: *GA*, 4:146-7; *HA*, 4:52, Asher ben Yehiel: *GA*, 1:53, 4:140; *NM*, p. 25. Aderet: *DH*, pp. 46, 308; *TY*, p. 158; *NY*, p. 64; *HA*, 1:32. Mordecai: *NO*, 2:81 Ishbili: *DH*, p.274; *HA*, 1:151. Gerondi: *OH*, p. 208; *HA*, 3:18; *NO*, 2:90-93. Habib: *NO*, 2:52.

61. Hai: *GH*, p. 198. Moses of Coucy: *GA*, 3:139; *TY*, p. 113; Jacob ben Asher: *GA*, 3:143; *GH*, pp. 195, 282; *DH*, pp. 14, 105, 242, 268; *NO*, 1:115, 2:90-93; *TY*, p. 206; *HA*, 1:94.

62. Abraham ben David: *NO*, 2:90-93; *GH*, p. 289. Karo to Maimonides: *GA*, 3:71. Karo to *Tur*: *NO*, 2:90-93; *GH*, pp. 195, 282. Cohen: *GH*, p. 304. Shem Tov ben Abraham: *GA*, 2:25. Eliezer Menahem: *GH*, pp. 200, 209.

63 Jacob Tam: *GA*, 1:68; 5:90. Isaac ben Sheshet: *DH*, p. 155. Moses ben Nahman: *GA*, 3:131, 134.

64. Saadya: *GA*, 2:12, 135; see A. Weiss, p. 35. Gersonides: *GH*, pp. 6-9. Abraham Shalom: *DH*, pp. 234-35. Albo: *DH*, p. 324; *TY*, pp. 67, 194; see A. Weiss, p. 34.

65. Maimonides' *CM*: *GA*, 1:21, 34, 177; 3:75, 92, 131; *GH*, pp 40, 183; *DH*, pp. 90, 92, 148, 204, 288; *NO*, 2:98; *TY*, p. 18; *HA*, 3:176. Maimonides' *Sefer Ha-Mizvot*: *GA*, 2:114; *NO*, 2:98; *TY*, p. 113. Maimonides' *MT*: *GA*, 3:13, 46, 64, 75, 88; 5:11, 82; *GH*, p. 196. Maimonides' *Guide*: *GA*, 3:135; 4:93, 99; *GH*, pp. 15, 131; *SOT*, p. 36, *DH*, pp. 57, 68, 143, 207, 232-33, 322-24; *NO*, 1:59, 61, 224; 2:108, 206; *NY*, p. 170; *TY*, pp. 21, 25, 40, 96; *BG*, p. 49; *HA*, 2:17, 3:32, 73, 109, 202, 215; 4:123. See A. Weiss, pp. 29-32.

66. The term *ha-inyan ha-elohi*, for example, is peculiar to Ha-Levi. Loew uses this term in the following places: *GA*, p. 41; *GH*, p. 78; *DH*, p. 322; *HA*, 1:21. See A. Weiss, p. 36; A. Kleinberger (1962), pp. 35, nos. 33, 38, 40, 58, 108, 111, 116, 120; Gross (1974), pp. 16, 21, 77, 89-90, 93, 150-153; Kariv, 1:34-35.

67. A. Weiss, pp. 35-36.

68. Gottesdiener (1972), pp. 269, 282-83.

69. *SOT*, p. 26; *NY*, p. 180; *TY*, p. 98; *HA*, 3:210.

70. *GA*, 2:20; *GH*, p. 109; *DH*, p. 30; *BG*, p. 89; *NY*, p. 178; *HA*, 1:101, 112; 2:1; 3:88.

71. *BG*, p. 86.

72. *GH*, p. 315; noted here by its alternative title, *Sefer Marot Elohim*.

73. *DH*, p. 235.

74 *SOC*, pp. 59, 61; *GH*, p 298; *NO*, 2:118, 166; *BG*, pp. 86, 95; *HA*, 1:117-18; 3:34; 4:113.

75. *BG*, p. 34; *HA*, 1:108.

76. See Gottesdiener (1972), p. 299; A. Weiss, pp. 40-41; Neher, (1966), p. 16.
77. In *BG*, ch. 5, Loew quotes Averroës; see Weiss, pp. 27-29. Also see Neher (1965), 14:301.
78. *GA*, 2:21.
79. *NY*, pp. 32-33; *HA*, 2:105.
80. *NO*, 2:98.
81. *DH*, p. 306; see Kleinberger (1962), p. 132, no. 15.
82. *GH*, p. 141.
83. *GA*, 1:51; *NO*, 1:82, 207; *HA*, 3:89.
84. *GA*, 2:86.
85. *GA*, 1:148; 2:102.
86. *NY*, p. 35; *BG*, p. 133; *HA*, 2:108.
87. *DH*, p. 234.
88. *DH*, p. 287. Many places in *NY*. See Gross (1974), pp. 19-34, 56, 70-71, 144, 216-17, 227-28, 250-51.
89. See Gottesdiener (1962), p. 291, no. 9; A. Weiss, p. 37.

Chapter 5

1. See, for example, the many possible definitions listed in Inge, "Appendix."
2. Jones, p. xv, defined "mysticism" as "immediate awareness of relation with God . . . intimate consciousness of the Divine Presence . . . religion in its most acute, intense and living stage." Underhill (1920), ch. 1, defines "mysticism" as "the direct intuition or experience of God."
3. See, for example, "Mysticism is the act of union with reality." Underhill (1915), p. 3; (1911), pp. 35, 68, 72, etc.; Watts (1947), part 1, chs. 2 and 3.
4. Scholem (1941), p 5.
5. Ibid., p. 6.
6. Ibid.
7. Scholem (1957), 1:173; (1973), p. 212.
8. Scholem (1971), p. 98.
9. See Gottesdiener, p. 255. On the influence of Loew upon Kook, see Lipshitz, p. 171; compare Rosenbluth, pp. 325-31. Also note the references in Yaron, pp. 13, 118.
   To a lesser extent than he influenced Hasidism, Loew also had an impact upon the *musar* movement. Israel of Salant, the founder of *musar*, was apparently influenced by Loew in the formulation of his philosophical-pietistic apprehension of Judaism; see D. Katz, 2:33. Simha Zesel Breida (b.1824), an important Lithuanian figure in the nineteenth-century *musar* movement, claimed to be a descendant of Loew; see Katz, 2:28.
10. Scholem (1941), p. 339. Also see Rabinowitz (1944), p. 49. According to Bunam of Przysucha, Loew expressed ideas similar to those of the sixteenth-century Lurianic school, but in a more accessible fashion; see *Siaḥ Sarfei Kodesh* 3:28, para. 110.
11. Fox, pp. 93-94. Rabinowitz (1944), p. 49, no. 16, suggests that Bunam's style in his *Kol Simḥa* appears to have been influenced by that of Rabbi Loew.
12. Langer, p. 27.
13. Rabinowitz (1944), p. 49, no. 16.
14. Rabinowicz, pp. 95-96.
15. Rabinowitz (1947), p. 59, no. 47.
16. Ibid., p. 61.

17. Ibid. See also Alfasi, p 16. Alfasi claims that the Rabbi of Kotsk was encouraged to enter the Hasidic fold by Israel of Koznitz.
18. Rabinowitz (1947), p. 61.
19. Samuel of Shinow, 18:163; according to another tradition, so did Mendel of Kotsk, see Langer, p. 251.
20. *Siah Sarfei Kodesh,* 3:27, par 110.
21. Samuel of Shinow, 18:163.
22. Rabinowitz (1944), p. 42
23. See J. Kula's introduction to Israel of Koznitz's *Geulat Yisrael.*
24. Fox, pp. 93-94; Gottesdeiner, p. 254; Heschel (1973), *Kotsk,* 1:62, 65; Heschel (1973), *A Passion for Truth,* p. 58.
25. *Siah Sarfei Kodesh,* 3:11.
26. Gottesdiener, p. 254.
27. Araten, p. 11.
28. Kula's introduction to *Geulat Yisrael.*
29. Ibid ; also see Fox, p 94 There is also a tradition attributing this complaint to Mendel of Kotsk, see *Emet Mi-Kotsk Tizmah,* p. 249, par. 81.
30. Gottesdiener, p. 254.
31. Kasher (1958), 1:31.
32. Schneersohn, 2:18-19. According to Langer, pp. 6, 33, Shalom of Belz also claimed to be a descendant of Loew.
33. In the foreword to his *Sidrei Taharoth* the prominent nineteenth-century Rabbi of Lemberg (Lwow), Joseph Saul Halevy Nathanson writes the following:
    "I was pleased to have the opportunity to meet the young and wise Gaon Rabbi Gershon Hanokh Leiner. . . . I must admit that in my later years I, too, had considered preparing a work such as this and indeed had copied copious notes on the Tractate *Kelim.* However, nothing came of it, firstly because of my constant preoccupation with other matters, and also because of the praise I had read of the Maharal who also had commenced a similar work, but had to abandon it when his manuscripts and notes were destroyed in a fire."
    Quoted by Kon (1971), p. 205; (1964); p. 202. Nathanson authored a volume *Torat Moshe* defending Moses Isserles's *Torat Hatat* from the attacks of Rabbi Hayyim of Friedberg, Judah Loew's brother, in his *Vikuah Mayim Hayyim.* Despite his apparent dislike of Rabbi Hayyim, Nathanson was apparently an admirer of Rabbi Loew. He wrote a very enthusiastic endorsement (*haskama*) to an edition of Loew's collection of glosses on a number of talmudic tractates–*Hidushei Gur Aryeh Al Shabbat, Eruvin, Pesahim.* It may not be a coincidence that most of Judah Loew's works were reprinted at Lwow during Nathanson's tenure as chief rabbi there. In his commentary to Perles's *Megillat Yuhasin,* Noah Hayyim ben Moshe Levin of Kobrin mentioned that Joseph Saul Nathanson once told him that when he visited Prague, he requested to see the golem's remains at the Altneushul. An elderly man who served as beadle of the synagogue informed him that when the great Rabbi Ezekiel Landau, Chief Rabbi of Prague, wanted to do likewise, he fasted that day, immersed himself in a *mikveh,* wrapped himself in the *tallit* and *tefillin,* and ascended to the loft (where the remains of the golem were stored). When he descended, he said that it was improper for anyone else to ascend there. When he (Nathanson) heard these words he trembled and was afraid to ascend.

Chapter 6

1. Wolfson (1924), 1:575-99.
2. *GH*, p. 181, without mentioning Albo by name. See Albo, 1:4, p. 64. Note Guttmann (1955), p. 170. Guttmann suggests that Albo's three principles of the faith, existence of God, revelation, and providence, were not original with Albo but that Albo adapted them from Simeon ben Zemah Duran's (1361-1444) *Commentary on Job* ("Introduction": chapter 8) and that Duran in turn had adapted them from the Islamic philosopher Ibn Roshd (Averroës). Nevertheless, Loew undoubtedly adapted this position directly from Albo, whom he often quotes, paraphrases, and implies, usually with no mention of his source.
3. See, e.g., *HA*, 3:9.
4. *TY.* pp. 50-51.
5. *NO*, 1:223-24; *HA*, 2:17. See Maimonides, *Guide*, 2:1 Loew's views concerning Maimonides are ambivalent Though he often singles out Maimonides' views for attack, he nevertheless expressed great reverence for Maimonides. In an apologetic aside Loew claims that Maimonides was forced to express certain undesirable views in order to save the tradition from outright rejection as a result of the intellectual onslaught upon Judaism then being made by Gentile philosophers. In the very same work (*BG*) where Loew often has occasion to attack Maimonides, he refers to Maimonides as "the great master who was as full of wisdom as the ocean is of water in all the natural, metaphysical and mathematical sciences. . . . All his writings, in general and in particular, require no re-enforcement or support" (*BG*, p. 149). Elsewhere, Loew apologetically notes: "In the generation of the Master [Maimonides], [Jewish] people were attracted by the views of gentile scholars upon whom the light of the Torah did not shine, i.e., the philosophers. Had he not explained Scripture to them in a manner which corresponded with their opinions, there was a threat of even greater harm–their outright rejection of Scripture altogether–heaven forfend. For this reason, he interpreted Scripture to them in harmony with their opinions" (*DH*, p. 323).
6. The following studies by H. Wolfson provide an evaluation of the centrality of the predication of divine attributes for medieval Jewish philosophy. See Wolfson, 1916, 1938, 1953, 1954.
7. *GH*, pp. 9, 99; *DH*, p. 233; *NY*, p. 213; *BG*, pp 64, 69
8. Scholem (1974), p. 88.
9. *HA*, 2:87.
10. *GH*, p. 9.
11. Loew refers to Gersonides by name and to Maimonides by inference; see *GH*, pp. 8-9. The accuracy of Loew's presentation of Maimonides' and Gersonides' views is not of central concern here. The present discussion aims rather at revealing Loew's attitudes toward Jewish philosophical speculation. In the case of Gersonides, it is not clear which of his works Loew might have read. Loew seems to have read Gersonides' *Commentary on the Torah*, but does not seem directly familiar with his major philosophical work, *Milhamot Ha-Shem* On Gersonides' views regarding the issues under discussion, see Bleich; Kellner; Samuelson (1969).
12. Maimonides, *Guide*, 1:51, 54. Note Guttmann (1964), p. 161.
13. Loew argues against Gersonides on epistemological grounds. Loew assumes that human beings cannot know the essence of God, that God is called "holy" (Hebrew: *kadosh*), which literally means "completely different" because God is different from all things and therefore His essence cannot be conceived. The assertion that one of God's essential attributes is intellect or knowledge purports some kind of knowledge

of God's essence, which is impossible. Loew maintains that all we know about God is that He is "holy," which means we cannot know anything about His essence. All we can know is how we apprehend God and not what He is. In a satirical aside, Loew recites that, if we followed the advice of the philosophers, instead of referring to God as the "Holy One, blessed be He," we would refer to Him as the "Intellectual One, blessed be He"; see *GH*, pp. 8-9.

The assumption that God's knowledge is part of His essence led a number of medieval Jewish philosophers to question the biblical and rabbinic notion of divine knowledge of particulars in particular and divine providence in general. Changes in God's knowledge would imply changes in God. Knowledge of imperfect things, they argued, would imply imperfection in Him. For God to know and exert providence over imperfect individuals would entail a compromising of His perfection. Loew, who rejected the notion that God's knowledge is part of His essence, also rejects the notion that God cannot know particulars. Having rejected the philosophers' premise, he rejects the conclusion which emanates from it. For Loew, God knows everything. Nothing is unworthy of His knowledge or of His providence. See *DH*, pp. 68, 233, *HA*, 3:73.

Without mentioning Maimonides by name, Loew discounts his view that God's providence extends only to the human species, and not to individual human beings save those who, because of their having attained a level of intellectual perfection, have effected a relationship with the Active Intellect. For Loew, God knows all. To say less is to attribute deficiences to Him. In opposition to Maimonides, who limited the possibilities for divine knowledge and providence in the sublunar sphere, Loew asserts that God knows everything and every event existent in the lower world Loew rejects the view he identifies with "some men who philosophize," that God does not know things in this world directly but only knows them through a knowledge of Himself. He rejects the position of those who argue that God can know only necessary existents and not accidental ones. See Maimonides, *Guide*, 3:17, 18. In Loew, see *GA*, 3:136; *HA*, 4:22, 24; *BG*, p. 69.

14. E. Ashkenazi (1583), *Ma'aseh Ha-Shem*, "Ma'aseh Avot," chapter 21. Loew is not mentioned by name in Ashkenzi's work. Scant scholarly attention has been paid to Ashkenazi. One may, however, consult Ben-Sasson (1959), pp. 34-37, and (1970), pp. 20-22; Neher (1966), pp. 129-144, provides an analysis of the controversy between Loew and Ashkenazi.

15. Unless otherwise stated, the immediately following discussion will be an analysis of *DH*, pp. 233-35.

16 *DH*, p. 234; see *GH*, pp 8-10.

17. Some additional conjecture ought to be mentioned as to why Loew responded to Ashkenazi so vigorously. Ashkenazi had served as Chief Rabbi of Posnań, a position later held by Loew. Ashkenazi's radically different view as to the nature of Judaism may have enjoyed a support in Posnań which Loew felt obliged to provoke. Ashkenazi had died in 1586, and Loew in *Derekh Ḥayyim* (published in 1589) speaks of Ashkenazi in the past tense. It is therefore reasonable to assume that Loew wrote his rejoinder to Ashkenazi sometime between 1586 and 1589. As was mentioned above, not only was Rabbi Loew probably born in Posnań, but it is also likely that he served as rabbi there from 1584-87. It may be that Loew's attack on Ashkenazi reflects a conceptual conflict which then obtained in Posnań between rationalists and mystics. It may have been the rationalist sentiment which drove Loew to leave Posnań, while the emergence of a more receptive view toward mysticism in the 1590s may have encouraged him to return to Posnań.

18. Dei Rossi, "Imrei Binah," chapter 6, p 124. On Loew and dei Rossi, see Neher (1966), pp. 98-116. Loew harshly attacks dei Rossi in a number of places, see, e.g., *BG*, esp. pp. 126-133; *NY*, p. 35; *HA*, 2:108.

19. Ashkenazi's position is clearly stated in the "Introduction" to his work and in "Ma'aseh Avot," chapter 21

20. *TY*, pp 50-51.

21. *SOT*, p. 36.

22. Also see *GH*, p. 10. Note A. Weiss, pp. 122-124, 219-22.

23. Scholem (1974), p. 69. Also see Ben-Shlomo, pp. 127-35.

24. Loew incorrectly cites this source as ch. 11, when in fact it is found in ch. 12.

25. Ibn Gabbai, "Helek Ha-Yihud," ch. 1.

26. Maimonides, *Guide* (1963), 1:53, p. 120. See Guttmann (1964), p. 161. Describing Maimonides' view, Guttmann writes, "God thus appears as the essentially incomprehensible cause of the most perfect actions." This statement may similarly be applied to the kabbalists

27. Isserles (1858), 3:4. On Cordovero, see Scholem (1974), p. 401; Ben-Shlomo, pp. 31-36; Horodetzky, 3:60.

28. Kariv, 1:13, deemphasizes the kabbalism of Loew on the grounds that Loew does not use kabbalistic terminology. Kariv unjustifiably minimizes Loew's use of the idea of the *sefirot*. On Cordovero's view, see Scholem (1974), p. 401.

29. On the *sefirot* and the kabbalistic notion of God, in Jewish mystical literature which preceded Loew, see Scholem (1941), pp. 205-43; Tishby (1957), 1:95-117, 131-61.

30. *DH*, p. 142

31. See Guttmann (1964), p. 226, on Crescas.

32. On Shalom, see Davidson (1964).

33. See Wolfson (1916), pp. 179-221.

34. Ibid., p. 209.

35. Ibid., pp. 198-221; see Davidson (1964), pp. 26-43.

36. Shalom, 13, 1:4, p. 207b; see Davidson (1964), p. 36.

37. Shalom, 5, p. 81b. Albo, 2:11, p. 63, likewise identifies the *sefirot* with celestial intelligences. Note Davidson (1964), p 12.

38. Scholem (1974), p. 61.

39. *HA*, 3:33. Kariv, 1:13, claims that Loew only directly refers to the *sefirot* once in his work; however, many citations from Loew's writings rebut this claim. Kariv does not seem acquainted with *HA*, where these references appear with greater frequency than elsewhere in Loew's writing.

40. In the Zohar and elsewhere, the *sefirot* were identified with the limbs of the "Primordial Man" (*Adam Kadmon*). See Tishby (1957), 1:150-58

41. *GH*, p. 324.

42. *DH*, p. 231.

43. *HA*, 1:105.

44. Jacob: *GA*, 1:254-55; *HA*, 2:117. Joseph: *HA*, 2:73, 3:35. David: *HA*, 1:128. Rachel: *GA*, 1:148. For an example of a "code" for identifying individual biblical characters with individual *sefirot*, see, e.g., *Ma'arekhet Ha-Elohut*, chapter 4. Note Scholem (1974), p. 111.

45. *HA*, 4:1-5, for Torah with *hesed*; *DH*, p. 272, for Bible with *hokhmah*, and Mishnah with *da'at*, and Talmud with *binah*.

46. *HA*, 2:30, 100; 3:90. Elsewhere, he specifically notes the *sefirah* of *Keter*: *HA*, 3:221. Also note the references collected by Elbaum, 22:39, no. 36.

47. Neher (1966), p. 137.

48. *GH*, p. 6; *TY*, pp. 50-51. See Davidson (1974), pp. 53-69; Rawidowicz, pp. 305-17 Some medieval Jewish philosophers had attempted to argue that the Jewish philosophical tradition is actually a distorted version of what once was an essential part of Jewish tradition, and that one is obligated to attempt to reclaim this "lost" Jewish heritage. See, e.g., Maimonides, *Guide*, 1:71, 3:Introduction; Ha-Levi, *Kuzari*, 2:66; Isserles, *Torat Ha-Olah* (1858), 1:1. Note Ginzberg, 5:197 Loew may have been trying subtly to refute this approach.

49. Isserles (1858), 3:4, p 3. In apparent opposition to Isserles, Loew's brother, Hayyim of Friedberg, wrote, "The Torah speaks in one language while philosophy speaks in another language"; see Sherwin (1975), pp. 51-55. Loew's view approximates that of his brother, see *DH*, p. 234 Loew may have also had Gersonides in mind. Gersonides had claimed that when there is a conflict between the Torah and philosophy, one should reinterpret the Torah according to the teachings of philosophy See *NO*, 1:61. On Gersonides' position, see Samuelson (1969), "Philosophic and Religious Authority," pp. 30-44. Loew's contemporary, Joel Sirkes, expresses the most clear, unambiguous statement of this generation in opposition to philosophy, Sirkes (1697) p 4b writes, "Philosophy is the epitome of heresy" [*Ha-filosofia hi ha-minut b'azmah*].

50. *DH*, p. 234.

Chapter 7

1. Though other works have identified Loew's theory of opposites, they have not made the present distinction between these two kinds of opposites. See, e.g., Kariv, 1:14-15; Gross (1974), pp. 62-74.

2. *GH*, p. 31.

3. *GA*, 3:137. On the relationship between form and matter in Loew's writings, see A. Weiss, pp. 72-77.

4. *HA*, 1:154; see also *GH*, p. 29; *TY*, p. 91; *HA*, 1:17.

5. On polarity in Judaism, see Heschel (1966), *God in Search of Man*, pp 341-42, and sources noted on p 347, no. 10.

6. *GH*, pp 162, 181, 245, 264; *NO*, 1:96, 1:213; *DH*, p. 259; *HA*, 4:153

7. *HA*, 2:89: "Everything which exists in the world is either of a certain essence or of its opposite "

8. *NY*, pp. 9, 37-38; *OH*, pp. 50-51; *HA*, 2:38, 111.

9. *OH*, p. 227: "It is impossible for opposites [i.e., Haman and Mordecai] to exist at once." Compare this statement to Loew's example of Mordecai and Esther as complementary opposites; see *OH*, pp. 50-51: "Mordecai and Esther are united opposites. There cannot be one without the other, for it is known that knowledge of one pole infers knowledge of its opposite." On Mordecai and Haman as exclusive opposites, see *OH*, p. 172; *HA*, 4:116. Also see *NO*, 2:107, for additional examples: good and evil, wholeness and privation, etc On truth and falsehood as irreconcilable opposites, see *BG*, p. 51.

10. The proto-Hegelian quality of this motif has been noted in the secondary literature on Loew. See Neher (1966), p. 177; Kariv, 1:55; Gross (1974), p. 68. It is interesting to note that Loew portrays "master" and "slave" as polar opposites, not requiring a synthesis. See *OH*, p. 185; compare Hegel, pp. 228-40. One might also note Watts (1969) on the theme of polarity in the religious literature of various traditions. He identifies complementary as well as contradictory opposites.

11. *GH*, p. 249: "Everything that God made in this world, He created in male and female pairs. For the male is form and the female is matter.... God couples them and binds them

together." Speaking of male as form and female as matter, in *OH*, p. 104, Loew writes: "There is no joining comparable to that of form to matter by which they become one, single entity." See also *GA*, 1:16, 31, 237; *HA*, 1:135, 3:83. Note A. Weiss, pp. 108-11.

12. Matter as related to change, etc., see *NO*, 1:48; *DH*, pp. 162, 198, 262; *OH*, p. 144; *HA*, 1:12, 66; 3:191. On matter as a Gentile, "this-worldly" trait and form as an "other-worldly" Jewish trait, see *GA*, 4:164; *NY*, pp. 14, 106; *HA*, 4:17, 128. On this world as being fragmented, see *GA*, 1:248; *OH*, p. 72; *DH*, p. 46.

13. *HA*, 1:82.

14. *GA*, 5:118; *GH*, pp. 161, 238; *OH*, p. 213; *HA*, 1:2.

15. *NY*, p. 128.

16. Gen. 25:22; *NY*, pp. 87, 90; *DH*, p. 247; *HA*, 2:53. Loew identifies Esau with "this world" and Jacob with the World to Come. Esau represents Christendom and Jacob represents Jewry.

17. See Sanh. 21b; *HA*, 3:140.

18. *GA*, 2:93; *OH*, pp. 50-51, 90, 127, 227.

19 Neher (1966), was the first to identify the centrality of this concept of the "center" in the thought of Judah Loew. A. Weiss has carefully examined the implications of this concept in Loew's moral philosophy and psychology. It is reasonable to assume that the roots of Loew's theory of the "center" are found in earlier Jewish mystical literature. Theories of the thirteenth century in particular seem to be a likely place to look, specifically the writings of Ibn Latif and Joseph Chikitilla, as well as the Zohar. See Scholem (1974), p. 224.

20. *GA*, 1:40; *SGS*, p. 201.

21. *GH*, p. 242.

22. *OH*, pp. 74, 86.

23. See Weiss, p. 15, no. 32.

24. Trachtenberg (1961), p. 119.

25. *GH*, p. 58.

26. *TY*, p. 156; *GH*, p. 119.

27. *DH*, pp. 23, 119; *TY*, p. 58; *HA*, 3:100.

28. *GH*, pp. 119, 241; *DH*, p. 125; *SOT*, p. 25; *BG*, p. 34; *HA*, pp. 112, 210.

29. *TY*, p. 33; *DH*, p. 131; *HA*, 2:81, 4:13.

30. *SOT*, p. 33; *Eulogy*, p. 190.

31. *SOT*, pp. 11-12, 15; *NO*, 1:22, 2:36, 148; *DH*, p. 25; *HA*, 3:227.

32. *GA*, 2:126, 3:72; *GH*, p. 192; *SSR*, p. 68; *DH*, pp. 48, 77, 131, 275, 281; *NO*, 1:39, 2:52; *TY*, pp. 4, 32 167; *NY*, p. 13; *BG*, p. 19; *HA*, 2:22, 3:229, 4:13, 89.

33. The themes of the relationship of the Torah to the sefirotic realm, the Torah as part of that realm, the Torah as a supernatural entity, and other related themes in Jewish mystical tradition, are examined in the following: Scholem (1974), pp. 168-174, and (1965), pp. 32-87; Tishby (1957), 1:144-48, and (1961), 2:363-98.

34 *HA*, 2:25.

35. *NO*, 1:58, 2:20. See A. Weiss, pp. 182-95. On God as the "Cause of the Torah," see *TY*, p. 2.

36. *DH*, p. 116. Loew appears to be referring to the following midrashic sources which identify the Torah as the "daughter of God," see Ex. R. 33:1; Tan. "Pekudei," 4.

37. *DH*, pp. 7-8. See Scholem (1965), p. 46.

38. E.g., *DH*, p. 272; *HA*, 4:105.

39. *BG*, p. 37; *HA*, 2:72; 4:86.
40. *TY*, p. 50; *HA*, 3:233 Also A. Weiss, p 187.
41. *HA*, 3:39.
42. *TY*, p. 44.
43. Zohar 3:152a. An English translation is found in Scholem (1949), pp. 121-22.
44. *TY*, p. 74.
45. *DH*, pp. 78, 309; *SOT*, p. 23; *SOC*, p. 53; *HA*, 2:118.
46. *TY*, p. 72; *NY*, p. 46.
47. *NO*, 1:72.
48. *NO*, 1:153; *DH*, p. 7; *TY*, p. 39; *NY*, p. 134; *HA*, 3:1.
49. *TY*, p. 161.
50. *GA*, 4:127; *DH*, p. 47; *TY*, p. 179.
51. *GA*, 2:203; *TY*, pp. 28, 80, 179; *BG*, p. 24.
52. See, Albo, 1:7-12; note Lerner (1964), pp. 143-44. On the whole question of rational "justifications for the commandments" (*ta'amei ha-mizvot*), see Heinemann.
    An analysis of Loew's discussion of this matter demonstrates his reliance upon Albo. Much of the terminology is identical, though Albo is not mentioned by name. Loew even repeats Albo's misreading of Plato on the question of communal marriage; see Albo, 1:8, p. 82, no. 1; *TY*, p. 51. This further demonstrates our assumption that Loew did not know the writings of the Greek philosophers either in the original or in translation but acquired his knowledge of what was represented to be their ideas in the writings of the medieval Jewish philosophers, especially Maimonides and Albo. For Loew's distinction amongst rational (or natural), conventional, and divine law, see *DH*, p. 123, and note *BG*, pp. 31-32; *OH*, p. 99; *HA*, 1:28
53. See, e.g., *TY*, pp. 21, 25, 28, 79.
54. *TY*, p. 20.
55. *TY*, p. 22.
56. *TY*, pp. 12, 14, 46.
57. *TY*, p. 5
58. *HA*, 3:229.
59 *DH*, p. 26.
60. Goldin, pp. 278-80; Teeple, pp. 36-41. Note Heschel (1965), 2:33-58, 123-146, 166-181, 299-344.
61. Maimonides, *CM*, Sanh. 10:1; *MT—Sefer Shofetim*, ch. 11.
62. *MT*, 1891, 90:5, p. 388.
63. The text in brackets is a paraphrase summary of what precedes the literally translated text.
64. *TY*, pp. 67-68; *HA*, 2:56; see also *TY*, p. 74. By interpreting the term from Ps. 90:1, *ish ha-elohim* as "man-God," Loew goes beyond even the Zohar's bold description of Moses as the husband of the *Shekhinah* (the lowest of the *sefirot*). The Zohar interprets *ish ha-elohim* to be the man, i.e., the husband, of God (i.e., of the *Shekhinah*). As such, Moses is said to have had sexual intercourse with the *Shekhinah* This sexual image seems to be the Zohar's way of saying that Moses experienced the most intimate experience of God humanly possible. See Zohar, 1:216b, and 1:236b. Note Scholem (1941), pp. 199-200, 226-27.
65. *SOT*, p. 23; *GH*, p. 77; *TY*, p. 156. Torah as "three": *TY*, p. 76; *HA*, 4:82-83.
66. *GA*, 1:100-101.
67. *GA*, 2:100; *GH*, pp. 76-77, 83, 103; *DH*, pp. 20, 282; *HA*, 4:116. According to Loew, when Moses ascended to receive the Torah, his form was detached from its matter; see *TY*, p. 73.

68. *GH*, p. 76.
69. *HA*, 4:116.
70 *DH*, p. 20.
71. Compare the above discussion of the Torah and Moses to Dreyfus's discussion.

Chapter 8

1. *GH*, p. 76; *HA*, 1:33.
2. *GH*, pp. 76-78.
3. *GH*, pp. 76-78, 83; *DH*, pp. 20, 282; *TY*, p. 73; *HA*, 2:56, 4:116.
4. *GH*, p. 76.
5. *GA*, 2:10; *GH*, p 77.
6. *GA*, 2:100-101, 4:115; *GH*, pp. 87-88; *TY*, p. 42; *NY*, pp. 17, 177, 199; *BG*, p. 96; *OH*, p. 111; *HA*, 4:82-83.
7. *GA*, 5:18; *GH*, pp 147, 150, 261; *TY*, pp. 136, 168.
8. *GH*, p. 327.
9. *TY*, pp. 156-58.
10. *SGS*, p. 105; *NY*, pp. 68-72. For a detailed analysis of Loew's position on the election of Israel, see Gross (1974), pp. 86-118.
11 *NO*, 1:59; *NY*, p. 71; *TY*, p. 9; *OH*, p. 46; *HA*, 2:12. See discussion on "conversion" in the following chapter
12. See the relevant discussion and documentation in the chapter below on human perfection.
13. *GH*, p. 147.
14. *NY*, p. 62.
15. See *NY*, pp 62, 106.
16. *GH*, pp. 45, 57; *NY*, pp. 66, 72-73, 81, 191.
17. See Sherwin (1975), pp. 55-60.
18. Shab 88a.
19. *GA*, 2:120; *NY*, p. 71, *TY*, p 94; *OH*, p 46.
20. *NO*, 1:39.
21. *GA*, 2:4; *SGS*, p. 105; *NY*, p. 65. Also see Gross (1974), pp. 80-81.
22. Shab. 88a
23. *TY*, p. 136.
24. See, e.g., *NY*, p. 62.
25. *OH*, p. 180.
26. *OH*, p. 174.
27. See, e.g., *GA*, 1.69-70, 96, 5:13; *GH*, p. 27, *NO*, 2:109; *NY*, p. 10, *BG*, p. 14; *OH*, p. 63; *HA* 3:138. See the discussion in the following chapter on wine.
28. *NO*, 1:88; *NY*, pp 9, 121-22; *BG*, p. 67.
29. *GA*, 1:7; *TY*, p. 55; *NY*, p. 205; *HA*, 1:36, 4:82-83.
30. *NY*, pp. 14, 60-61, 210; *HA*, 1:62.
31. *HA*, 1:62. See *NY*, pp. 14, 210; *BG*, p 64; *OH*, p. 178; *HA*, 4:114.
32. *GA*, 5:118.
33. *GH*, pp. 29, 35, 238.
34. *HA*, 1:2.
35. *GH*, p. 36.

36. *GA* 5:118; *GH*, p. 161; *OH*, p. 213.
37. See, for example, *GH*, p. 238; *DH*, p. 247; *OH*, pp. 141, 154; *HA*, 2:53, 3:140. Also note relevant discussion and documentation in the preceding chapter.
38. *OH*, p 113, see esp. pp. 51-52, 127. In rabbinic literature, see, for example, Est. R. 7:4.
39. *GA*, 2:93; *GH*, p. 161; *OH*, pp. 50-51, 127, 172, 213, 227; *HA*, 4:116.
40. *OH*, pp. 50-51.
41. *DH*, p. 247; *NY*, pp. 87, 90; *OH*, pp. 50-51, 127, 141; *HA*, 2:53. Note the relevant discussion in the preceding chapter. For Loew, peoples other than Amalek properly exist as part of the natural order. Amalek, however, has only accidental existence. Properly, it should not exist. See *OH*, p. 150. For Loew, Amalek represents the privation of existence. It is akin to the demonic, which Loew similarly describes as a privation of existence.
42. See, e.g., G. Cohen, 1967, "Esau as Symbol," pp. 19-49; Ginzberg, 5:272, no. 19, 6:68, no. 350, and, 6:462-63, no. 93.
43. On Loew's thought as a response to the exile of 1492, see Neher (1965), 14:299. The breakdown of Jewish mysticism in the modern age was significantly due to a rejection of the powerful tendency found in classical Jewish mysticism to stress Jewish uniqueness and the "metaphysical" difference between Jew and Gentile. If the intensity of one's claim of Jewish exclusivity is indicative of one's mystical tendencies, then Loew, who, more than virtually anyone else in the history of Judaism, stressed Jewish physical and metaphysical exclusivity, is certainly to be considered a central figure in the history of Jewish mysticism. In periods following traumatic events in Jewish history such as the Spanish expulsion, an intensification of Jewish mystical speculation and its corollary–an emphasis upon Jewish exclusivity–almost always seems to occur. Such, for example, has been the case in response to the European holocaust during World War II. It should not be surprising, therefore, that a parallel has been drawn between Loew's mysticism and his claim to Jewish exclusivity and that made by Leo Baeck in his *This People Israel: The Meaning of Jewish Existence*, written during and after World War II Also see Altmann (1973), p. 28, no. 83

Chapter 9

1. Av. Zar. 2:3.
2. See Eisenstein, pp. 168-69.
3. Katz (1961), *Exclusiveness and Tolerance*, pp. 27-41. See, for example, Maimonides: *SM* (1967), 2:189-91, Negative Commandment no. 194, and *MT–Sefer Kedushah* (1965), "Laws of Forbidden Foods," 17:19: "There are other things which the sages have forbidden, these prohibitions, although without root in the Torah, having been decreed by them in order to keep the people away from heathens, so that Israelites might not mingle with them, lest such commingling should lead to intermarriage. These things are as follows: drinking with heathens, even in circumstances where no apprehension need be felt for libation wine; and eating their bread or cooked food, even when no concern need be had for heathen cooking utensils."
4. E.g., Isserles glosses to *SA-YD*, 123:1.
5. Av. Zar. 31b. For a discussion of changing attitudes in the sixteenth century, see Katz (1961), *Tradition and Crisis*, pp. 19-26.
6. Isserles (1971), pp. 484-88, no 124. Ziev, the editor of Isserles's responsa, notes that the Amsterdam, 1611, and Sudlikow, 1835, editions deleted parts of this responsum

because of the lenient position on Jewish use of Gentile wine taken therein; see ibid., p. 484, no. 1. Also see Isserles's glosses to *SA-YD*, 123:1, 132:1, 133:1. See the discussion of Isserles's position in Ben-Sasson (1959), pp. 22-23

7. Gold, pp. 50, 267.
8. Halperin, p. 89, no. 272.
9. In 1603, in Frankfurt, efforts were taken to stem abuse of the prohibition. See the records of the "Synod of Frankfurt" in Finkelstein, p. 260.
10. See *SOC,* pp. 53, 61-64. Also see *NO,* 2:198.
11. See Schochet, pp. 124, 128, no. 22, 23.
12. See *SOC,* pp. 53, 56.
13. See *SOC,* p. 61; *GH,* pp. 331-32; *NY,* p. 129; *OH,* p. 137; *NM,* p. 31.
14. *NM,* pp. 30-31. See Zohar, "Shemini," 3:40a-b. Note Tishby (1961), 2:477-78, and (1957), 1:285-90.
15 See Katz (1961), *Tradition and Crisis,* pp. 26-27.
16. *SOC,* p. 61.
17. *OH,* p. 137; see also *NY,* pp. 126, 129
18. See also *SOC,* pp. 53, 56.
19. See Bokser, pp. 42-44.
20. *GH,* p. 333.
21. Katz (1961), *Exclusiveness and Tolerance,* p. 147
22. J. Katz and Kleinberger read Loew as being in effect opposed to conversion, while Gross and Weiss claim that Loew actually favored the possibility of conversion. Katz notes that he consulted Kleinberger's work in manuscript "with considerable profit." Weiss attempts to unravel what he believes to be the difficulty with Kleinberger's presentation of Loew's position. Gross also takes issue with Kleinberger and with Katz. Without going into laborious details concerning these arguments and counter-arguments, it is the present hope that our analysis of Loew's position is both comprehensive and correct. See Katz (1961), *Exclusiveness and Tolerance,* pp. 146-149. Kleinberger, p. 41; Gross, 1974, pp. 77-79 no. 45, Weiss, pp. 100-101. It ought to be noted that failure adequately to consult Loew's views in *HA* on this issue, as on many other issues, may have led the authors just noted to have formulated an inadequate statement of Loew's views.
23. See, e.g., *GA,* 1:69-70, 96, 3:60-61, 5:13; *GH,* pp. 47, 165; *NO,* 2:109; *NY,* p. 10; *BG,* p. 14; *OH,* p. 63; *HA,* 3:138. See Buber, pp. 77-89.
24. *GH,* p. 160; *HA,* 3:156.
25. *HA,* 3:156, 4:71. See Katz (1961), *Exclusiveness and Tolerance,* pp. 70-73, 149-50.
26. *TY,* p. 10. Note *NY,* p. 149. See Weiss, p. 100.
27. *SOT,* p. 6; *NY,* p. 149; *HA,* 2:150. Loew may have been alluding to the following citation in the Zohar, "Mishpatim," 2:95b: "It is a great humiliation for the holy soul, characteristic of Jews, to enter into a 'stranger'; namely, into a convert. For then it has to fly from paradise into a habitation built from an uncircumcised and impure source."
28. *HA,* 4:71. Also, with minor variations, *GH,* p. 160. The talmudic referrent at the end of the citation is Yev. 22a.
29. For Loew, circumcision represents a metaphysical as well as a physical change for the better. See *GH,* pp. 151, 184; *NY,* p. 100; *BG,* p. 95; *HA,* 2:5.
30. *GA,* 1:190; *HA,* 3:136. According to Loew, the Messiah, who represents a "new creation," is destined to be a descendant of converts because converts represent a "new creation." See *NY,* p. 149.
31. *GA,* 3:169, 172; *TY,* p. 10.
32. Yev. 47b, 109b; Ned. 13b.

33. See Lev. 13:2.
34. For a discussion of Rabbi Helbo's meaning, see Moore, 1:346-47.
35. Yev. 109b.
36. Kid. 70b-71a, "Tosafot."
37. *HA*, 1:130. See Also *HA*, 1:136; *SOT*, p. 6; *NY*, p. 149.
38. Braude, p. 42.
39. See Katz (1961), *Exclusiveness and Tolerance*, p. 145.
40. Ibid., p. 145, quoting Luria's *Yam Shel Shelomo*, "Yevamot," 4:49.

Chapter 10

1. For a careful and thorough analysis of Loew's theory of human nature, see A. Weiss, especially pp. 43-231. Also note the helpful discussion in Kleinberger (1962), pp. 30-72, 90-122.
2. Man as "form" of the lower world: *GA* 1:31, 5:31, *HA*, 1:135, 3:55; also see *TY*, p 91. Everything created for man: *DH*, p 25; *TY*, pp. 15, 96; *BG*, p. 142; *HA*, 2:6. Man as the "basis" (*ikkar*) of the world: *GA*, 3:70. In many of these citations, Loew seems to be citing the Zohar 3:48a: "Everything in the world was only made for the sake of man, and all things were kept back until he that was called 'Adam' should appear, since his form was after the divine prototype, and when he was created all was complete, for he includes all."
3. *GA*, 1:21; *SGS*, p. 194; *HA*, 4:98.
4. *SGS*, p. 103; *DH*, pp. 58, 254; *NO*, 1:202; *HA*, 3:44.
5. *BG*, p. 9; see also *DH*, p. 143. On self-knowledge as a path to knowledge of reality as discussed in medieval Jewish mystical and philosophical literature, see Altmann (1969), pp, 1-41.
6. There is also another trend which minimizes man's place in the cosmos. On the idea of man in biblical and rabbinic thought, see Heschel (1960), pp. 108-57; Urbach, pp 189-226. Also see Eichrodt; Ringgren, pp. 121-26.
7. *ARN*, ch. 7, p. 127.
8. On the microcosm motif in Jewish medieval philosophical and mystical literature, see Altmann (1969), pp. 19-28; A. Weiss, pp. 58-64.
9. Saadya, 4:2, pp. 182-83. Also see Malter, p. 186.
10. Albo, 1:102-104.
11. Shalom, 1:2, pp. 1b-2a; see Davidson (1964), p. 55, no. 1
12. On anthropocentricism in medieval Jewish mystical tradition, see Altmann (1969), pp. 14-19; Tishby (1961), 2:3-11; Heschel (1949), 2:934-36.
13. See Scholem (1974), p 69.
14. Husik, p. 125.
15. Maimonides, *Guide*, 3:13, (1963), p. 455.
16. Ibid., ch 12, p. 443.
17. Ibid., ch. 13, p. 452.
18. Ibn Gabbai, 3:3.
19. *TY*, p. 40, *HA*, 4:124; see Kleinberger, p. 36 no. 36.
20. See, e.g., *DH*, pp. 58, 254; *NO*, 1:202. Though Loew distinguishes among these three dimensions of existence, the division is not absolute. Since one dimension acts as the "form" of the one which precedes it, there is a certain degree of interrelation and fluidity. There is also a class of beings which specifically bridges the natural and supernatural realms, having qualities of both. These are beings created at dusk on the

sixth day of creation, between the creation of the natural world and that of the sacred Sabbath, which Loew identifies with the supernatural realm, the realm of static perfection; e.g., see *GH*, p 171. Such beings are, for example, the donkey upon which the Messiah will ride into Jerusalem, and disembodied spirits (*shedim*); see *GA*, 2:26, 117; *HA*, 2:124. Loew apparently had in mind Gen. R. 7:5. In that text God is described as creating the souls of the spirits, but because of the oncoming Sabbath, he had to cease his labor and could not create their bodies as well. See also Trachtenberg (1961), pp. 29-30.

Loew's description of the universe as consisting of three gradually descending worlds appears to be drawn from the earlier Jewish mystical tradition. The direct source may have been Isaac Ibn Latif (13 c.) whom Loew is known to have read. See Wilensky, p. 204; Scholem (1931), 2:415-92 Maimonides also posited three dimensions of existence though he ascribed to each world different qualities than those ascribed by Loew; see *MT-Sefer ha-Madda, "Yesodei Ha-Torah" 2:3, and Guide of the Perplexed*, 2:10. Maimonides' position is adopted by Abraham Shalom, of whom Loew was not particularly fond. See Davidson (1964), p. 43; Weiss, p. 49. Already in the late thirteenth and early fourteenth century the Jewish mystical tradition had begun to develop a portrait of reality consisting of *four* worlds. Only in the sixteenth century, with the writings of Cordovero and Luria, did this notion take root and further develop; see Scholem (1941), p. 272, and (1974), p. 119. Loew was apparently influenced by Cordovero, though not by Luria, whose teachings became popular after Loew's death. Because Loew consistently mentions three worlds and not four, it has been claimed that he opted for the three-world view of the philosophers over the four-world view of the mystics and is therefore not to be considered a devotee of mysticism, but of philosophy; see Kariv, 1:13, 17-23. This claim does not stand up to analysis for the following reasons: (1) As was noted above, the four-world theory was not fully developed until Loew's own time; (2) the earlier kabbalists upon whom he apparently relied did posit a three-world universe; (3) the four worlds of the sixteenth-century kabbalists, Cordovero included, were *olam ha-aẓilut* (the world of emanation), *olam ha-beriah* (the world of creation), *olam ha-yeẓirah* (the world of formation), and *olam ha-asiyyah* (the world of action). Though characterizations of the two middle worlds differed from system to system, the first world is most often identified with the sefirotic realm and the last world is most often identified with the terrestrial realm. In one text, apparently overlooked by Kariv, Loew describes his tripartite universe as follows: The material realm is called "action," the realm of matter implanted in form is called "formation," and the world of form without matter is called "creation"; see *DH*, pp. 254-56. Loew therefore apparently does accept the kabbalistic scheme, using the descriptions of the three lower realms often found in kabbalistic literature as well as the terms used by the literature, most specifically by Cordovero, to describe them (see Cordovero's *Pardes Rimonim*, chapter 16)

Loew's understanding of the three worlds, therefore, does not support the claim that he was not a mystic but helps to refute it Furthermore, it should be noted that Loew's thought consistently reiterates the notion of contradictory opposites and their synthesis. To be consistent, Loew must develop a portrait of the universe consisting of two opposite dimensions: material and spiritual and the synthesis between them–the "intermediary world." The fourth world does not fit into his "system" of thesis, anthithesis, synthesis. That highest world, representing the essence of God, is above all three worlds, above the "system." God is the form of all of reality, of all three worlds, and cannot therefore be counted as one of them. Note Tishby (1957), 1:386-90.

21. *DH*, p. 58.

22. *TY*, p 216.
23. *HA*, 1:119, "Each man by himself is all men." Compare Cordovero (1960), 1:4, p. 52. Note Scholem (1974), p. 404.
24. *DH*, p. 51.
25. *DH*, p. 58.
26. *DH*, p. 254.
27. Though Loew does not clearly articulate this analogy between the aspects of man and the dimensions of existence, such an identification emerges out of a careful reading of his works. Loew's distinction amongst the three aspects of the human being–intellect, soul, and body–is explicitly stated throughout his writings. See, e.g., *SSR*, pp. 72, 78; *DH*, pp. 79, 118; *NO*, 1:12, 2:43, 168, 233, 239; *TY*, pp. 8, 164; *NY*, pp. 88, 99; *OH*, p 55; *HA*, 2:34, 4:68 Loew utilizes this tripartite division as a rubric for discussing other issues. For example, the Talmud denotes three cardinal sins. "In every other law of the Torah, if a man is commanded–transgress and suffer not death–he may transgress and not suffer death, excepting idolatry, illicit sexual relations [i.e., incest or adultery] and murder" (Sanh. 74a). Loew relates each of these sins to a different aspect of man. Illicit sex is the sin peculiar to the body and most damaging in the quest for perfection of the body. Murder is the sin peculiar to the soul and most damaging for one seeking to attain perfection of the soul. Idolatry is a sin committed by the intellect; it is wrong perception, mistaken thought, and as such is particularly damaging to one seeking perfection of the intellect. See *SSR*, p. 70; *NO*, 2:239; *HA*, 4:68. Loew also identifies these three sins with three kinds of relationships man may have: with the self, with one's fellow, with God. Illicit sex is a sin against the self. Murder is a sin against one's fellow human being, and idolatry is a sin against God. Since all sins are against one of these three, these three sins are paradigmatic for all sins; see *NY*, p. 36. Elsewhere, Loew identifies these three relationships–to oneself, to other people, to God–to the three varieties of human perfection one may achieve. Each variety corresponds to each of the three aspects of man. One may achieve perfection of the body, which is perfection of man in relationship to himself; perfection in relationships with others, which is perfection of the soul; perfection of relationship to God, which is perfection of the intellect. See *DH*, p. 9, *NO*, 1:210; *HA*, 3:4.

   Loew also compares the three parts of man to the three trimesters of gestation of the human embryo and to the three stages of human life: youth, when the body is dominant; middle age, when the soul is dominant; and old age, when the intellect is dominant; see *NY*, p. 88. Loew also utilizes this tripartite division of man in expressing his philosophy of history. The exile of Israel is compared to a long night, divided into three watches. In each watch a different kingdom rules and suppresses Israel. Each kingdom concentrates upon a different aspect of the person. Babylonia represents physical suppression. Media (Persia) represents suppression of the soul and murder, which is the sin peculiar to the soul. The Hellenists represent suppression of the intellect, personified by the Torah. They forbade Jews to study the Torah. The contemporary rule by the Fourth Kingdom, "Rome" or Christendom, Loew claims, combines the other three varieties of oppression; see, e.g., *GH*, p 51; *NY*, p. 99; *NM*, p. 11.
28. *GA*, 1:23, 5:31; *GH*, p. 321 Loew's source seems to be Albo, 3:1, pp 3-6.
29. *NO*, 1:184-85.
30. *GA*, 5:31. Similarly, Loew claims that in the Messianic Age, gross matter will no longer exist, but a more refined variety of matter will replace it; see *NY*, p. 196.
31. *GA*, 1:94, 4:164, 5:32.
32. *BG*, p. 126.

33. *BG*, pp. 9-10

34. *GH*, p. 155; *DH*, p. 94; *SSR*, pp. 81-82.

35. *DH*, p. 126; *NO*, 1:92. On "form" and "matter" in Loew's thought, see A. Weiss, pp. 72-75.

36. *DH*, pp. 196, 262; *HA*, 1:146.

37. *DH*, pp. 126, 162, 182; *HA*, 4:66.

38. *DH*, pp. 78, 182; *HA*, 1:66, 4:26, 31. "The more material an entity is, the more despicable it becomes"; see *NY*, p. 48.

39. *HA*, 4:26, 31. Hell is described as the privation of existence; see *DH*, p. 30; *TY*, p. 59. Satan is also identified with the privation of existence, *NO*, 2:214.

40. *DH*, pp. 126, 255; see A. Weiss, p. 73 and sources noted there.

41. *HA*, 4:160.

42. *GH*, p. 155; *HA*, 4:92. A. Weiss, p. 135, no. 96, correctly disagrees with Kleinberger (1962), p. 50. Kleinberger identifies the businessman with the bodily aspects of man, rather than with the soul. Both Weiss and Kleinberger overlook *HA*, 1:92, where it is clearly stated that men concerned with business achieve perfection of the soul

43. *HA*, 1:10.

44. For Loew, sin and the consequential perversion of the natural sphere have their roots in matter; see *DH*, p. 262; *BG*, pp. 21, 106; *OH*, p. 144; *HA*, 1:12, 3:95. See A. Weiss, pp. 77-86, on Loew's idea of "man's material nature."

45. *SSR*, p. 85; *NO*, 1:39, 2:22; *TY*, p. 163; *HA*, 1:82. Loew identifies various opportunities for weakening the body as a means for attaining human perfection; e.g., affliction (*yisurim*), *NO*, 2:153, 174; humility, *NO*, 2:2. Loew also believed that as a person ages, his progressively weakened body permits his soul to become dominant, except during very old age, when body and soul would be considerably weakened; see *DH*, pp. 203, 273-74; *OH*, p. 116. Compare Maimonides, *Guide*, 3:51 (1963), p. 627. Loew's direct sources for the idea that matter is an impediment for human perfection and by limiting its influence one may strengthen the soul and the intellect may be Maimonides, *Guide* 3:8 (1963), pp. 433-34; Albo, 3:32, pp. 301-2.

46. *GA*, 3:123; *NO*, 2:112; *NY*, p. 87. Loew insists that one must suppress the desires of the body for the sake of the intellect; otherwise, the body will suppress the powers of the intellect never allowing it, and consequently never permitting the individual, to achieve perfection; *NO*, 1:12.

47. *DH*, pp. 220-21.

48. *GH*, pp. 151, 187; *NY*, p. 100; *BG*, p. 95. See also *NY*, p. 58, where circumcision is noted to be the sign of the covenant and transgression of the commandment of circumcision is considered a cause of the exile of the Jewish people. Loew, as well as some of his contemporaries, tends to stress the importance of circumcision. It may be that this expression of concern was in response to a contemporary lapse of observance; see also *SSR*, p. 68, where Loew notes that every slave bears the sign of his master and that of the Jew is the mark of circumcision. As might be expected, Loew identifies circumcision with a number, the number eight, which signifies the beginning of the supernatural realm.

49. *BG*, pp. 93-95; see also *HA*, 3:33, where Loew distinguishes between human and animal sex. Loew's reference is to Maimonides' *Guide*, 2:40 (1963), p. 384: "The strongest of the indications you should pay attention to is constituted by his renunciation of, and contempt for, the bodily pleasures, for this is the first of the degrees of the people of science and, all the more, of the prophets. In particular this holds good with regard to the sense that it is a disgrace to us as Aristotle has set forth and especially in what belongs to it with regard to the foulness of copulation." See also *Guide*, 3:8

(1963), p. 432; note 3:49, p. 604. Maimonides' reference is to Aristotle's *Ethics* 3, 10, 1118 B2 (1962), p. 79. On Maimonides' attitude to sex, see Sherwin (1974), pp. 32-35. Loew, of course, follows the Hebrew translation of the *Guide*, but was unaware of any nuance this specific text may have in its Arabic original; see A. Weiss, p. 158, no. 25.

50. Bokser, p. 75, and A. Weiss, p. 159, no. 26, correctly notice the similarity between Loew's position and that adopted in the tract *Iggeret Ha-Kodesh*, traditionally ascribed to Nahmanides. The treatise asssumed by Bokser and Weiss to have been written by Nahmanides actually is of anonymous authorship. On the possible identity of the author, see Scholem (1974), p. 67, and (1945), 21:179-86, and (1948), p. 148, no. 2. For an analysis of this text, see Harris, 33:201-3.

51. On women and marriage as a necessary means for man to achieve human perfection, see *GA*, 1:31; *TY*, p. 53; *OH*, p 121; *HA*, 1:12, 4:164. As man's "matter," woman is both a potential source of corruption of male "form" as well as for the fulfillment of male "form." Loew notes that the first sin was brought on because of a woman, because women enjoy a close relationship with matter, see *BG*, p. 21. Loew identifies woman with the material world. He therefore charges a man to heed his wife in "this-worldly" affairs since she is more involved than he is with them; see *DH*, p. 36. For Loew, though women have bodies, souls, and intellects, theirs are flawed when compared to those of men. Women therefore have less potential than men to realize in order to attain perfection; see *OH*, p. 55 Like the kabbalists, Loew perceives everything to be characterized by an interplay between masculine and feminine forces. The relationship between male and female, especially during sexual intercourse, is identified with the paradigmatic relationship between polar, complementary opposites; see *GA*, 1:16, 31, 237; *GH*, p. 249; *OH*, p. 104. Also see A. Weiss, pp. 108-11, and sources noted there. Loew, like the mystics, sees the sex act as the paradigm of the unity which obtains in the higher worlds which man must attempt to infuse in the natural world; see *BG*, pp 83-84; *HA*, 1:135.

52. *TY*, p. 17. See Altmann (1969), pp. 14-17. A hint of this notion is found in *DH*, p. 143. "When man considers the configuration of his body, he is able to reach an understanding of God."

53. *NY*, pp. 102, 104.

54. *GH*, p. 277; *OH*, p. 93.

55. *GA*, 1:94; *HA*, 2:50.

56. For Loew, only the Jew is truly "man," because only he has the "divine soul," and only in him can the soul dominate the body. The Gentile has but a semblance of humanity; see *GA*, 2:157; *GH*, pp. 96, 157, 167; *DH*, p. 146; *TY*, pp. 56, 92; *NY*, p. 74; *NM*, p. 10; *HA*, 4:20, 103. To express this notion, Loew often has recourse to Ha-Levi's claim that only Jews possess the "divine element" (*ha-inyan ha-elohi*). See Ha-Levi, especially 2:24-49. For Loew's use of this term peculiarly unique to Ha-Levi, see *GA*, 5:32; *GH*, p. 78; *DH*, p. 322; *TY*, p 16; *NY*, pp. 40, 63; *HA*, 4:97. It is significant that though Loew appears extraordinarily influenced by Ha-Levi, especially in his notion of the nature of the Jewish people, Ha-Levi is never mentioned by name in Loew's writings. A. Weiss, pp 83-103, laboriously attempts to distinguish between the use of the term in Loew's writings and its use in Ha-Levi's writings. It may be suggested that Loew's use of ideas originally found in Ha-Levi may have been drawn from sources other than Ha-Levi; specifically from Jewish mystical sources emanating from thirteenth-century Provence. Ha-Levi's ideas, especially those concerning the nature of Israel, were quickly adapted by the mystics of Lunel; see Scholem (1948), pp. 80-84. Also note Altmann (1944).

57. *NY*, pp. 26, 106

58. *SSR*, pp. 81-84.

59. *GA*, 4:164.

60. *GH*, pp. 167, 312.

61. *NY*, p. 14; *OH*, pp. 93-94; *HA*, 4:100.

62. *DH*, p. 86; *NO*, 2:43; *TY*, p. 7; *HA*, 3:227, 4:121. "The soul which resides in the body gravitates towards the natural [i.e., the material]"; see *TY*, p. 26.

63. *DH*, p. 95; *NO*, 1:124; *NY*, pp. 29, 116; *HA*, 1:96. Sometimes he places the intellect in the heart, but usually he places it in the brain; see *GA*, 5:5; *DH*, pp. 25, 33, 49, etc. Also see A Weiss, pp. 148-49; Kleinberger (1962), p. 49, no. 101, and sources gathered there.

64. Loew's theory of the soul is not consistent and is therefore difficult to represent. His often indiscriminate use of a variety of terms, e.g., *nefesh, neshama, ruah*, etc., only confuses matters. A most adequate presentation of his theory of the soul and intellect is provided by A. Weiss, pp. 118-99. Besides outlining Loew's thinking, Weiss also discusses the roots of Loew's ideas on the soul in medieval Jewish philosophy and mysticism. Kleinberger (1962), p. 47, also notes Loew's indiscriminate use of terms. Nevertheless, Kleinberger (1962), pp. 45-57, also manages an admirable reconstruction of Loew's theory of the soul.

65. *SSR*, p. 85. Loew ascribed will to animals; however, he claims that their will is dominated by their bodies while humans' wills are dominated by their intellects; see *GH*, p. 156; *DH*, p. 149; *HA*, 3:227. See A. Weiss, pp. 167-68. On Loew's idea of freedom, see L. Ashkenazi, 5:432-39; Neher (1965), 14:290-304; Kleinberger (1962), pp. 32-36.

66. For an exhaustive discussion of the notion of the "evil inclination" in Loew's writings, see A. Weiss, pp. 201-12. On the "evil inclination" in the Zohar, see Tishby (1961), 2:81-89. Loew does not adopt the Zohar's understanding of the "evil inclination" as being utterly demonic. His notion that it may serve as a prelude to the good is very protohasidic This is not to say that the notion of evil as a possible prelude to good is totally absent in the Zohar; see, e.g , Zohar 2:162b-163b.

67. *GA*, 1:65; *NO*, 2:133.

68. See Schechter, pp. 219-345.

69 Loew identifies slavery with matter, with the body, and freedom with the soul; see *TY*, p. 108; *HA*, 2:48. The "evil inclination" is not related to the intellect, but to the soul, see *NO*, 2:70-71, and is especially identifiable with matter, see *DH*, p. 110 It is therefore identifiable with Satan and with death; see BB, 16a; *NO*, 2:126. Note Weiss, p. 203, no. 22, and sources noted there.

70. *NO*, 2:112.

71. *GA*, 1:17; *GH*, p. 167; *DH*, pp. 142, 148; *NY*, p.110; *HA*, 4:110. In *NO*, 2:116, Loew is in the midst of discussing the propriety of reciting certain liturgical hymns on the High Holidays. With specific reference to a prayer entitled "Angels of mercy, bring our supplications to the Lord of mercy," Loew argues that, even though "it is our custom to recite the prayer," it is better not to do so since man does not need the intercession of angels. When the prayer is recited, however, the intention should not be that man, who is presumably superior to the angels, should *supplicate* them to intercede. Man rather *commands* them to do so! Discussion of Loew's view on recitation of this prayer may be found in the *Responsa* of Moses Schreiber (1762-1839) known as Hatam Sofer, *Orah Ḥayyim*, no. 165; note discussion, Jacobs (1975), pp. 215-16 and pp. 193-94.

72. *TY*, p. 73; see also *DH*, pp. 144, 148.

73. *TY*, pp. 10-14, 27; *BG*, pp. 35, 73.
74. Loew considered *derekh erez*, or what may be termed "natural morality"–moral law grounded in rationality or convention, rather than in revelation–as the means to perfection of the body, which is the perfection peculiar to the Gentile, to natural, worldly existence. This is how Loew interprets the statement in Av. 2:2, "*Derekh erez* precedes the Torah"; see *DH*, p. 71; *NO*, 2:250. Also see *BG*, p. 19. Note Kleinberger (1962), p. 103.
75. On observance of the commandments as a specific means to perfection of the soul, see *NO*, 1:209; *TY*, pp. 10, 27, 31-32. As a means to perfection in general, see *SOT*, pp. 10-11; *NO*, 1:75, 216; *TY*, p. 31.
76. *TY*, p. 27; *HA*, 2:83. Loew's analogy of man's soul with a seed from above seems to have been drawn from Jewish mystical tradition. He uses the kabbalistic description of man as an upside down tree with its roots above; see *NY*, p. 47; *HA*, 4:158.
77. *SOC*, p. 53; *SOT*, pp. 23 35; *NO*, 1:3; *TY*, p. 90; *HA*, 2:7, 39.
78. The Torah as a means to human perfection, see *SOT*, pp. 10, 12, 15; *GH*, p. 176; *DH*, pp. 25-26; *NO*, 1:4, 22, 34, 2:148, 150, 153; *TY*, pp. 5, 16, 89, *IIA*, 2.7, 3.227.
79. For Loew perfection is a static state. Therefore, the spiritual realm, the realm of the intellect which is the realm of the Torah, is static. Movement, space, time, change, fragmentation, etc., are all characteristics of the natural, material dimension of existence. Potential characterizes the natural; actuality or reality portrays the spiritual.
80. On Loew's understanding of the notion of human perfection in early medieval Jewish philosophy, see A. Weiss, pp. 236-44; Kleinberger (1962), pp. 90-92, 101-17.

For Loew, to claim that intellectual perfection equals human perfection is to claim that a part of man–the intellect–is the whole man.

According to Loew, the strength of one's innate intellectual ability is an accident of birth. How therefore, he asks, can the philosophers assume that that which is eternal–life after death–might be secured solely by means of that which is accidental? Even if one were to admit that the intellect is the essence of man, intellectual perfection would not entail human perfection. For the intellect, by its nature, is always in potential in this world. The intellect can always be improved and can therefore never realize the static condition of perfection. Furthermore, Loew queries, what about those who, because of their innate capabilities, are unable to achieve intellectual perfection? Is one to assume that they are to be denied some kind of existence after death? See *TY*, pp. 32, 36; *HA*, 1:16; 3:109.

In a number of discussions in his writings, which may be aimed at certain Protestant notions as well as certain philosophical ones, Loew articulates his main objection to the equation of human perfection with intellectual perfection. The idea that human perfection may be acquired through intellectual reflection rather than through specific physical deeds Loew perceived to be a threat to an act-oriented Judaism. Loew viewed the claim that acts are inconsequential as the logical corollary of the assertion that the way to God is by means of the mind. He believed that a stance which denigrated physical deeds, which argued that not human acts but intellectual speculation, is the way to attain eternity, is a danger to basic Jewish teaching. He writes, "The [human] task in this world is to perform the required deeds. Though these be physical acts they are desired by God and by doing them man attains eternal bliss in the World to Come"; see *DH*, p. 314.

In one specific passage, Loew's position on the philosopher's equation of human perfection with intellectual perfection is comprehensively stated. He writes: "It is well known that the philosophers claim the essence [of man] is the intellect. They believe that the soul of man cannot survive death save for the intellect and that without the intellect man is not man. According to the scholars of Israel, however, this notion is absolute falsehood. . . . They argue that human perfection is attained by acquiring intellectual perfection. . . . The belief of the sages of blessed memory is that the soul [neshamah] is of a divine essence. It knows and perceives and in this is similar to God. It is not as they [the philosophers] think that the soul is nothing and that after death only the intellect, which in itself is the person, survives." HA, 4:123; see also DH, p. 124; HA, 3:109.

81. See, e.g., DH, p. 51; NO, 2:67; TY, pp. 12, 14; OH, p. 155.

82. TY, p. 13.

83. NO, 1:22; TY, p.176; HA, 3:39. As the body is essentially material, it is the contradictory opposite of the Torah, which is essentially spiritual; see HA, 2:118.

84. See especially TY, pp. 161-63; also see DH, p 106, NO, 1:50; HA, 3:39, 4:82.

85. Ex. 32:15-34:5. According to the biblical narrative, the first set was divine, "the work of God"(Exod.: 34-15), while the second set was the work of man, i.e. of Moses (Exod. 34:1). According to Loew, the sin of the Golden Calf compromised the degree of the spiritual then (at Sinai) existent in "this world." Consequently, the first set of tablets, which were fitting only for such a realized world, had to be broken and a second set had to be given to correspond to the more material level of existence of the world engendered by the sin of the Golden Calf; see SOT, p. 14; TY, pp. 102-3; HA, 3:10.

86. DH, p. 194; NO, 1:20; TY, pp. 101, 103; HA, 2:43, 3:30.

87. Loew claims that "there is no truth in the terrestrial realm." Being always in potential and never totally actual, the natural realm must be bereft of truth; see NO, 1:204.

88. According to Loew, the world was created with an innate flaw so that human beings may have the opportunity to effect repair. For example, wheat grows unrefined, uncooked, because it requires human effort to "complete" it, to perfect it; see, e.g., NY, p. 28. On the rabbinic roots of the notion that there is a flaw in the fabric of creation, see Heschel (1962), pp. 87-93. This notion played a central role in Lurianic mysticism.

89. DH, p. 6.

Chapter 11

1. E.g., Psalm 102:6, Job 19:20.

2. E.g., Lam. 4:4, Job 29:10, Ezek. 3:26

3. E.g., Gen. 2:24, 34:3; I Kings 11:2.

4. E.g., Deut. 4:4, 10:20, 11:22, 13:5, 30:20; Josh. 22:5, 23:8; II Kings 18:6, Jer. 13:11.

5. Sif. Deut. (1939), "Ekev," pp. 114-15, no. 59.

6. Sota 14a; see MT 25:11

7. Ket. 111b; Num. R. 22:1; Tan., "Mattot," no. 1.

8. Tishby (1961), 2:184-85.

9. Sanh. 64a.

10. SSR 6, 4:2; PR, ch. 1.

11. PR, 11:7.

12. Gen. R. 80:7.

13. Tan., "Va-Yishlah," no. 20. See Tan., ed. S. Buber (1964), 1:174.

14. See Heschel (1962), 1:153-56.

15. On love and fear of God in Biblical and rabbinic literatures, see Bamberger, 6:39-55; Buchler, pp. 118-70; Moore, 2:98-100; Urbach, pp. 350-70. Bamberger, p. 150, claims that in the biblical view, terms for fear and love are used interchangeably.

Urbach, p. 368, claims that in the rabbinic view, fear or awe, was a necessary prerequisite for love of God and that love of God was considered a higher manner of worshipping God. Urbach's position approximates that of Rabbi Loew.

16. Maimonides, *SM*, "Positive Commandments," no. 6. In this source Maimonides quotes the source from Ket. 111b, noted above. Also see his *MT—Sefer ha-Madda*, "Hilkhot De'ot," 6:1-2; compare "Hilkhot Teshuvah," 10:9-10.

17. See Maimonides, *Guide* (1963), 3:51-54; especially pp. 620-29.

18. See Tishby (1961), 2:286-87; Scholem (1974), p. 44.

19. Scholem (1948), pp. 115-22.

20. Scholem (1974), p. 50.

21. Nahmanides, *Commentary to the Torah*, Lev. 18:4; compare Exod. 16:6, 33:14.

22. Compare *Ma'arekhet Ha-Elohut*, chapter 8

23. Chone, 11:86-99, especially p. 89.

24. G. Scholem has repeatedly denied the presence of this motif in Jewish mystical literature, but has been challenged with adequately documented sources by I. Tishby. See Scholem (1941), p. 5, and (1971), p. 203; Tishby (1961), 2:289.

25. This position was held, for example, by Azriel of Gerona. See Scholem (1974), p. 175.

26. See Tishby (1961), 2:291.

27. Ibid., 2:293-97. Compare Cordovero (1960), p 117.

28. Scholem (1941), pp. 225-29, 235.

29. Tishby (1961), 2:293-306.

30. Scholem (1971), p. 208. Scholem does not mention the Zohar as a source for the notion of a variety of *devekut* attainable by all.

31. See, e.g., Scholem (1973), p. 208; Dresner, pp. 185-86. Compare Tishby (1961), 2:304, no. 160, who challenges this notion by quoting Judah Loew.

32. See Scholem (1973), p. 212. Compare the almost exact wording commenting on the identical biblical verse which appears in Loew's *TY*, p. 165, with that which appears in the first Hasidic book, *Toledot Ya'akov Yosef;* see sources noted by Dresner, p. 186.

33. *TY*, p. 165; *HA*, 4:9; see also *NO*, 1:208; *GH*, p. 152.

34. Mak 23b-24a.

35. *TY*, p. 30.

36. See *TY*, p. 26.

37. *NO*, 1:209.

38. *TY*, p. 32.

39. *SSR*, pp 81-85.

40. *NO*, 2:153.

41. *NO*, 2:2.

42. *NY*, p. 101; *NO*, 2:175.

43. Altmann (1969), p. 25.

44. *NY*, p. 21; *NO*, 1:104.

45. Man: *BG*, p. 120; Temple: *NY*, p. 196.

46. *NO*, 1:88.

47. Ibid., 1:104; see 1:81; note Weiss, pp. 364-70.

48. The Zohar, especially, holds prayer as a means to *devekut;* see Zohar 2:213b.

49. *HA*, 3:101.

50. *NO*, 1:104. See Scholem (1971), pp 176-203. For a very different notion of *devekut* in Hasidism, see J. Weiss (1955), 6:87-99.

51. *HA*, 1:6, commenting on Shab. 118b.

52. *TY*, p. 4.

53. See *NO*, 2:52.

54. See Kleinberger (1962), p. 11.
55 *NO*, 2:29. It is to be noted that Loew identifies martyrdom, the ultimate expression of self-sacrifice, with love of God, see *NO*, 2:48.
56 See A. Weiss, p. 344.
57. *NO*, 2:41.
58. Scholem (1974), p. 175. For Loew, man's awe of God is monolithic; however, love of God differs from person to person; see *HA*, 1:19. Also see Kleinberger (1962), p. 110, no. 96.
59. *HA*, 1:131; *NO*, 2:22. On love and awe of God in Loew's writing, see A. Weiss, pp. 330-47.
60. *NO*, 2:22. Elsewhere, Loew warns that love of God should not eclipse awe of God; see *DH*, p. 32.
61 *SSR*, p. 68; *GH*, p. 192; *DH*, pp. 48, 131; *TY*, p. 167; *NY*, p. 13; *BG*, p. 19; *HA*, 3:229, 4:13. See *GA*, 2:126; *NO*, 1:9.
62. *HA*, 2:22.
63 *NO*, 1:31. See Kleinberger (1962), p. 108
64. *NO*, 1:62; see A. Weiss, pp. 188-89, no. 142.
65. See A. Weiss, p. 189. On the basis of this assumption, Loew's philosophy of education assumes the notion of learning as recollection. Though the theory of recollection derives from Plato, Loew's source is the Talmud Nid. 30b. See Kleinberger (1962), p. 102.
66. *DH*, p. 116
67. *TY*, p. 31.
68. *NY*, p. 47; *HA*, 4:158; see *Eulogy*, p. 187; *HA*, 3:165.
69. *NY*, p. 195; see *NY*, p. 20. Loew compares the spark of divinity within man to the presence of the divine within the sanctuary.
70. *DH*, pp. 13, 144-45.
71. *HA*, 2:95; *TY*, p 31.
72. Wolfson (1947), 1:389-95.
73. *PR*, 11:7.
74. The Zohar posited three aspects of the human soul: *nefesh, ruah, neshamah*. The last was considered the most exalted part of the soul. On the Zohar's psychology, see Scholem (1974), pp. 152-65. According to some authorities, only *neshamah* is a spark of God and is even above sin. See also Tishby (1961), 2:3-42.
75. Scholem (1941), p. 406, no. 124.
76. Ibid., p. 241.
77. To Gen. 2:7; Bahya identifies the soul with *hokhmah* while Nahmanides identifies the soul with *binah*.
78. See Scholem (1974), p 175.
79. Neher (1966), p. 17.
80. On this whole issue, see Jacobs (1966), "The Doctrine of the 'Divine Spark' in Man," pp. 87-115, especially p. 111, no. 48.
81. Ibid., p. 105.
82 See discussions of this motif in Jacobs (1966), *Seeker of Unity*, especially pp. 130-33, and (1973), p. 21.
83. *NO*, 2:39.
84. The term "normal mysticism" was coined by M. Kadushin to describe a basic characteristic of rabbinic thought. Utilizing "ordinary, familiar, every-day things and occurrences" to experience God is "normal mysticism." See Kadushin, p. 203.
85. *NO*, 2:35.

86. *DH*, p. 215. This claim may be Loew's attempt to refute what he understood to be the view of the medieval Jewish philosophical tradition which held that philosophy was a way to *devekut*. Loew's position may derive from Albo and indirectly from Crescas, whom Loew did not closely identify with "the philosophers." See Kleinberger (1962), p. 92.
87. Ket. 111b. Loew quotes this source in *BG*, p. 142.
88. *NO*, 1:34.
89. *DH*, p. 34. See *DH*, p. 36, where Loew states that attachment to the scholars is a "branch of the love of God." Since love of God is a means to *devekut*, attachment to scholars is an indirect way to *devekut*.
90. *NO*, 1:42; *HA*, 3:167, 4:105; *DH*, p. 34.
91. *NO*, 1:39.
92. *NO*, 2:193.
93. *NO*, 2:81.
94. *HA*, 3:66-67.
95. *BG*, p. 142.
96. Ibid., p. 144.
97. *SSR*, p. 70.
98. According to Loew, the *zaddik's devekut* has three sources: his own desire to be with God, God's desire to have the *zaddik* with him, and the propriety of the *zaddik's* being with God by his very nature; see *HA*, 1:161.
99. *BG*, p. 122.
100. *GA*, 2:87.
101. *Eulogy*, p. 191.
102. *DH*, p. 222.
103. *GA*, 4:102.
104. See Gottesdiener, p. 302.
105. See *OH*, p. 65.
106. *GA*, 1:155.
107. On human perfection, see, e.g., *SGS*, p. 127; *TY*, p. 13-14; *NO*, 1:63, 203; *HA*, 2:98, 3:182
108. *DH*, p. 194; see *DH*, pp. 20, 124-25; *HA*, 2:43.
109. *NY*, p. 101.
110. *HA*, 2:43. For Loew, *devekut* causes "eternal existence," see *NO*, 2:206; note *BG*, p. 19.
111. See A. Weiss, p. 343.
112. Scholar: *NO*, 2:124-25; *Zaddik*: *OH*, p. 130. See *NY*, p. 103.
113. *NY*, pp. 56, 94-95.

Chapter 12

1. *SOT*, p. 23; *TY*, p. 79. For Loew, time is related to space which signifies matter, change, degeneration. Time and space cannot therefore be eternal. Loew's theory of time has been compared to that of Henri Bergson; see Thieberger, p. 54; Gross (1974), p. 241. Kariv, 1:55, relates Loew's identification of space and time to "modern physics," presumably to relativity theory.
2. This is known as the doctrine of "cosmic cycles" (*shemitot*). See, e.g., Scholem (1974), pp. 116-22.
3. See the discussion in A. Weiss, pp. 330-47.

4. See Scholem (1973), pp. 65-66.
5. *DH*, pp. 219-21; *GH*, pp. 32-35. Also see Neher (1965), 14:291-93; Gross (1974), p. 92.
6. *GA*, 1:80; *SGS*, p. 105; *GH*, p. 103; *DH*, p. 262. See Gross, pp. 86-94.
7. *NY*, pp. 68-70.
8. *GH*, pp. 35-36.
9. *SGS*, p 232; *GH*, p. 45; *NY*, pp. 72-73, 146; *HA*, 1:163, 3:100, 212.
10. *GH*, pp. 53-56; see Gross (1974), pp. 128-29.
11. On Gen. 12:10, 15:12.
12. Ned. 32a.
13. See also PRE, chapter 43; and Bahye ben Asher's commentary to Gen. 12:13.
14. *GH*, p. 56; *NY*, p. 139.
15. *NO*, 1:208-12.
16. *GH*, pp. 38-39.
17. See *NY*, chapters 8-9 for a discussion of the "desert generation."
18. See, e.g., *GH*, p. 191; *NY*, pp. 196-98 Note Gross (1974), pp. 141-42.
19. *GH*, p. 191.
20. *GA*, 2:86-87; *DH*, p. 270.
21. *GA*, 1:27, 158; 2:129; *GH*, pp. 18, 52, 325; *TY*, p. 68; *NM*, p. 8; *HA*, 1:164, 2:82; 4:25. Loew's multivalent use of the term *emza* to describe such things as the Temple, is a perfect illustration of M. Eliade's notion of "the symbolism of the center." For Loew, *emza* may refer to a physical, moral, or metaphysical state, simultaneously. See Eliade (1965), pp. 27-57.
22. *HA*, 2:89.
23. *GA*, 1:27; *HA*, 1:10, 25. See, e.g., Gen. R. 14:8; MT, 92:6; PRE, ch. 11.
24. *DH*, p. 271; *NO*, p. 104; *NY*, p. 21. For medieval sources, see Altmann (1969), pp. 25-26; Malter, pp. 186-88.
25. On Loew's views concerning the king and his function, see *GA*, 1:93; *SSR*, p. 72; *GH*, pp. 20, 71; *DH*, pp. 10, 115, 173, 296; *NO*, 2:13, 169; *TY*, p. 65; *OH*, p. 63; *HA*, 1:2, 93, 2:37, 3:139, 146, 195. Throughout his writings, Loew repeatedly discusses the king's relation to his people. The king is essentially different from his people just as God is from man, just as the human intellect (*seikhel*) is from the human body. "The king differs from the people. He is not similar to other men." The king represents the perfection, the form, the purpose of his people. He unifies them, and directs them. He cares for them and improves them morally The king is the heart of the body–the nation–over which he rules.

   Though Loew's description of the king as the soul of his people and his analogy of the king's rule over his people to God's rule over the world is identical to the description of the monarchy found in the writings of St. Thomas Aquinas, it is doubtful that Loew was aware of Thomas's views; see Gilson, p. 332. Loew's promonarchial attitude may have been derived from his Jewish predecessors who favored monarchial rule both in the present and in the expected messianic future. Loew, however, seems to go further in his praise of the monarchy than his predecessors. There are a number of reasons this may be so. First, as has been noted, he was well aware that the existence and stability of his community [i.e., Prague] depended upon the monarchy. Second, the expulsion of the Jews from Spain had left doubts in Jewish minds concerning the trustworthiness of the monarchy vis-à-vis the Jews. The monarchs of Iberia who expelled and persecuted the Jews had been the same monarchs who employed Jews as counsellors at court. The recent antimonarchist writings of Don Isaac Abravanel, who served as advisor to Ferdinand of Spain, cautioned Jews against seeking their salvation in monarchs. Loew may have been responding to Abravanel's challenge. Loew may have believed that a strong unified promonarchist stance, especially where the Hapsburgs were concerned, could only be to the advantage of his insecure co-religionists.

Loew's assertions concerning the monarchy are representative of the exact position opposed by Abravanel. In his *Commentary to Samuel* (I 8:4-7), Abravanel writes: "All of those commentators [i.e., Maimonides, David Kimhi, Gersonides, Nahmanides] accepted the establishment of the monarchy as the fulfillment of a positive commandment. But I am not of their opinion. . . . Those who have investigated the question [of whether the monarchy is intrinsically necessary] think that this is so and that the relationship of the king to the community is like the relationship of one's heart to one's body and like the relation of creation to God. They believe kingship entails three things: 1. unity and the absence of the relationship [with his subjects]; 2. continuity and the absence of change; 3. absolute power." See Lerner (1972), pp. 215-16; Netanyahu, pp. 150-95.

26   *NY*, pp. 19, 64, 113, 143; *BG*, pp. 67-68.

27.   *GA*, p. 120; *NY*, pp. 19-20; *HA*, 2:99.

28.   *NY*, p. 132. See Gross (1974), p. 190.

29.   *NM*, pp. 7-21; see also *GH*, p. 51; *NY*, chapters 17-18.

30   *NM*, p. 18 On Christendom and later Islam as the Fourth Kingdom, see Cohen (1967), "Esau as a Symbol," pp. 47-48.

31.   Loew does not clearly enunciate this view; nevertheless, it is certainly implied in his work. His veiled language may be for reasons of caution. It would seem that Loew's theory of contradictory opposites would require the triumph of Israel in messianic times to entail the annihilation of its contradictory opposite during historical times; i.e., Esau-Amalek-Christendom. It seems that he views the Messianic Age as one in which Israel will destroy its contradictory opposites and will dwell in its own land while peoples representing its complementary opposites such as Ishmael-Arabia will dwell in their lands Second, Loew's insistence that each of the four kingdoms must pass out of existence before messianic redemption can be accomplished would strongly suggest that Christendom must disappear as history reaches its resolution. For Loew, the very existence of the four kingdoms indicates a flaw in nature which must be eliminated for messianic redemption to commence, see *NM*, pp. 7-8. This would bespeak the elimination of Christendom, represented by the Fourth Kingdom. Finally, Loew specifically notes that Esau; i.e., the Fourth Kingdom, has no portion in the Messianic Age; see also *NY*, p. 152; *OH*, p. 186.

32.   It is interesting that Sabbatean writers found what they considered cryptic references in Loew's writings to the notion that the Messiah would be bound to the world of Islam; see Scholem (1971), p. 98.

33.   *OH*, pp. 58, 60, 124-25. The significance of the role of a woman–Esther–in this redemption is a symbol of the incomplete nature of this specific act of redemption. For Loew, the female element signifies imperfection, incompleteness. Therefore, incomplete redemptions, such as Purim (*OH*, p. 113), and the Exodus (in which Miriam played a role; see *NY*, p 200), must contain a feminine element, signified by the role of a woman. The final redemption, Loew claims, will contain only a masculine element–a masculine Messiah–signifying its total completeness.

34.   *NY*, chapter 4

35.   *GH*, p. 51; *NY*, p. 99, *NM*, p. 11.

36.   *NM*, pp. 19-22.

37.   *NM*, p. 31-32. See chapters 8 and 9 above and chapter 13 below on Loew's position regarding the need for Jews to retain cultural isolation.

38. *GH*, p. 51; *NY*, p. 99.

39. Yom. 9b; Git. 55-56; *NY*, chapter 5; *NO*, 2:211. Also see Gross (1974), pp. 141-44.

40. According to Loew, time was created by God. It functions as a feature of the historical dimension. It is peculiar to "this world" and to matter; it is unrelated to the World to Come, to spiritual entities, or to essences. Time also determines the proper point for the actualization of a given entity in the world; the dialectic of history and the messianic redemption are dependent upon time flowing toward its point of resolution. The process of history requires time to work itself out. Just as everything in the world has its natural place, each entity has its "natural time," the specific moment in history corresponding to its particular realization. Loew writes, "Everything depends upon time. And because this is so, time actualizes everything intended to become actual in the world because everything depends on the time process, everything becomes actual at the proper time"; see *NY*, p. 134. That history will become actual at a specific time is the corollary of Loew's dialectic of history. Messianic redemption must occur at a specific time, i.e., at the end of time. The end, signifying completion, perfection, realization, is the proper time for messianic redemption. See *NY*, p. 188; *HA*, 3:209. It is important to note that, though Loew held this position, he did not attempt to calculate the time of the messianic advent but inveighed against such calculation. For Loew, the Messiah cannot come *before* the "proper time"; however, he need not come *at* the proper time. Whether or not the Messiah comes at the first available juncture depends upon human preparation and receptivity. Though he cannot come before his time, the Messiah may come afterwards, depending upon the state of human preparation for his advent. Loew's notion of a proper time for the Messiah and his opposition to calculating the time for the messianic advent are not, therefore, contradictory.

41. The present position agrees with Gross and not with Thieberger. The latter claims that grace without any action or merit will secure messianic redemption. Thieberger seems to have chosen his data selectively and to have overlooked many textual references. Loew's position on human perfection and social action become all but meaningless once the human element is removed from the messianic drama. Secondly, Loew claims that a "prepared receipient" is required for messianic redemption. It is man's function, in his view, to make the world a prepared recipient for messianic redemption. See Thieberger, p. 69; Gross (1974), pp. 206-10 According to Loew, historical times were divided into three periods of two thousand years each. The proper time for the Messiah to come is at the beginning of the third trimester. This is the first point, before which he cannot come. For Loew, when he comes during that trimester depends upon human action, human preparation of the world for the messianic advent. See especially *NY*, pp. 135-36.

42. See above, chapter 7.

43. *HA*, 3:219.

44. *NY*, p. 178; *HA*, 3:219.

45. *NY*, p. 196.

46. *NY*, chapter 35.

47. *NY*, chapters 35-36; see Gross's discussion (1974), pp. 173-78. The term "birth-pangs of the Messiah" is derived from Hos. 13:13. In the Talmud, see especially Sanh. 97-98. For a good summary of this notion in rabbinic literature, see Klausner, pp. 440-51. The material on the Geonic era is collected by J.E.S. Kaufmann in *Midreshei Geulah*.

48. Saadya, 7:6, pp. 304-12.

49   Maimonides, *MT–Sefer Shofetim*, "Laws of Kings," 11:1-12:3; (1949), pp. 238-41.

50. For Abravanel, see Netanyahu, pp. 195-261. In the thought of many important figures of the Protestant Reformation, the Reformation and messianic expectation were interrelated. With the particular exception of Calvin, many reformers believed their times to be the harbinger of the messianic advent. Roland Bainton, for example, writes, "Here is one of the most significant differences between Calvin and the previous reformers. He rejected their expectation of the speedy coming of the Lord and projected the final cataclysm into an indefinite future. Luther looked wistfully for the end of the age before his own demise and the Anabaptists often set dates." Bainton (1952), p. 114. Luther, like Muentzer, it has been claimed, "performed all his deeds in the conviction that the Last Days were at hand." See Bainton (1952), pp. 42-43; also see Bainton (1950), p. 109. The sufferings of the Anabaptists during the Peasants' War were interpreted as the "Messianic woes" which would usher in the Millennium. See Cohn, p. 254. Servetus also apparently believed the messianic advent was fast approaching, and that it would occur either in 1565 or 1585; see Bainton (1953), pp. 145-47. Some early Anabaptists, such as David Joris, even considered themselves to be messianic figures; see Cohn, pp. 234-81; Bainton (1951), p. 129

51. *NY*, chs. 44-45; *HA*, 1:163. See Gross (1974), pp. 210-21; Kleinberger (1962), p. 74; Silver, pp. 110-30, 231-33.

52. On Loew's *NY* as the culmination of Ashkenazic messianic speculation, see Scholem (1971), p. 33, and (1941), p. 308. Note Scholem's comment (1941), p. 419, no. 43, "Far too little account has been taken in the literature on Messianism of his [i.e., Loew's] great book, *Neẓaḥ Yisrael.*" On the divergent messianic postures of the Ashkenazic and Sefardic communities, see Cohen (1967), "Messianic Postures."

53. The biblical roots for this notion are found in Ezek. 37-39 where "Gog and Magog" first appear. In Talmud, see, e.g., Av. Zar. 3b. In Geonic literature, see J.E.S Kaufmann, *Midreshei Geulah* especially pp. 83, 93. In Geonic literature Gog and Magog are replaced by a monster named "Armilus." No reference to "Armilus" appears in Loew's writings. Also see Jellinek in *Beit Ha-Midrash*, vol. 3; Klausner, pp. 127-32, 483-502.

54. *NY*, chapters 37-38; see Gross (1974), pp. 178-83.

55. The idea of the Messiah ben Joseph first appears in rabbinic literature, see, e.g., Suk. 45b, 52a; Sanh. 97b; Lam. R., II, 2. Note discussion in Klausner, pp. 483-502. In one source, the Messiah ben Joseph is the final Messiah PR, 36:1.

56. See Netanyahu, pp. 228-35

57. See, e.g., PR, chapters 37-38, and Lieberman, pp. 58-59. Note Silver, p. 98. Compare Zohar 2:212a.

58. See Scholem (1973), pp 55, 70.

59. *NY*, ch 53. In biblical literature see Mal. 4:5-6 as the basis for the development of the role of Elijah in later messianic literature. Note discussions of Klausner, pp. 451-58; Friedmann, pp. 2-44.

60. PR, 4:2.

61. On this motif in biblical literature, see Klausner, pp. 15-19. In rabbinic literature, see, e.g., Deut. R. 2:23; YS, "Torah," para. 827, and "Psalms," para. 865. See also Saadya, 8:1, p. 291.

62. *NY*, p. 189

63. According to Loew, everything has its particular "natural place." When all things are in their respective natural places, the natural order is as it should be; if not, the natural order is in disarray. See, e.g., *DM*, p. 122; *TY*, p. 27; *BG*, p. 67. For Loew, each people has its natural place, its particular spot on the globe. The natural place of the people of Israel is the land of Israel. Exile, therefore, represents an unnatural situation for the

people of Israel and for the world. See *GA*, 1:27, 5:27, 136; *NO*, 1:88; *NY*, ch. 24; *BG*, p. 67; *HA*, 4:124; see Scholem (1973), p. 65. Loew's notion of natural place is Aristotelean in origin. Kleinberger suggests Loew's source for this Aristotelean notion was medieval Jewish philosophy, specifically, Maimonides' *Guide of the Perplexed*, 1:71. One may suggest, however, that Loew's use of the idea of natural place to develop a theodicy, i.e , evil means things are not in their natural place, seems more directly derived from the writings of the thirteenth-century kabbalist Joseph Chikatilla; see Scholem (1974), p. 126. On the Aristotelean roots of the notion of "natural place," see Aristotle, *Physics*, Book Delta, note Bokser, pp. 191-92.

On the basis of Loew's discussion of the Land of Israel as the "natural place" of the Jewish people, Loew has been identified as a "Zionist " See, e.g., Buber, pp. 77-89. The claim that Loew was a "Zionist" is anachronistic Furthermore, his views on many issues are very different from those which later were adopted by various Zionist ideologies. Unlike most Zionists, and unlike some of his contemporaries, Judah Loew did not encourage immigration to the Land of Israel; nor did he consider migrating to Israel himself. According to Loew, the people of Israel are fated *not* to be restored in the Land of Israel until messianic times. He therefore would have been more likely to discourage immigration to Israel. Furthermore, he asserts only diasporan existence is proper for Jews in historical times; such is their fate. The centralization of Jews in one geographical area would make them a ripe candidate for complete genocide. Dispersion guarantees their safety. For Loew, the people of Israel is the "form" of the world; it is only proper, therefore, that it be dispersed throughout the width and breadth of the world; see *GH*, p. 265; *NY*, pp. 122, 206. Loew, unlike the Lurianic School, did not expect an immediate messianic advent. Therefore, he, unlike the Lurianic mystics, did not immigrate to the Land of Israel to prepare for the initiation of the Messianic Era.

64. In biblical literature, see Klausner, pp. 5, 15-19.
65. See, e.g., the sermon preached in 1560 at Jerusalem by Solomon of Turiel, published by Scholem (1957), 1:77.
66. See, e.g., Nathan Shapira, *Megaleh Amukot*, "Va-et-ḥanan," quoted in Levin, p.4. Note discussion in Tishby (1963), pp. 134-35.
67. See, e.g.. Aggadat Bereshit, chapter 67; Zohar 1:25b.
68. See Gross (1974), pp. 187-90.
69. Zohar 2:8a
70. See above, chapter 7 end, chapter 8 beginning.
71. *GA*, 1:25; *NY*, pp. 138, 170.
72. *NY*, chapters 37, 41.
73. *HA*, 3:221.
74. *NY*, chapter 42. Loew does not explicitly draw these comparisons between Moses and the Messiah. They are only implicit in a comparison between his discussions of the nature of Moses and his discussions of the nature of the Messiah.
75. *SOT*, p. 49.
76. *HA*, 4:70.
77. *NY*, pp. 185, 188, 226.
78. *HA*, 3:218.
79. *TY*, p. 161. On the question of the eschatological role of the Torah as viewed in early rabbinic literature, see Davies.

Chapter 13

1   In Christian mysticism, see Ozment and Underhill (1920), pp. 25-43; (1915), p. x. In Jewish mysticism, see Scholem (1967), 53:1-24.

2.   Scholem (1967), pp. 13-15; (1965), p. 236.

3.   See Weintraub's discussion of Johann Huizinga's analysis of the late medieval mentality. Weintraub, p. 236.

4.   Loew influenced a number of his younger contemporaries in the field of education, for example, Ephraim Luntshitz, his successor as Chief Rabbi of Prague; Yom Tov Lipmann Ha-Lev Heller, mentioned below; Joseph ben Elhanan Halperin; Issachar Eulenberg, who wrote textbooks under his influence; eminent members of the Horowitz family, a well-established Prague dynasty whose sixteenth-century members such as Isaiah Horowitz, his brother, Jacob, and his son, Sheftel Horowitz, as well as Abraham Horowitz, enriched Jewish mystical and moralistic literature of the age. For literature and discussion, see Assaf, 1:45-72; Fishman, pp. 13, 82, 99, 100, 114; Gottesdiener, pp. 320, 335-36; Kleinberger (1962), pp. 9, 157; Trachtenberg (1939), 11:122; Pollack; Newman, pp. 96-97 Many of the views expressed by Loew in his critique of contemporary Jewish life, specifically on the questions of education and rabbinic leadership, were reiterated by his successor to the position of Chief Rabbi of Prague, Ephraim Luntshitz, see Bettan, pp. 443-81.

    Loew was the first to undertake a systematic inquiry into the education of European Jewry and to protest against its defects. His didactic principles bear startling resemblance to the revolutionary changes advocated by the "realist" reformer-educators of the sixteenth and seventeenth centuries, specifically John Amos Comenius. Though a direct relationship between Loew and contemporary Christian educational policies is possible, it is not probable. On Loew and Comenius, see Kleinberger (1962), especially chapter 9, pp. 156-81; English translation, Kleinberger (1963), 13:32-55; Fishman, p. 87; Stransky, pp. 104-16. Trachtenberg (1939), 11:121, suggests that Loew was influenced by humanists and Protestant reformers in Prague, but adduces no evidence to support the claim. Note the discussion in Berman, pp. 60-68, 94-100

5.   *HA,* 3:138.

6.   For further documentation and elucidation of Loew's model for rabbinic leadership, see the end of chapter 11 above and the sources noted there.

7.   Katz (1961), *Tradition and Crisis,* pp. 86-90, 107-8, 169-75.

8.   E. Roth, p 51, no. 62.

9   *NO,* 1:194.

10.   *DH,* p. 174. On the whole question of a salaried rabbinate, see Reines, 7:84-90, especially the reference to Loew, p 98 Maimonides' position is stated in his *Commentary to the Mishnah-Avot,* 4:5; English translation (1968), pp. 71-79.

11.   *SOC,* p. 63; *DH,* p. 38; *NM,* p. 33; especially *DH,* p. 171.

12.   *DH,* p. 43.

13.   *DH,* pp. 36, 74. Specifically concerning preachers who tell the people what they want to hear and misinterpret sacred texts in their sermons, see *DH,* p. 74; *NO,* p. 195; *BG,* p. 44.

14   *NM,* p. 33.

15.   E.g., see *NO,* 2:198.

16.   *GA,* 5:39-41.

17.   *NO,* 2:12.

18.   See above, chapter 9.

19. The term "Nadler" is apparently a translation of the Hebrew term "shuma," meaning a "birthmark." Gottesdiener, p. 274, no. 11, makes this suggestion based upon Solomon Luria, *Yam Shel Shelomo* "Bava Kama," chapter 8. Luria records a story of a brother and sister, separated at birth, who through a strange series of circumstances are reunited, not knowing they are related, and who then marry. After they have already had children, they notice a common birthmark and establish that they are brother and sister, bound by an incestuous marriage, making their children illegitimate according to Jewish law. From then on, the term "birthmark" (Hebrew: *shuma;* Yiddish: *Nadler*) became an epithet suggesting illegitimacy. See also Isaac Rivkind (1935), 2:60-65. Rivkind's article is entitled "Families of the Dice" because he contends that Nadlerism is connected with gambling. When one dice player was angry at another, he would call him a "Nadler," i.e., a bastard.
20. *SSR*, p. 80.
21. *NO*, 2:81-94.
22. *NO*, 2:82, *NY*, chapters 8 and 9. See Gross (1974), pp. 133-41.
23. *NO,* 2:81.
24. Ibid., 2:84-94.
25. Schochet, 198-99
26. Ibid., p. 15.
27. *Yam Shel Shelomo*, "Kiddushin," 4:7, where Luria rules that he who libels others is himself to be treated as if the libel were true of him; also Luria's *Responsa*, nos. 12, 101.
28. Luria (1969), no. 12.
29. Loew's notion of slander is rooted in Jewish mystical tradition. In kabbalistic literature, slander is equated with the primordial serpent, the personification of evil. Loew notes, for example, that the last letter in *lashon* ("tongue" or "speech") points downward, away from God. It is also at the left of the word *lashon* and in Jewish mysticism "the left side" is synonymous with the demonic. Thus, for Loew slander is a metaphysical and mystical notion and not just a moral one. See A. Weiss, pp 449-55. In kabbalistic literature, see, for example, Zohar, 3:46b-47a.
30. Neher (1965), 14:297
31. *DH*, p. 303.
32. *SOT*, p. 8. On translating "began to think independently" as "since I began to pursue my own mystical way," see Jacobs (1976), p. 154.
33. *SOT*, p. 46; *TY*, pp. 169-70.
34. *NO*, 1:25.
35. *NO*, 1:26; *DH*, p. 305.
36. See Kleinberger (1962), pp. 118-21, 164-68
37. *SOT*, pp. 43-44; *DH*, p. 304.·
38. *SOT*, p. 46.
39. Kleinberger (1973), p. 48.
40. *GA*, 5:40.
41. *TY*, p. 170.
42. *DH*, p. 305.
43. *NO*, 1:24-25. Loew notes that it is an accident of fate that the *tosafot* were printed together with the talmudic text. If some other commentary would have been printed there, it would have been studied too, simply because of a printer's quirk. Loew minimizes the importance of the *tosafot* See also *BG*, p. 93; compare *GH*, p. 194.
44. *DH*, p. 305
45. *SOT*, p. 46.

46. *SOT*, p. 47; *DH*, p. 305; *TY*, p. 169.
47. Kleinberger (1962), p. 148, no. 92. See also Suler, 7:411-20.
48. *GA*, 5:40; *SOT*, pp. 46-47
49. *TY*, p. 171.
50. Kleinberger (1963), p. 52.
51. Loew considered the study of grammar essential in order for one to be able to understand the literal meaning of a text. However, he rebuked those who obscure the ideational content and message of a text by their overzealous morphological critiques of individual words. See *BG*, p 47. Note Kleinberger (1962), pp. 146-47. Furthermore, while Loew favored the study of grammar, he did not agree with the practice of the "grammarians" to make emendations in sacred texts on the basis of their grammatical analysis. Such emendations, or corrections, assume the Torah is flawed, an assumption Loew would not admit; see *TY*, p. 198. Loew also opposed the claim that the Sefardic pronunciation of Hebrew is grammatically superior to the Ashkenazic pronunciation. For Loew, tradition is the final standard, not grammar. See *TY*, pp. 201-204. Knowledge of Hebrew grammar amongst Jewish scholars reached such a low ebb in Loew's time that Christian Hebraists mocked Jewish scholars for their ungrammatical manner of writing Hebrew. Loew's brother, Hayyim of Friedberg, was also an advocate of grammatical study and wrote a textbook for the study of Hebrew grammar. See Sherwin (1975), 37:42-43.
52. For Loew's views on the importance of the Mishnah, see *GA*, 5:40, 66; *SOT*, p. 43-44; *SOC*, p. 54; *SGS*, p. 228; *DH*, p. 303. *NO*, 1:44, 2:247; *HA*, 2:67. See Heller, "Introduction."
53. For Loew's negative views on counterproductive *"Pilpul,"* see *GA*, 5:40; *SOT*, pp. 43-47; *SOC*, p. 53; *SGS*, p. 228; *NO*, 1:54, 2:236; *DH*, pp. 22, 303; *TY*, p. 168-71; *HA*, 3:226. On "good" or "true *pilpul,"* see *SOT*, p 42; *NO*, 1:26, 54; 2:248; *DH*, pp. 297, 305; *TY*, p. 171; *BG*, p. 50; *HA*, 2:13, 3:40, 144. Note Kleinberger (1962), pp. 136-43.
54. *NO*, 1:54; 2:248; *HA*, 3:144.
55. *SOT*, p. 46
56. For Loew's views on the codes, see *SOT*, p 48; *DH*, p. 305; *TY*, p. 170, and especially *NO*, 1:69. Note Kleinberger (1962), pp. 100, 132-35, 145. For Loew's brother's views, see Sherwin (1975), pp. 43-47. The following literature concerning the publication of the *SA* and the reaction to it by contemporary scholars may be consulted with profit: Tchernowitz, vol. 3; Cahana, pp 89-96; Twersky, 16:141-59; Ziev, pp. 286-96.
57. On Ganz and Loew, see Neher (1974).
58. See especially Grün.
59. *HA*, 4:85.
60. *NO*, 1:60.
61. *NO*, 1:61.
62. See Kleinberger (1962), p. 81, and Neher (1977), pp 211-27.
63. *BG*, p. 114. See also *TY*, p. 39. Loew's anticipation of Kant has already been noted by Neher (1966), p. 120, and Weiss, pp. 181-81.
64. *NO*, 1:60.
65. Heinrich Graetz, for example.
66. See Baron (1927), pp. 12-52, especially p. 21. Note the following discussions of dei Rossi's views: C. Roth, pp. 318-29; Shulvass, pp. 253-58. On Loew's critique of dei Rossi, see Neher (1966), pp. 98-119.
67. *GH*, pp 6-17. Note *DH*, p. 232 (against Maimonides' theory of miracles); *BG*, pp. 106-12.
68. Dei Rossi, 1:15, 27-28, 57-59.

69. *NO*, 1:61.
70. *BG*, pp. 126-41. See also *NY*, p. 35; *HA*, 2:108.
71. Maimonides (1963), 3:43, pp. 572-73
72. Elbaum, 22:32-35.
73. *BG*, p. 86. See Elbaum, 22:35-45
74. *BG*, p. 23.
75. *BG*, p. 87. See also *DH*, p. 77; *NY*, p. 47.
76. Elbaum, p. 39.

Bibliography

1. Primary Sources — The Writings of Judah Loew

Loew, Judah ben Bezalel. *Gur Aryeh* (GA). 5 vols., Prague, 1578; Bnai Brak, 1972.

——. *Gevurot Ha-Shem* (GH). Cracow, 1582; *Kol Sifrei Maharal Mi-Prag,* vol. 3, New York, 1969. English translation (of introductions) by Shlomo Mallin, *Book of Divine Power: Introductions,* New York, 1975.

——. *Derekh Ha-Ḥayyim* (DH). Prague, 1589; *Kol Sifrei Maharal Mi-Prag,* vol. 2, New York, 1969.

——. *Be'er Ha-Golah* (BG). Prague, 1598; *Kol Sifrei Maharal Mi-Prag,* vol. 4, New York, 1969.

——. *Hesped* (Eulogy). Prague, 1598; *Gur Aryeh,* vol. 4, Bnai Brak, 1972.

——. *Netivot Olam* (NO). Prague, 1595; *Kol Sifrei Maharal Mi-Prag,* vols. 7 and 8, New York, 1969.

——. *Neẓaḥ Yisrael* (NY). Prague, 1599; *Kol Sifrei Maharal Mi-Prag,* vol. 6, New York, 1969.

——. *Tiferet Yisrael* (TY). Venice, 1599; *Kol Sifrei Maharal Mi-Prag,* vol. 5, New York, 1969.

——. *Or Ḥadash—Ner Miẓvah.* Prague, 1600; Bnai Brak, 1972.

——. *Ḥidushim L'Arba'ah Turim.* Fürth, 1775.

——. *Ḥidushei Gur Aryeh Al Shabbat, Eruvin, Pesaḥim.* Lemberg, 1862.

——. *Ḥidushim L'Arba'ah Turim—Even Ha-Ezer.* Jerusalem, 1955.

——. *Perushei Maharal Mi-Prag.* Edited by M. Kasher. 4 vols., Jerusalem, 1958.

——. *Kitve Maharal Mi-Prag.* Edited by A. Kariv. Jerusalem, 1960.

——. *Sefer Derashot Maharal Mi-Prag.* Edited by M. Kasher. Jerusalem, 1968.

——. *Derashot; Kol Sifrei Maharal Mi-Prag,* vol. 4, New York, 1969.

——. *Hagadah Shel Pesaḥ (Kol Sifrei Ha-Maharal Mi-Prag,* vol. 3). New York, 1969.

——. *Ḥidushei Aggadot* (HA). 4 vols.; *Kol Sifrei Ha-Maharal Mi-Prag*, vols. 9-12, New York, 1969.

——. *Kol Sifrei Maharal Mi-Prag.* 12 vols., New York, 1969.

2. Other Primary Sources

Albo, Joseph. *Sefer Ha-Ikkarim.* Edited by I. Husik. 6 vols., Philadelphia, 1946.

Aristotle. *Physics.* English translation by R. Hope. Lincoln, Nebraska, 1961.

——. *Nicomachean Ethics* (Ethics). English translation by M. Ostwald. New York, 1962.

Araten, I. J. *Emet v'Emunah.* 3rd ed., Jerusalem, 1969.

Ashkenazi, Eliezer. *Ma'aseh Ha-Shem.* 1583; reprint, New York, 1962.

——. *Damesek Eliezer.* Piotrkov, 1905.

Ashkenazi, Zevi. *She'elot U'Teshuvot.* Amsterdam, 1812.

Avot De-Rabbi Nathan. Edited by S. Schechter. Vienna, 1887; English translation by Judah Goldin. *The Fathers According to Rabbi Nathan.* New Haven, 1955.

Babylonian Talmud. Vilna, various dates; English translation edited by I. Epstein. London, 1948-52.

Bachrach, Yair. *Ḥavvot Yair.* Frankfurt 1699.

Bahye ben Asher. *Al Ha-Torah.* Edited by C. Chavel. 3 vols., Jerusalem, 1968.

Beit Ha-Midrash. Edited by A. Jellinek. 2 vols., 2nd ed., Jerusalem, 1967.

Batei Midrashot. Edited by A. Wertheimer. 2 vols., 2nd ed., Jerusalem, 1958.

Cordovero, Moses. *Tomer Devorah.* Venice, 1588; English translation by Louis Jacobs. *The Palm Tree of Deborah.* London, 1960.

——. *Pardes Rimonim.* Salonika, 1584.

dei Rossi, Azariah, *Sefer Me'or Enayim.* Edited by D. Cassel. Berlin, 1866.

Ganz, David. *Ẓemaḥ David.* Prague, 1592; reprint ed., Jerusalem, 1966.

Hayot, Isaac. *P'nei Yiẓḥak.* Cracow, 1591.

Hayyim ben Bezalel. *Vikuaḥ Mayim Ḥayyim.* 1712.

——. *Be'er Mayim Ḥayyim.* 3 vols., London, 1964.

Hegel, G. W. F. *The Phenomenology of Mind.* English translation by J. B. Baillie. New York, 1967.

Heller, Yom Tov Lipmann. *Tosfot Yom Tov.* Cracow, 1644.

The Holy Scriptures. Philadelphia, 1917.

Ibn Gabbai, Meir. *Avodat Ha-Kodesh.* Venice, 1567.

Ibn Zaddik, Joseph. *Sefer Ha-Olam Ha-Katan.* Hebrew translation by Moses Ibn Tibbon. Leipzig, 1854.

Iggeret Ha-Kodesh (author unknown, traditionally ascribed by Moses ben Nahman). Rome, 1546; English translation by S. J. Cohen. *The Holy Letter.* New York, 1976.

Israel of Koznitz. *Sefer Geulat Yisrael.* Warsaw, 1865.

Isserles, Moses. *Torat Ha-Ḥatat.* Cracow, 1569.

——. *Torat Ha-Olah.* Lwow, 1858.

——. *She'elot U-Teshuvot.* Edited by A. Ziev. Jerusalem, 1971.

Jacob ben Asher. *Arba'ah Turim.* Vilna, 1900.

Jacob Joseph of Polnoye. *Toledot Yaakov Yosef.* Korets, 1780.

Jerusalem Talmud. Krotoschin, 1886.

Judah ben Samuel Ha-Levi. *Kuzari.* Hebrew translation by Judah Ibn Tibbon. Venice, 1547; English translation by H. Hirschfeld. London, 1905.

Karo, Joseph. *Shulḥan Arukh.* Vilna, 1911.

Levi Ben Gerson (Gersonides). *Perush Al Ha-Torah.* Mantua, 1475.

——. *Milḥamot Ha-Shem.* 2nd ed., Leipzig, 1866.

——. *Commentary on Job.* English translation by A. Lassen. New York, 1946.

Luria, Solomon. *Yam Shel Shelomoh—Bava Kamma.* Prague, 1616.

——. *Yam Shel Shelomoh—Ḥullin.* Cracow, 1633.

——. *Yam Shel Shelomoh—Beẓah.* Lublin, 1636.

——. *Yam Shel Shelomoh—Yevamot.* Altona, 1740.

——. *Yam Shel Shelomoh—Gittin.* Berlin, 1761.

——. *Yam Shel Shelomoh—Kiddushin.* Berlin, 1766.

——. *Yam Shel Shelomoh—Ketuvot.* Warsaw, 1850.

——. *She'elot U'Teshuvot.* 7th ed., Jerusalem, 1969.

Ma'arekhet Ha-Elohut. Mantua, 1558.

Midrash Aggadot Bereshit. Vilna, 1802.

Midrash Rabbah. Venice, 1545; English translation by H. Freedman and M. Simon. 10 vols., London, 1939.

Midrash Tanhuma. Edited by S. Buber. 2 vols., Vilna, 1885.

Midrash Tehillim (MT). Edited by S. Buber. Vilna, 1891; English translation by W. G. Braude. New Haven, Conn., 1959.

Midreshei Geulah. Edited by J. E. S. Kaufmann. Jerusalem, 1954.

Mishnah. Various editions; English translation, H. Danby. Oxford, 1933.

Moses ben Maimon (Maimonides). *Mishneh Torah* (MT). Various editions.

——. *Mishneh Torah—Sefer Shofetim.* English translation by A. M. Hershman. *The Book of Judges.* New Haven, Conn., 1949.

——. *Mishnah im Peirush Ha-Rambam* (CM). Hebrew translation by J. Kafih. 3 vols., Jerusalem; vol. 1, 1963; vol. 2, 1964, vol. 3, 1967; English translation of *CM-Avot, The Commentary to Mishnah Aboth* by A. David. New York, 1968.

——. *Moreh Nevuḥim* (Guide). English translation by S. Pines. *Guide of the Perplexed.* Chicago, 1963.

——. *Sefer Ha-Miẓvot* (SM). English translation by C. Chavel. 2 vols., New York, 1967.

Moses ben Nahman (Nachmanides). *Peirush Al Ha-Torah.* 2 vols., Jerusalem, 1969.

Pesikta D'Rav Kahana. Lyck, 1868; English translation by W. G. Braude and I. J. Kapstein, London, 1975.

Pirke De-Rabbi Eliezer (PRE). Venice, 1608; English translation by Gerald Friedlander. London, 1916.

Pesikta Rabbati (PR). Prague, 1654; English translation by W. G. Braude, London, 1968.

Saadya Gaon. *Book of Beliefs and Opinions.* English translation by S. Rosenblatt. New Haven, 1948.

Samuel of Shinow. *Ramatayim Ẓofim.* Jerusalem, 1963.

Schreiber, M. *She'elot U'Teshuvot Ḥatam Sofer.* Vienna, 1885.

Seder Eliahu Rabba-Seder Eliahu Zutta. Edited by M. Friedmann. Vienna, 1904.

Sefer Teshuvot Geonim. Prague, 1597.

Shalom, Abraham. *Neve Shalom.* Venice, 1575; reprint ed., Jerusalem, 1967.

She'elot U'Teshuvot Ha-Geonim Batrei. Turka, 1764; Prague, 1816.

Sifre on Deuteronomy. Edited by L. Finkelstein, Berlin, 1939; New York, 1969.

Sirkes, Joel. *Bayit Ḥadash.* Frankfurt, 1697.

Yalkut Shimoni (YS). Cracow, 1595.

Zohar. Vilna, 1882; partial English translation by H. Sperling and M. Simon. 5 vols., London, 1933; selections in English translation by G. Scholem. *Zohar: Book of Splendor.* New York, 1949.

3. Secondary Sources

Alfasi, I. *Ha-Rav Mi-Kotzk*. Tel Aviv, 1952.

Altmann, A. "Torat Ha-Aklimim L'Rabbi Yehudah Ha-Levi." *Melilah* (1944), 1:1-17.

——. *Leo Baeck and the Jewish Mystical Tradition*. New York, 1973.

——, ed. *Studies in Religious Philosophy and Mysticism*. Ithaca, 1969.

Ashkenazi, L. "Nature, Société et Liberté d'après le Maharal de Prague." *Targoum* (1954), 5:432-39.

Assaf, S., ed. *Mekorot L'Toledot Ha-Hinukh Be-Yisrael*. 4 vols., Tel Aviv, 1954.

Azulai, H. D. *Ma'arekhet Gedolim*. 2nd ed., Jerusalem, 1967.

Baeck, L. *This People Israel*. English translation by A. H. Friedlander. Philadelphia, 1965.

Bainton, R. *Here I Stand*. Nashville, 1950.

——. *The Travail of Religious Liberty*. Philadelphia, 1951.

——. *The Reformation of the Sixteenth Century*. Boston, 1952.

——. *Hunted Heretic*. Boston, 1953.

Bamberger, B. "Fear and Love of God in the Old Testament." *Hebrew Union College Annual* 6:39-55.

Baron, S. W. "Azariah de Rossi's Attitude to Life." *Jewish Studies in Memory of Israel Abrahams*. Edited by A. Kohut. New York, 1927.

——. *The Jewish Community*. 3 vols., Philadelphia, 1945.

——. *A Social and Religious History of the Jews*. 12 vols., New York, 1969.

Barzilay, I. *Between Reason and Faith: Anti-Rationalism in Italian Jewish Thought*. Paris, 1967.

——. *Shlomo Yehudah Rapoport and His Contemporaries*. Israel, 1969.

Ben-Sasson, H. H. *Hagut Ve-Hanhaga*. Jerusalem, 1959.

——. *The Reformation in Jewish Eyes*. Jerusalem, 1970.

Ben-Shlomo, J. *Torat Ha-Elohut Shel R. Moshe Cordovero*. Jerusalem, 1965.

Bergman, S. H. "Prague." *Keneset* (1942-44), 8:110-18.

Berman, A. *Toledot Ha-Ḥinukh*. Tel Aviv, 1968.

Bettan, I. "Ephraim Luntshitz: Champion of Change." *Hebrew Union College Annual* (1931-32), 9-10: 443-81.

Bin Gorion, Emanuel, editor. *Mimekor Yisrael: Classical Jewish Folktales*. 3 vols., Philadelphia, 1976.

Bleich, J.D. *Providence in the Philosophy of Gersonides*. New York, 1973.

Bloch, C. *Der Prager Golem.* Berlin, 1920. English translation by H. Schneiderman. Vienna, 1925.

Bokser, B. Z. *From the World of the Cabbalah: The Philosophy of Rabbi Judah Loew of Prague.* New York, 1954.

Borges, J. L. "The Golem." *A Personal Anthology.* New York, 1967.

Braude, W. G. *Jewish Proselyting* [sic] *in the First Five Centuries of the Common Era.* Providence, 1940.

Brod, M. *Tycho Brache's Weg Zu Gott.* Munich, 1915.

Buber, M. *On Zion: The History of an Idea.* English translation by Stanley Goodman. New York, 1973.

Büchler, A. *Studies in Sin and Atonement.* 2nd ed., New York, 1967.

Cahana, I. Z. *Meḥkarim Be-Sifrut Ha-Teshuvot.* Jerusalem, 1973.

Chavel, C. B. *Rabbi Moshe ben Nahman.* Jerusalem, 1967.

Chone, H. "Sod Ha-Devekut Eẓel Ha-Ramban." *Sinai* (1942-43), 11:86-99.

Cohen, G. D. "Esau as Symbol in Early Medieval Thought." *Jewish Medieval and Renaissance Studies.* Edited by A. Altmann. Cambridge, Mass., 1967.

——. "Messianic Postures of Ashkenazim and Sefardim." *Leo Baeck Memorial Lecture No. 9.* New York, 1967.

Cohn, N. *The Pursuit of the Millennium,* New York, 1961.

Collectio Davidis. Hamburg, 1826.

Davidson, H. A. *The Philosophy of Abraham Shalom.* Berkeley, 1964.

——. "The Study of Philosophy as a Religious Obligation." In *Religion in a Religious Age.* Edited by S. D. Goitein. Cambridge, Mass., 1974.

Davies, W. D. *Torah in the Messianic Age and/or the Age to Come.* Philadelphia, 1952.

Dresner, S. H. *The Zaddik.* New York, 1960.

Dreyfus, T. *Dieu Parle aux Hommes.* Paris, 1969.

Eichrodt, W. *Man in the Old Testament.* Chicago, 1951.

Eisenstein, J. D. *Oẓar Dinim U-Minhagim.* New York, 1938.

Elbaum, J. "Rabbi Judah Loew of Prague and His Attitude to the Aggadah." *Scripta Hierosolymitana* (1971), 22:28-48.

Eliade, M. *The Myth of Eternal Return.* English translation by W. R. Trask. Princeton, 1965.

——. *Images and Symbols.* English translation by P. Mairet. New York, 1969.

Encyclopedia Judaica. Jerusalem, 1972.

Evans, R. J. W. *Rudolf II and His World.* Oxford, 1973.

Finkelstein, L. *Jewish Self-Government in the Middle Ages.* New York, 1964.

Fishman, I. *The History of Jewish Education in Central Europe from the End of the Sixteenth Century to the End of the Eighteenth Century.* London, 1964.

Flesch, H. "Anmerkungen zur Geschichte der Mahrischen Landesrabbiner." In *Die Juden und Judengemeinden Mahrens in Vergangenheit und Gegenwart.* Edited by H. Gold. Brünn, 1929.

——. "Geschichte der Juden in Kanitz." In *Die Juden und Judengemeinden Mahrens in Vergangenheit und Gegenwart.* Edited by H. Gold, Brünn, 1929.

Fox, J. *Rabbi Menaḥem Mendel of Kotzk.* Jerusalem, 1960.

Friedberg, H. B. *Bet Eked Sepharim.* 4 vols., 2nd ed., Tel Aviv, 1951.

Friedlander, M. H. *Kore Ha-Dorot: Beiträge zur Geschichte der Juden in Mahren.* Brünn, 1876.

Gilson, E. *The Christian Philosophy of Saint Thomas Aquinas.* English translation by L. K. Shook, New York, 1956.

Ginzberg, L. *The Legends of the Jews.* 7 vols., 2nd ed., Philadelphia, 1938.

Gold, H., ed. *Die Juden und Judengemeinden Mahrens in Vergangenheit und Gegenwart.* Brünn, 1929.

Goldin, J. "The First Chapter of *Abot de Rabbi Nathan.*" In *Mordecai M. Kaplan Jubilee Volume.* Edited by Moshe Davis. New York, 1953.

Goldschmied, L. "Geschichte der Juden in Prossnitz." In *Die Juden und Judengemeinden Mahrens in Vergangenheit und Gegenwart.* Brünn, 1929.

Gottesdiener, A. "Ha-Ari She-be-Ḥakhme Prag." *Azkara,* vol. 3. Edited by J. L. Fishman. Jerusalem, 1937.

Graetz, Ḥ. *Geschichte der Juden.* 11 vols., Leipzig, 1891.

Gross, B. *Le Messianisme Juif.* Paris, 1969; *Neẓaḥ Yisrael,* Tel Aviv, 1974.

Grün, N. *Der Hohe R. Löw und sein Sagenkreis.* Prague, 1885.

Guttmann, J. *Dat U-Mada.* Hebrew translation by S. Esh. Jerusalem, 1955.

——. *Philosophies of Judaism.* English translation by D. W. Silverman. New York, 1964.

Halevi Pardes, H. *Derekh Ḥayyim—Peirush L'Masekhet Avot—Ha-Maharal.* Tel Aviv, 1975.

Halperin, I., ed. *Takkanot Medinat Mahren 1650-1748.* Jerusalem, 1952.

Harris, M. "Marriage as Metaphysics: A Study of the *Iggereth Ha-Kodesh.*" *Hebrew Union College Annual* (1962), 33:197-221.

Heinemann, I. *Ta'amei Ha-Mizvot be'Sifrut Yisrael.* 2 vols., Jerusalem, 1942.

Heschel, A. J. "The Mystical Element in Judaism." In *The Jews: Their History, Culture and Religion.* Edited by L. Finkelstein. Philadelphia, 1949.

——. "The Concept of Man in Jewish Thought." In *The Concept of Man.* Edited by S. Radhakrishnan and P. Raju. London, 1960.

——. *Torah min Ha-Shamayim.* 2 vols., New York, vol. 1, 1962; vol. 2, 1965.

——. *God in Search of Man.* New York, 1966.

——. *Kotsk.* 2 vols., New York, 1973.

——. *A Passion for Truth.* New York, 1973.

Horodetzky, S. A. *Ha-Mistorin B'Yisrael.* 4 vols., Tel Aviv, 1961.

Horovitz, M. *Rabbanei Frankfurt.* Hebrew translation by J. Amir. Jerusalem, 1972.

Husik, I. *A History of Medieval Jewish Philosophy.* Philadelphia, 1940.

Inge, W. R. *Christian Mysticism.* London, 1899.

Ish Kishor, S. *The Master of Miracle.* New York, 1971.

Jacobs, L. "The Doctrine of the 'Divine Spark' in Man in Jewish Sources." In *Studies in Rationalism, Judaism and Universalism.* Edited by R. Loewe. London, 1966.

——. *Seeker of Unity.* New York, 1966.

——. *Hasidic Prayer.* London, 1973.

——. *Theology in the Responsa.* London, 1975.

——. *Jewish Mystical Testimonies.* New York, 1977.

Jerábek, L. *Der Alte Prager Judenfriedhof.* Prague, 1903.

Jones, R. *Studies in Mystical Religion.* London, 1909.

Kadushin, M. *The Rabbinic Mind.* New York, 1952.

Kahana, I. Z., ed. *Sefer Aggunot.* Jerusalem, 1954.

Kahane, J. S. "Ha-Maharal B'Moravia." *Ba-Mishor* (1941), pp. 11-12.

Kamelhar, M. "Rabbi Avidgor Kara." *Sinai* (1940), 5:122-48.

Katz, D. *Tenuat Ha-Musar.* 4 vols., Tel Aviv, 1952.

Katz, J. *Exclusiveness and Tolerance.* New York, 1961.

Kaufman, D. "Rabbi Jair Chaim Bacharach." *Jewish Quarterly Review* (Old Series, 1891), 3:292-313, 485-536.

Kaufmann, J. *Rabbi Yom Tov Lipman Mulhausen.* New York, 1927.

Kellner, M. M. "Gersonides, Providence and the Rabbinic Tradition." *Journal of the American Academy of Religion* (1974), 42:673-86.

Kisch, G. "Linguistic Conditions Among Czechoslovak Jewry." *Historica Judaica* (1946), 8:19-32.

——, ed. *The Jews of Czechoslovakia,* vol. 1. Philadelphia, 1968.

Klausner, J. *The Messianic Idea in Israel.* English translation by W. F. Stinespring. New York, 1955.

Kleinberger, A. F. *Ha-Maḥashavah Ha-Pedagogit Shel Ha-Maharal Mi-Prag.* Jerusalem, 1962.

——. "The Didactics of R. Loew of Prague." *Scripta Hieroslymitana* (1963), 13:32-55.

Klemperer, G. "The Rabbis of Prague." *Historica Judaica* (1950), 12:33-66, 143-52; (1951), 13:55-82.

Kohen-Yashar, J. "Bibliografia Shimushit Shel Kitve Ha-Maharal." *Ha-Ma'ayan* (1967), 7:66-71.

Kolitz, Z., ed. *Yahadut Tchekoslovakia,* Jerusalem, 1959.

Kon, A. *Siaḥ Tefilah.* Jerusalem, 1964; English translation *Prayer,* London, 1971.

Landshuth, E. L. *Amudei Ha-Avodah.* Berlin, 1857; 2nd American ed., New York, 1965.

Langer, J. *Nine Gates.* English translation by S. Jolly. London, 1961.

Lerner, R. "Natural Law in Albo's *Book of Roots.*" In *Ancients and Moderns.* Edited by J. Cropsey. New York, 1964.

——. "Moses Maimonides." In *History of Political Philosophy.* Edited by L. Strauss and J. Cropsey. Chicago, 1972.

Levine, N. H. *Gevurot Ari.* Warsaw, 1864.

——. *Kol Demamah Daka.* Piotrkov, 1905.

Lieben, K. *Gal-Ed.* Prague, 1856.

Lieberman, S. *Shki'in.* Jerusalem, 1970.

Lion, J., and Lukas, J. *Das Prage Ghetto.* Prague, 1959.

Lipshitz, A. M. "Ha-Rav." In *Azkara,* vol. 1. Edited by J. L. Fishman. Jerusalem, 1937.

Malter, H. *Saadya Gaon.* Philadelphia, 1926.

Markus, A. *Ha-Ḥasidut.* Hebrew translation by M. Sheinfeld. Tel Aviv, 1954.

Mauskopf, A. *The Religious Philosophy of the Maharal of Prague.* 1949; 2nd ed., 1973.

Meyrink, G. *The Golem.* English translation by M. Pemberton. New York, 1928.

Michael, H. J. *Or Ha-Ḥayyim.* Frankfurt, 1891; 2nd American edition, 1965.

Moore, G. F. *Judaism in the First Centuries of the Christian Era.* 3 vols., Cambridge, Mass., 1927.

Muneles, O. *Bibliographical Survey of Jewish Prague.* Prague, 1952.

——, ed. *Prague Ghetto in the Renaissance Period.* Prague, 1965.

Neher, A. "The Humanism of the Maharal of Prague." *Judaism* (1965), 14:290-305.

——. *Le Puits de l'Exil.* Paris, 1966.

——. *David Ganz.* Paris, 1974.

——. "Copernicus in Hebrew Literature, Sixteenth to Eighteenth Century." *Journal of the History of Ideas* (April-June 1977), 38:211-227.

Netanyahu, B. Z. *Don Isaac Abravanel.* Philadelphia, 1953.

Newman, E. *Life and Teachings of Isaiah Horowitz.* London, 1972.

Ozment, S. *Mysticism and Dissent.* New Haven, 1973.

Perles, J. "Geschichte der Juden in Posen." *Monatsschriften für Geschichte und Wissenschaft des Judentums* (1864), 13:361-73.

Perles, M. *Megilat Yuḥasin.* Prague, 1864; German translation by S. H. Leiben. "Megillath Juchassin Maharal Mi-Prag." *Jahrbuch der Jüdisch-Literarischen Gesellschaft* (1929), 20:315-36.

Pollack, H. *Jewish Folkways in Germanic Lands, 1648-1806.* Cambridge, Mass., 1971.

Rabinowicz, H. M. *The World of Hasidism.* London, 1970.

Rabinowitsch, W. Z. *Lithuanian Hasidism.* English translation by M. B. Dagut. New York, 1971.

Rabinowitz, Z. M. *Rabbi Simḥa Bunam Mi-Przysucha.* Tel Aviv, 1944.

——. *Ha-Maggid Mi-Koznitz.* Tel Aviv, 1947.

Rawidowicz, S. *Studies in Jewish Thought.* English translation by B. Ravid. Philadelphia, 1974.

Reines, C. W. "Public Support of Rabbis, Scholars and Students in the Jewish Past." *YIVO Annual of Jewish Social Studies* (1952), 7:84-90.

Ringgren, H. *Israelite Religion.* Philadephia, 1966.

Rivkind, I. "Mishpetei Kubyustusim." *Horeb* (1935), 2:60-65.

——. *L'Ot U'L'Zikaron.* New York, 1942.

Rosenbluth, P. "Ha-Maharal V'Rav Kook." *Proceedings of the Fifth World Congress of Jewish Studies,* vol. 3. Jerusalem, 1969.

Rosenfeld, A. "Human Identity: Halakhic Issues." *Tradition* (1977), 16:3, pp. 58-75.

Rosenfeld, B. *Die Golemsage und ihr Verwertung in der deutschen Literatur.* Breslau, 1934.

Roth, C. *The Jews in the Renaissance.* Philadephia, 1959.

Roth, E., ed. *Sefer Takkanot Nikolsburg.* Jerusalem, 1962.

Rothberg, A. *The Sword of the Golem.* New York, 1971.

Samuelson, N. "On Knowing God: Maimonides, Gersonides and the Philosophy of Religion." *Judaism* (1969), 18:64-78.

——. "Philosophic and Religious Authority in the Thought of Maimonides and Gersonides." *Central Conference of American Rabbis Journal* (1969), 16:30-44.

Sarashohn, E. *Nishmat Hayyim.* Jerusalem, 1961.

Sassoon, D. *Ohel David: A Descriptive Catalogue of Hebrew and Samaritan Manuscripts in the Sassoon Library.* 2 vols., Oxford, 1932.

Schechter, S. *Aspects of Rabbinic Theology.* New York, 1961.

Schneersohn, J. *Lubavitcher Rabbi's Memoirs,* vol. 2. New York, 1966.

Schochet, E. J. *Bach: Rabbi Joel Sirkes.* New York, 1971.

Scholem, G. "Notes." *Kiryat Sefer* (1924), 1:1-10.

——. "Hitpathut Torat Ha-Olamot Be-Kabbalat Ha-Rishonim." *Tarbitz* (1931), 2:415-92.

——. *Major Trends in Jewish Mysticism.* New York, 1941.

——. "Notes." *Kiryat Sefer* (1945), 21:179-86.

——. *Reshit Ha-Kabbalah.* Jerusalem, 1948.

——. "Derush Al Ha-Ge'ulah." *Sefunot* (1957), 1:62-80.

——. *On the Kabbalah and Its Symbolism.* English translation by R. Manheim. New York, 1965.

——. "Mysticism and Society." *Diogenes* (1967), 53:1-24.

——. *Shabtai Zevi.* 2 vols., Tel Aviv, 1957; English translation by R. J. Z. Werblowsky. *Sabbatai Sevi: The Mystical Messiah.* London, 1973.

——. *Kabbalah.* New York, 1974.

Schwenger, H. "Geschichte der Juden in Ludenberg." In *Die Juden und Judengemeinden Mahrens in Vergangenheit und Gegenwart.* Edited by H. Gold. 1929.

Sheinfeld, M., ed. *Emet Mi-Kotzk Tizmah.* Bnai Brak, 1961.

Sherwin, B.L. "Moses Maimonides on the Perfection of the Body." *Listening* (1974), 9:28-38.

——. "In the Shadows of Greatness: Rabbi Hayyim ben Betsalel of Friedberg." *Jewish Social Studies* (1975), 37:35-61.

Shulvass, M. A. *The Jews in the World of the Renaissance.* English translation by E. Kose. Leiden, 1973.

Siah Sarfei Kodesh. Lodz, 1928-31.

Silver, A. H. *A History of Messianic Speculation in Israel.* Boston, 1959.

Stein, A. *Die Geschichte der Juden in Böhmen.* Brünn, 1904.

Steinhartz, S. "Gerush Ha-Yehudim Mi-Behm Bi'Shnat 1541." *Zion* (1950), 15:70-92.

——, ed. *Die Juden in Prag.* Prague, 1927.

Steinschneider, M. *Catalogus librorum Hebraeorum in Bibliotheca Bodleiana.* Berlin, 1852-60.

Stern, S. *Josel of Rosheim.* Philadelphia, 1965.

Stransky, H. "Rabbi Judah Loew of Prague and J. A. Comenius–Two Reformers in Education." *Comenius.* New York, 1972.

Suler, B. "Ein Maimonides-streit in Prague im 16 Jahrhundert." *Jahrbuch der Gesellschaft für Geschichte der Juden in der Czechoslovakischen Republik* (1935), 7:411-20.

Tchernowitz, H. *Toledot Ha-Poskim.* 3 vols., New York, 1946-47.

Teeple, H. *The Mosaic Eschatological Prophet.* Philadelphia, 1957.

Thieberger, F. *The Great Rabbi Loew of Prague.* London, 1955.

Thomson, S. H. *Czechoslovakia in European History.* Princeton, 1953.

Tishby, I. *Torat Ha-Ra Ve-Ha-Klipot B'Kabalat Ha-Ari.* Jerusalem, 1963.

——. *Mishnat Ha-Zohar.* 2 vols., Jerusalem, vol. 1, 1957; vol. 2, 1961.

Trachtenberg, J. "Jewish Education in Eastern Europe at the Beginning of the Seventeenth Century." *Jewish Education* (1939), 11:121-37.

——. *Jewish Magic and Superstition.* New York, 1961.

Twersky, I. "*The Shulḥan Arukh:* Enduring Code of Jewish Law." *Judaism.* (1967), 16:141-59.

Underhill, E. *Mysticism.* 1911; reprint, New York, 1961.

——. *Practical Mysticism.* New York, 1915.

——. *The Essentials of Mysticism.* 1920; reprint, New York, 1960.

Urbach, E. *Ḥazal: Pirkei Emunot Ve-De'ot.* Jerusalem, 1971.

Wachstein, B. "Zur Biographie Löw ben Bezalels." In *Feschrift zu Simon Dubnow.* Berlin, 1930.

Watts, A. *Behold the Spirit.* New York, 1947.

——. *The Two Hands of God: The Myths of Polarity.* New York, 1969.

Weiner, N. *God and Golem, Inc.* Cambridge, Mass., 1964.

Weinryb, B. D. *The Jews of Poland.* Philadelphia, 1973.

Weintraub, K. J. *Visions of Culture.* Chicago, 1966.

Weiss, A. "Rabbi Loew of Prague: Theory of Human Nature and Morality." Ph.D. diss., Yeshiva University, 1969.

Weiss, J. G. "Rabbi Abraham Kalisker's Concept of Communion with God and Men." *Journal of Jewish Studies* (1955), 6:87-99.

Wilensky, S. H. "Isaac Ibn Latif." In *Jewish Medieval and Renaissance Studies*. Edited by A. Altmann. Cambridge, Mass., 1967.

Willman, A. "Die Mahrischen Landesrabbiner." In *Die Juden und Judengemeinden Mahrens in Vergangenheit und Gegenwart*. Edited by H. Gold. Brünn, 1929.

Wolfson, H. A. "Crescas on the Problem of Divine Attributes." *Jewish Quarterly Review* New Series, 1916-17, 3:1-44, 175-221.

——. "Notes on Proofs of the Existence of God in Jewish Philosophy." *Hebrew Union College Annual* (1924), 1:575-99.

——. "The Amphibolous Terms in Aristotle, Arabic Philosophy and Maimonides." *Harvard Theological Review* (1938), 31:151-173.

——. "The Aristotelean Predicables and Maimonides' Division of Attributes." In *Essays and Studies in Memory of Linda Miller*. New York, 1938.

——. *Philo.* 2 vols., Cambridge, Mass., 1947.

——. "Maimonides and Gersonides on Divine Attributes as Ambiguous Terms." In *M. M. Kaplan Jubilee Volume*. New York, 1953.

——. "Maimonides on Negative Attributes." In *Louis Ginzberg Jubilee Volume*. New York, 1954.

——. *Studies in the History of Philosophy and Religion*. Cambridge; Mass., 1973.

Yaron, Z. *Mishnato Shel Rav Kook*. Jerusalem, 1974.

Ziev, A. *Ramo*. New York, 1972.

Zimmels, H. J. *Magicians, Theologians and Doctors*. London, 1952.

Index

248

Breinigsville, PA USA
16 December 2010
251605BV00001B/9/A